ADDICTION SURVIVAL GUIDEBOOK

TO BUILD BRIDGES FOR BETTER UNDERSTANDING
FOR FRIENDS, FAMILY AND FELLOW ADDICTS

Theodora Saddoris

Trilogy Christian Publishers
A Wholly Owned Subsidiary of Trinity Broadcasting Network
2442 Michelle Drive
Tustin, CA 92780

Cover design by: Cornerstone Creative Solutions

For information, address Trilogy Christian Publishing
Rights Department, 2442 Michelle Drive, Tustin, Ca 92780.
Trilogy Christian Publishing/ TBN and colophon are trademarks of Trinity Broadcasting Network.

For information about special discounts for bulk purchases, please contact Trilogy Christian Publishing.

Manufactured in the United States of America

Trilogy Disclaimer: The views and content expressed in this book are those of the author and may not necessarily reflect the views and doctrine of Trilogy Christian Publishing or the Trinity Broadcasting Network.

10 9 8 7 6 5 4 3 2 1

Library of Congress Cataloging-in-Publication Data is available.

ISBN 978-1-63769-302-5 (Print Book)
ISBN 978-1-63769-303-2 (ebook)

DEDICATION

I want to dedicate this book to my son, who struggles with this problem of addiction. God had used you for me to become a guiding light to all who are in need of help.

ACKNOWLEDGMENTS

I would like to thank God for giving me the inspiration, motivation, and desire to do the book. For guiding me and having the right people cross my path.

I want to thank my sisters Priscilla Pierce and Juliana Dickson for all their help and to my friends Sharon Waters, Pat McClendon, and Debbie Teike for their guidance. I also want to thank my husband John for his understanding and help during the process of writing this book.

Most importantly,

I want to thank Christ Jesus, my Heavenly Father, and the Holy Spirit for allowing me to go through the process of dealing with a loved one's addiction and giving me the wisdom and insight to help others caught in this journey of addiction.

CONTENTS

PREFACE

In life, it is difficult to understand why certain things happen to us and to our loved ones. I traveled the difficult journey of finding treatment for my son, who became addicted to opioids after sustaining an injury from a motorcycle accident.

Addiction causes a lot of grief for anyone suffering from it and the family dealing with the problem. It was devastating to see my son's hopes, dreams, and potential destroyed by this problem. I understand the frustration people experience when dealing with their child suffering from addiction and how it can cause all kinds of emotional turmoil in the family. It can range from guilt that we were somehow responsible for our child taking drugs and trying to find some way of fixing the problem. I remember wishing *if only he could get enough time away from the drugs, he would be back to normal again!* This kind of thinking led to a lot of poor choices of dipping into savings accounts in a desperate attempt to try and 'fix' him. Despite all these treatment programs, my child kept making the same mistakes over and over again. I was angry and frustrated that he didn't understand all the sacrifices we made trying to get him better—and none of it worked. All of us got caught in this downward spiral of hope turning to disappointment, to discouragement, frustration, anger, and then apathy.

I understand how easy emotional thinking can cause such torment and pain. Swamped from dealing with all the difficulties I encountered, trying to get help for my son that became a nightmare of roadblocks, I became exhausted from seeing the devastation, the loss, of all my son's potential destroyed by addiction. Right before my eyes, I saw him change from someone I trusted and believed into a person I didn't recognize anymore. Overwhelming grief filled my heart because everything I tried didn't work. I was alone in my misery and felt helpless. That is when I cried out to God, "Why can't I find anyone to help him?" In a very still voice, I heard God ask me, "*What are YOU going to do about it?*"

I was expecting God to fix this problem—but God had other plans. I had already experienced how the enabler thinks, the misguided thinking that kept all of us going in circles, the frustrations, the anger, the hurts, and realized—I need to do something different. How could I help anyone if I didn't understand what was really happening? I needed to learn what addiction was all about, so I could make better choices. No longer did I feel so lost and helpless—I had a God-inspired plan.

I enrolled in an ASAM (American Society of Addiction Medicine) addiction review course, and I continue to learn this very complex disease called addiction (officially called substance use disorder) and became board certified in Preventive Medicine—Addiction Specialist. I learned that addiction is more than just taking drug(s), and treatment is a whole lot more than just stopping drug use.

God allowed me to experience all the heartache and frustrations dealing with addiction that tried to destroy our lives. So God could change my heart and be a more compassionate and understanding person. A heart transplant was needed for me to become part of the process of restoring what addiction has taken from a person and teach them how to reclaim their lives back to wholeness. I had never fully understood what it meant, that all the angels rejoice when a person turns to God—until now. To see and be part of the transformation is truly fulfilling. I now know why God allowed me to experience all the pain, hurt, frustrations and disappointments—so I can understand and be a guiding light to all those in need of help.

It is easy to give up, wash our hands of helping our child or partner who doesn't seem to "get it." As frustrating as it is for family members to be caught in this snare, it is equally devastating for those with an addiction who wants to stay away from taking drugs—but can't. There is so much misinformation about addiction and treatment that it is difficult to know which way to turn. I understand the confusion and how wrong thinking leads to poor choices in both the family and in anyone who has the disease of addiction. I want to uncover some myths, shed light on the problem, and view addiction from a new perspective. So that both the family and their loved ones are going in the same direction—*forward* and not being hung up by the past, that leads to relapse and disappointment.

I remember feeling so ashamed that my son has an addiction and felt so alone in my struggles to find help. I couldn't tell any of my family members, friends, or even my pastor because of the shame I felt inside—I had failed my son. Only by breaking the silence was I able to become free from this condemnation and be healed. Family members should *never* be ashamed their loved one has an addiction. Condemnation keeps us from reaching out and getting help. Addiction can affect any walk of life, such as policemen, clergy, teachers, physicians, dentists, etc.

I understand the emotional and spiritual tow this disease has on both the family and a loved one who is struggling. God has shown me a new path to follow. A path that I want to share in this book—looking at both sides now. Sharing my experiences, I learned from treating people with addiction—the successes and heartaches.

May this book brings enlightenment, comfort, and healing for all those caught in this journey—*you are not alone*.

Theodora Saddoris M. D.

ABIM, FASAM, ABPM—Addiction Specialist

INTRODUCTION

This book is *not* meant to be a textbook on addiction. It is a book that can be read in order or out of sequence by providing enough background information for people to understand that section. Any Bible references will be placed in the End Note section. The Bible references will be placed in the order of the Bible sections. Since a verse may be used in different ways and sections, there will be no superscript number to note them.

This book is meant to give the fundamentals in a way that anyone who has an addiction problem and their family can understand:

- A new perspective on what causes addiction and how to deal with it.
- Why it is so difficult to change.
- How the family dynamics are affected by having a loved one dealing with addiction.
- When we understand the underlying problems and treat them—change is possible.

It is geared so that both the family members and those who have an addiction can *build bridges* for *better understanding*, so everyone is moving in the same direction—*forward*. Let us Begin.

SURVIVAL TIP # 1

PEOPLE, PLACES & THINGS, OH MY

Just like Dorothy said in the Wizard of Oz when she saw danger lurking everywhere, "Lions, and Tigers, and Bears, Oh My."

For people with addiction it is, People, Places and Things, Oh My. Danger is everywhere and can crop up out of nowhere to undermine all their efforts to stay clean. Avoiding the trilogy of People, Places, and Things is repeatedly pounded into everyone who is trying to recover from addiction and is found in almost every addiction manual produced. My book is no exception—*except* my book will explain *the WHY*.

- *The why*, some people get addicted, and others don't.
- *The why*, a person in recovery needs to avoid contact with anyone they used drugs with because their brain patterns have been altered by the addictive process that makes drug use change from a voluntary decision to an impulsive out-of-control reaction.
- *The why*, they need to avoid the places they previously used drugs or obtained drugs from that are essential to succeed in recovery. When anyone in early recovery comes across a drug-using environment, it triggers an intense *automatic reaction* to take drugs. Our memories are a powerful force, and for those with an addiction in order for them to effectively fight this problem—*they need a plan*. Addiction is a

battle, and if we are going to become successful, we have to understand the strategy and agenda of the addictive mindset.

- *The why*, they need to eliminate all of the paraphernalia they used to inject, snort or smoke the drug is essential for recovery. The mind has made powerful associations between using drugs and the devices to deliver them. Just seeing these objects triggers a compulsive desire to use them. In the following chapters, I will discuss the science, why this happens, and ways to help curb this learned response.

Avoiding People, Places, and Things seems like it should be an easy thing to do. So, why is it so hard? In my addiction group meetings, all of the patients who have been in recovery for a year or longer discovered *they would have never been able to get better without changing their friends and avoiding all the places they obtained drugs from.* They also shared; *it was one of the hardest things they ever had to do.* They never felt so lonely and, at times, desperate to be with someone/anyone to distract their thoughts from the torture of isolation. They had nowhere to go because all their friends used drugs. They felt like they were in solitary confinement with no way to escape—and no end in sight.

In one of my addiction group meetings, I had them write on an index card a title for the cause of their last relapse and how to avoid it. Several wrote, *can't go home again.* I wonder how easy it would be for all of us to avoid our mother, father, sister, brother, children, or other relatives? It is like telling them to cut off their arm—not to go home again. For some people, all their family members have an addiction problem, and to give up all that is familiar for the unknown is scary. But for them, to survive and avoid a relapse—that is exactly what they have to do.

Even people who have been in recovery for years have slipped when an old drug-using friend makes a surprise visit to their home. They were totally unprepared for the compulsive urge to use drugs again and ended up relapsing. I have patients that want to get together with one of their previous drug-using friends and think it's okay since they are now both in recovery. Even when I tell them why it might not be such a good idea, they still resume the relationship, thinking *it won't be a problem for them.* Later, they find out differently—when they relapse.

So, why is it so difficult for them to avoid taking drugs when they encounter someone they took drugs with in the past or be around someone who is currently using drugs? It all comes down to three main things:

1. What makes a drug addictive?
2. The changes in the reward system.
3. Learned automatic behavior.

What Makes a Drug addictive?

Our body has an ingrained, instinctive desire for survival. It is built into our DNA. If we didn't have the survival instinct built in, humans would be extinct along with the dinosaurs. The survival system *rewards* behaviors that promote the continuation of our species, such as eating, having sex, and protecting our children. The brain makes these activities a lot more enjoyable than removing dead, decaying leaves from our gutters.

When an activity is enjoyable, it triggers the reward center in our brain and stimulates the desire to repeat the experience more frequently than less enjoyable ones. Addictive drugs can stimulate the survival reward pathway *stronger* than any of the natural rewards and makes them want to *continue* taking more drugs.

Changes in the Reward System

Frequent use of addictive drugs alters the natural reward system and changes what is most important (valuable) for a person to survive. These changes occur because of the brain's response to the drugs taken. When the reward pathways become overly stimulated, the body tries to offset its effect by lowering the brain receptors' response to the drug and makes the drug become less effective. These adaptive alterations cause the drugs not to produce the same amount of pleasure or last as long. People will then increase the frequency and potency of the drugs they take in order to get the same benefit as before. The adaptive changes the brain creates can explain certain behaviors such as,

- Why those in active addiction can never cut back.
- Why their life revolves around acquiring and taking more drugs because their brain won't let them stop.

When anyone addicted to opioids suddenly stops using them, they develop intense withdrawal symptoms. Withdrawal is likened to torture and makes them think they are going to die. Some of the withdrawal symptoms they experience are:

- Profuse sweating
- Intense anxiety
- Heart racing so fast that it feels like it might explode
- Light-headed, feeling faint
- Nausea, severe abdominal cramping, and diarrhea
- Every bone in their body aches

The intense withdrawal symptoms are a form of negative reinforcement the brain and body creates in response to them stopping the drugs. It is also teaching them, the only way for all this misery to go away is to take more drugs. The addictive pathways view drug use as necessary for survival, and it will *intensify* the *suffering* until they relent and start using drugs again. Remember, the brain promotes behaviors that make a person *feel good* and *avoids* things that cause *pain*. Physical and/or mental pain is what a person will get when he or she tries to stop drug use.

When I asked people in my addiction recovery group, "When you found some drugs to take, how did it make you feel?"

They commonly told me, "*Just holding them in my hand made me feel better.*"

They hadn't even swallowed a single one—yet, they felt better. Knowing they were *going* to get *relief* was almost as powerful as taking the tablets or injecting the drug. *Addiction* delivers the one-two punch. First, when they try to stop using drugs they get withdrawal pain and escalating anxiety, and when they just have the drugs in their hand, their brain rewards them by making them feel better.

Learned Automatic Behaviors

When we learn a behavior such as walking, running, typing, these processes never fully go away and are difficult to eradicate. We all learn by repetition. When we first learned to walk, we fell down a lot. With practice, we became more proficient, and now we no longer think about how to walk—we just do it. Walking has now become an automatic behavior. In people who have an addiction, the repetition of constantly searching and acquiring drugs becomes hard-wired into their psychic. The great switcheroo has happened in people with an addiction. The natural survival reward pathways have been altered, making drug use the highest priority in their life—more important than their friends, family, job, or even their own life.

The *learned automatic* behaviors make it difficult for them to stay in recovery and avoid a relapse. When they see anyone they previously used drugs with, WHAM-O, an intense craving hits them. They can't control the sudden urge to use. They can be innocently driving down the road, going to work, and see a house that looks familiar. Suddenly, wheels screech to a halt as they race inside for a hit instead. They can be at a gas station filling their gas tank, and a previous drug-using buddy shows up—they relapse. Shopping in a grocery store can be equally hazardous when a former friend starts talking and walks with them to the car, and once there, they relapse.

In order to prepare for the *unexpected*, we need a *plan* on how to avoid a relapse. One of the most common causes for relapse is encountering an old friend. Part of our emergency plan is to find ways to *avoid or limit* the encounter. From experience, I have found a lot of relapses happen when my patients would get gas for their car or shop after work or early evening. Since most drug users wake up later in the afternoon, I recommend to avoid the unexpected meeting by having them buy their groceries or get their gas in the early morning before going to work. If, by chance, they do see an old drug-using friend, *stop* shopping immediately, run out the door, and leave. I don't c*are if the cart is full of ice cream—they got to leave—their recovery is at stake.* It's important: *Do Not engage in conversation.*

In recovery, when they bump into previous drug-using buddies, the *subconscious* addictive processes are actively triggering intense cravings and urges *geared* to make them relapse. They are *unaware* this is happening. This is why it hits them so *unexpectedly* and so *intensely*. They are unprepared for the powerful cravings that strike them like a guided ballistic bullet finding its mark and destroying all their efforts.

Recovery takes time. It doesn't happen with the snap of the fingers or when one's just out of a treatment program. There are so many things a person has to learn, such as,

- What is important to them?
- How to deal with stress?
- How to identify misguided thinking?
- How to change their thoughts and the words they say that are necessary to change their behaviors?
- Learn to let go of the past in order to move toward their future.
- How to rediscover what makes their life fulfilling?

This process can become a lifetime journey of self-discovery and fulfillment as they learn a new path to follow.

SURVIVAL TIPS

- Avoiding people, places, and things is a *must* to sustain recovery, but in the beginning stages, it can be very difficult to achieve.

- o We need to give a lot of encouragement and support during this period. Recognize they are trying, and we need to help them find ways to stay busy and not have time for them to feel lonely.
- o Drugs altered the natural reward pathways needed for survival. Drug use is now more important than their children, family, or even their own lives.
- o Remember, it is not their fault why they got addicted or ours for what has happened.
- Recovery takes time for both the family and their loved ones. It doesn't happen the first time we pray—it is a process of healing. Miracles can happen in an instant, but healing takes time.
  - o In recovery, a lot of changes need to be made, and time for the brain to heal from all the damage drug use has caused.
  - o In addiction treatment, people try to give too much information early in recovery—at a time, their brain can't process it. Ask God to give us guidance and start with small activities that can be accomplished with little effort. Give information that focuses on only one item. We can start by helping them clean their room to eliminate all their drugs and paraphernalia they used to take drugs. Do not have them do this alone because if they find any drugs, they will impulsively take them. At the beginning stages of recovery, just picking their clothes off the floor can be overwhelming for them. Do not ridicule or criticize—even if we are doing most of the work. We are here to help.
  - o When we ask Jesus to become our Lord and Savior, we become born again. Our nature has been changed, but our mind needs to be renewed. We have to replace our old thoughts with what God says. When I say, "I am weak." the Bible says, "I can do all things through Christ who strengthens me." The renewing of our mind requires diligence so that my thoughts become God's

thoughts. Changing the way I think is the only way to become all that God has for me.

○ One step at a time, one day at a time, to slowly build a strong foundation for recovery and restoring our relationships. Rushing the process will not make it happen any quicker and increases their risk to relapse by putting too many expectations and demands on them that they are not ready to handle.

• To sustain recovery, they need to get medical treatment to *remain* successful.

○ This is one disease they can't do alone. Their brain has been damaged by chronic drug use. They need support and guidance and, most importantly, acceptance—not judgment over past mistakes. Remember, God will judge us using the same standard we used to judge others. Will it be kind and merciful or condemning?

SURVIVAL TIP #2

IT AIN'T ALL MY FAULT

What exactly is addiction? Is it a disease—*or*—a character, moral, lazy, only want to get high, personal failure?

For people who think addiction is a character problem, believe—those with an addiction have the ability to choose between taking drugs and not taking drugs. Their argument is based on their observation: *if I can say no to drugs—then those that use drugs have a moral or character problem.* Many of them assume addicts are lazy, worthless people who spend all their time getting high and feel the public is too soft on them. I have heard some people argue:

- *Why should taxpayers pay for these ingrates?*
- *Spend billions of dollars on treatments for—'those kinds of people'—that never work anyway.*

Public records show that *more* than fifty percent of people in prison have some type of drug-related charge. Because of the rising numbers of criminal drug offenses, some people feel these 'addicts' are breaking the taxpayers' pocketbook to house all these lawbreakers. Some are even against using Narcan that is needed to keep them from dying from an opioid overdose. What really riles a lot of people's temper is when those addicted to opioids keep overdosing, and healthcare personnel keep using Narcan to revive them. Some of my patients have overdosed so many times they have lost count. It is not uncommon for the same person to be revived in the emergency room two or more times in one night. This recurrent overdosing and the expense of repeated Narcan administration makes many people angry and frustrated with the situation (yet, not enough to explore other solutions) and feel it is a waste of time and money.

There are some who are so vehemently against providing any Narcan to repeat offenders and feel, *why should I have to pay for their mistakes?* Some want all those who overdose to die, providing a great solution for treating the opioid epidemic—until it becomes their child or loved one.

Yet, I don't hear them wanting to refuse treatment to those who have other medical problems such as diabetes, high blood pressure, heart attacks, emphysema, or cancer. The same arguments can be made that they chose to eat too much sugar, salt, or fat, smoke cigarettes, or fail to see a physician for a yearly physical. If people have a heart problem or other health issue, we don't callously tell them to die and save the rest of us the expense of caring for their needs. If we did, I doubt very many people would be alive to complain.

I wonder is getting high what a person with addiction is really doing? Or is something else going on? Many people with addiction started taking pain pills that were prescribed to them by a physician or dentist, for an injury or for a procedure. Teenagers started drug use in a desire to fit in with their peers, unaware of how it could affect the rest of their lives. If we think back to our own childhood, how many of us tried alcohol, cigarettes, marijuana, or other drugs out of curiosity or by persuasion from our friends? This is a normal developmental response in teenagers to experiment in life to find out what they want, rather than to unquestioningly adhere to what is expected of them.

In all the years I have been treating people with addiction, I have *never* had a single individual say to me, *I want to grow up to be an addict.* Most people didn't realize the challenging path they were on until a practitioner suddenly stopped prescribing the pain pills, or they ran out of the drugs their friends gave them. They were unprepared for the horrible stomach cramping, nausea, diarrhea, sweats, severe muscle aches, anxiety, and heart pounding anguish that made them think—*I'm going to die.* Once this withdrawal is experienced, they never want to go through that again. So, once they are off drugs and the immediate symptoms of withdrawal are gone—*why* do they keep returning to take drugs again? What is wrong with them? Obviously, it must be a moral character flaw for them to keep going back to something that makes them feel physically, mentally, spiritually miserable and causes so much pain for them and their family.

For years, addiction was viewed as a moral failure. It allowed no hope for change or improvement because a moral or character failing will always be there and will never change. What evidence is there to substantiate this moral character flaw theory? There is absolutely none. It is an *opinion.* If the opinion was examined more closely, it is easy to see the flaws. *No one* in their right mind would continue taking drugs that caused so much pain and suffering. There must be another explanation.

I have found, no matter how many scientific studies are done or evidence showing addiction is a disease, I hear some say, *Don't bother me with the facts, my mind is already made up.*

If we are willing to keep an open mind, let us examine the evidence for an alternate idea. Addiction is a disease coupled with a learned behavior they used to cope with stress. So, what is a disease anyway? Most people are familiar with the diseases of Diabetes Mellitus (DM), Cardiovascular Disease (CVD), Chronic Obstructive Pulmonary Disease (COPD), and Hypertension (HTN). Let us see if there are any common features to these diseases and Addiction.

DM, CVD, COPD, HTN, and Addiction all have an inherited component and an environmental component for the disease to manifest. Evidence shows that genetic causes for Addiction range between forty to seventy percent depending on the drug. For Nicotine, it is fifty percent, Alcohol and Opioids, about sixty to sixty-five percent, and Cocaine seventy percent. The inherited components for developing DM, HTN, COPD, and CVD also have a similar range between forty to seventy percent. They all have a similar genetic tendency, and they all need to be exposed to the offending agent, i.e., excessive calories, starches, salt, cigarettes, high cholesterol foods, or an addictive substance, for the diseases to become manifested in the form of

DM, HTN, COPD, CVD or Addiction. Because of the high genetic predisposition to addiction, *every* practitioner needs to assess an individual's family history for addiction *before* any potentially addictive drug is prescribed to a patient.

Let me repeat: *anyone* with a family history of addiction to *any* addictive substance is at an increased risk for developing an addiction. The risk is *greatest* in *first*-generation relatives, which consist of parents, siblings, or children. Second generation relatives also pose a risk but not as great, and that includes grandparents, aunts, and uncles who have an *addiction* to any of the following:

- Nicotine in all its forms:
  - Smoking cigarettes
  - Chewing tobacco
  - Snuff
  - Vaping nicotine
  - Nicotine inhalers, patches, and gum can be addictive but less so than the other forms above.
- Marijuana, Spice
- Alcohol
- Stimulants
  - Methamphetamine
  - Cocaine
  - Ecstasy or other stimulants
- Narcotics
- Benzodiazepines and derivatives that stimulate the GABA receptors in the brain that can increase addictive behaviors:
  - Xanax, Valium, Ativan, Klonopin, etcetera
  - Sleeping medications: Ambien, Restoril, Dalmane, Halcion, Lunesta, etcetera.
    - Gabapentin and Lyrica (not as addictive as the other benzodiazepine derivatives, but can be for some people)

A family history of addiction increases the *risk* of developing an addiction to *any* addictive drug and puts any *future* generations at risk for developing it, too. *Important to note*: It does not mean they will develop the same type of addiction their relative has or had. The genetic component causes an *increased susceptibility* or vulnerability towards developing an addiction to *any* type of addictive substance. An alcoholic father or mother can have a daughter addicted to benzodiazepines, a son addicted to opioids, and another son addicted to alcohol. In the predisposed person, their brain is hardwired differently than other people who do not have the same genetic predisposition. The increased susceptibility has their brain respond *differently* to the drug compared to other people who don't have an increased risk.

It is critical that everyone knows how to take care of his or her own health needs. Practitioners prescribe a lot of opioids to patients. Patients need to become more assertive and ask what type of medication they are being prescribed. If anyone has any of the above risk factors, I urge them not to take an opioid and ask for alternative ways to control pain. We don't want to trade a temporary pain problem for a *lifetime* addiction problem.

While facilitating my support group, I asked the people present who had an addiction to narcotics to describe their reactions when they took an opioid the very first time. Group responses were:

- *I felt better.*
- *I no longer felt anxious or depressed.*
- *It gave me more energy.*
- *The hole I felt inside wasn't there anymore.*
- *So, this is how normal people feel.*
- *I felt like Superman, capable of handling any problem.*
- *The pain from being abused no longer hurts so much.*

Not one person in the group responded the way I did when I took my first narcotic pain pill after I had a C-section. I had such severe nausea and vomiting that the sutures in my belly almost popped open. I was so sick that I vowed to never take one again. Their responses clearly showed me, their brains reacted very differently to an opioid than mine did. I think anyone who takes an opioid and feels better—less anxious, depressed, or who has more energy, would likely take more, but if they felt worse like I did, they would avoid them. The brain works on the simple principle *of reward and punishment.* The brain wants to repeat any activities that make anyone feel good and to avoid situations that cause pain.

Scientific evidence confirms that people who have a *genetic* tendency toward addiction have brains that respond differently than those who do not have that tendency. These changes can be due to:

- Different proteins being produced.
- Changes in the configuration of the receptors in the brain, so they respond differently.
- Altered metabolism of the drug.
- Different pathways that are stimulated in the brain.

These changes cannot be altered by a person's willpower or self-control. It is like telling them to concentrate on changing the color of their eyes and expecting them to do it. If they can't—is it a moral failure?

So far, scientists have not found a *single gene* that causes addiction. I highly doubt we will ever find just *one* gene. What the evidence does show, *multiple* areas on *different genes* contribute to a *tendency* or increased risk for addiction.

Our *genes* (the genetic sequences of DNA) and the *environment* our parents and grandparents experienced are *both* inherited. Epigenetics is how the environment our relatives experienced affects how we respond to stressful events by the *regulation* of the *proteins our cells produce.* Epigenetics is a very difficult concept to understand, but it's important for us to know how difficulties of past generations can cause *future* problems. Studies have shown that *children* with *alcoholic parents* responded differently to benzodiazepines (Valium, Xanax, Klonopin, or Ativan) compared to children who don't have an alcoholic parent. Benzodiazepines usually cause relaxation, but in *female children* of an alcoholic parent(s), they experience a stimulant effect. The Benzodiazepines give them more energy, which increases their risk for developing an addiction to this drug class.

Chromosomes are structures that carry our genetic sequences (DNA). So, how can environmental factors *alter* gene expression (proteins produced) and change our behavior? They do this by:

- How the Histone proteins intertwine and *surround* the DNA like a protective package.
- Environmental factors can add or remove protein groups off the histones and cause them to change *shape* and the DNA that it packages (but *not* alter the sequence or order of the DNA base pairs).
- Changing the shape of the histones can make the DNA coil tight or open up and acts like a switch that can turn off or on protein production in the cells.
- The proteins produced or blocked affect how our immune and stress response system reacts to mental or physical events.

To help clarify how this happens, think of water as our DNA sequence. It is made up of one oxygen atom and two hydrogen atoms (H_2O). This ratio does *not* change (sequence) despite how many shapes water can become. It can become a gas that burns our skin; a liquid to take a drink, or ice that is cold, hard, and slick. Despite its many properties, all the forms are still (H_2O). Each of the shapes (gas, liquid and solid) has unique functions and properties.

Histones are like the different properties of water. As a histone changes their configuration (shape), it modifies what part of the DNA strand that is or is not available for protein production in our cells. All these alterations influence how our immune and stress response systems will react when we are exposed to either *physical* (infections, injury, and cancers) or *mental* (abuse, loss of job, partner, or grief over the death or loss of a loved one) events that occur in our life. *Let me repeat:* Stressful *living environments* (abuse, trauma, or hardships) change the histone configurations in us, and these changes can be passed onto our *children* and *future* generations. Even though the gene sequence and order have not changed, but—the *regulation* of what proteins are produced has been changed.

Even people, who have no genetic predisposition to addiction, when repeatedly exposed to addictive drugs, it *alters* their histone configurations. These changes modify the proteins produced in certain areas of their brain, which affects their behaviors or responses. For example, when an animal becomes repeatedly exposed to cocaine, this stimulates the production of certain proteins in the brain that increases drug-seeking behaviors in them.

Poor nutrition is also an environmental stressor and alters histone configuration. These changes can be passed onto future generations. This is especially true if a mother has a low vitamin D level. Vitamin D blocks the production of certain proteins that affect the immune system. Vitamin D deficiency increases the risk of schizophrenia, cognitive decline, and risk of developing cancer onto her progeny (children). When people are deficient in Vitamin D, it can no longer *block the production* of cancer-producing proteins and increases their risk of developing melanoma, breast, colon, pancreatic, and prostate cancer. Vitamin D regulates the genes like histones regulate gene expression (proteins produced or blocked), and these changes can be passed onto future generations.

The nature (our genes) or nurture (environment) arguments about why a person turns out a certain way shows: They both have an influence on our genes either in their sequence or changes in gene regulation. Epigenetics is a hard concept to fathom. How can my grandfather's living conditions affect my ability to respond today? Even if I were never around him, the changes in the histones configurations would still have an influence on my progeny and me. I wonder *can this be the cause of generation curses?* What we do with our life has a profound effect on future generations. If our family struggles with addiction, anxiety, depression, or other mental illnesses, we need to ask God to reveal how to change our thinking and emotional responses. As a Christian, I am already a new creation, but my previous attitudes and thoughts are still with me—until my mind is renewed by the word of God.

Let me repeat. Stressful events, neglect, low self-esteem, starvation, etcetera, that happened in our parent and grandparent's lifetime influence how we will respond to emotional or physical stress. The environment that our ancestors experienced will influence not only our lives but also our children's. The environment has a huge impact on the things we inherit, along with actual changes in our genetic code, making addiction a very complex problem. And like any complex problem, there are *no* simple solutions.

It is interesting to note, there are areas mapped on the genetic code that can influence whether we will develop a tendency toward addiction or have a protective effect that would make it less likely. The part I find incredible, there are gene sequences that determine how many packs of cigarettes a person will smoke a day and if they will develop lung cancer, even if they are a light smoker.

A study of twins that have been adopted by different families has shown that an individual's risk for addiction is directly related to how close the *genetic association* (biological parents) a person has to an addictive relative. It did *not* show an increased risk if the adopted family had addiction problems. If an individual has a mother, father, sister, or brother who has an addiction, they will have a much higher risk of developing an addiction than if the relative is an uncle, aunt, or grandparent. If a child has a mother or father who has an addiction, that person will have *eight* times increased risk for developing an addiction. Remember, it doesn't have to be the *same* addiction. A parent could be an alcoholic, and the child may be addicted to methamphetamines, benzodiazepines (i.e., Xanax), or opioids. The genetic vulnerability is to *any* addictive substances.

But genetics and environmental influences are not the only culprits that can lead to addiction. If they repeatedly abuse drugs or alcohol to deal with their problems *over time,* those addictive agents will *permanently* re-wire their brain, even in people who have a *low* genetic predisposition to addiction can still develop it.

Let me repeat. If anyone has *repeated* exposure to an addictive drug, it can induce adaptive changes in the brain's reward system that can lead to tolerance (the need to take more and more of the drug to get the same benefit) and habit formation. This can start the downhill spiral of drug craving (which is manifested in some people as increased pain, when in actuality the injury has not changed or is getting better), leading to more drug use and depression. Symptoms of cravings and depression can last long after they stop using the addictive drug and increases the risk for them to relapse.

Some people who are addicted to pain pills will tell family and friends, "*If you have as much pain as I do, then you would understand why I have to take more of them than what the doctor prescribes.*"

This is a sure sign they are headed down the wrong path, and alternate treatments for pain should be implemented.

Another feature for every *disease,* if left untreated, will eventually cause organ damage or failure. For example, some people with diabetes can control their blood sugars with diet and exercise, but over time their pancreas becomes damaged and starts to produce less and less insulin. It then becomes harder to keep their blood sugars under control, and they need to start oral medications to maintain normal glycemic control. Eventually, their pancreas can no longer produce enough insulin to meet their needs, and they will require insulin shots.

Addiction also has a chronic progressive course. As brain pathways become altered, it becomes more and more difficult to control the severe craving for the drug(s). They end up taking even more drugs leading to further damage to the brain and loss of control. What was once a choice to take drugs has now become a necessity— and they no longer have control.

In people with diabetes, the pancreas is the organ that is damaged, and, in addiction, the *brain* is the organ that is damaged. Both lead to the progression of the disease to the point they can no longer manage their problem with simple measures and *need medications* to help reduce the symptoms and to slow down or prevent progression of the disease.

Functional MRI (fMRI) scans can detect changes in blood flow patterns in a person's brain. When a certain area of the brain is activated, it will *light* up due to increased blood flow to carry extra nutrients to the part of the brain that is doing more work. When a recovering alcoholic is watching television and sees a beer commercial, the reward center of their brain lights up and triggers a craving. Another person who never had an alcohol problem and sees the same commercial has no increased blood flow or activity in the reward center. This is *not* something an individual can consciously control. It is an *unconscious* event. The addicted individual is not even aware this is happening. All they know, they have a sudden urge to drink for no apparent reason.

Many people don't realize changes in the brain reward pathway can make it extremely difficult for them to follow through with the decision to quit taking drugs. This is why the campaign slogan, 'Just say No to Drugs,' was so ineffective. If they could just say no, they would have done so long before they lost their job, family, friends, and their self-respect.

Essential to know: Just because a person has a genetic vulnerability to addiction *doesn't mean that person will develop it.* To prevent a problem is easier than treating one. That is why people have to be aware of their potential risk for addiction and avoid exposure to any addictive substances or limit the amount. If they have developed *good coping skills* to deal with life stressors such as loss of a job or a relationship, grief over loved ones, anxiety, worry, and depression, they will have less of a risk for developing an addiction.

Formula on HOW to Develop Addiction is:

Genetic vulnerability + use addictive drugs + poor coping skills dealing with stress = *High risk for developing an addiction*

Warning signs an individual is at risk to develop addiction are:

- If taking a drug or alcohol helps them cope with their day—or life.
- If they have more energy while taking the drug.
- If they feel less stressed or depressed while on the drugs.
- If they feel better about themselves and dulls the pain of previous abuse or emotional trauma.
- If they use the drug to escape painful experiences or thoughts.

Any one of these signs is an indicator they need to stop taking the drug(s) or alcohol *now*. They need help to learn better coping skills on how to deal with their stress, uncomfortable emotions, and painful situations. We need to stop relying on a substance to mask our problems. When we put a Band-Aid to cover our problems— they don't go away and only get worse.

Part of the Recovery Process is learning coping skills to reduce the stress response. Some of the modalities a therapist or treatment provider can teach them is learning to practicing daily mindful breathing, meditation, yoga, mind-body connections, or safe place visualization exercises daily. Anyone in recovery should practice one of these modalities for a minimum of ten to fifteen minutes a day. When they do this, it lowers their reaction to daily stressors and helps them cope better when painful events occur. When not overwhelmed with strong emotions, they can make better choices and reduce the need to take a drug to make them feel better.

It is worth repeating: Anyone who developed an addiction (substance use disorder) did not plan on having this problem. Many times the drugs were prescribed to them for an injury, and they were unaware of their own vulnerability for developing an addiction. We all need to stop blaming them for their addiction problem and start getting them *the help* they need to get better. So easy to judge another and give poor advice over something we don't understand. Just like Job in the Bible experienced when his friends made assumptions that caused him more pain than good.

Let us start treating addiction like the disease it is and realize that many people need to take medication to control the changes that drug use has created in their brains. Just like people who have hypertension needs to take a medication(s) to get their blood pressure into a safe range.

Medication alone is less effective for those in recovery to avoid a relapse if they are not practicing ways to lower their stress level. Their brain is already hardwired to have an *exaggerated stress response* to even *minor* problems or situations. This magnified response to minor stressful events makes it difficult for other people to understand why insignificant conflicts cause so much emotional distress for them and for others around them.

SURVIVAL TIPS

- Family history of addiction to any addictive substance increases the *vulnerability* of family members to addiction.
  - If taking an opioid makes them experience more than just pain relief, they need to stop the medication.
  - It is better to avoid a problem than try to fix it.
- Life struggles in past generations influence current and future generations in how they respond to physical and emotional stress.
  - It is important for me to effectively deal with problems now than allow them to be passed onto my children.
  - We lack because we don't ask. Ask God every day to give us wisdom and guidance to handle whatever comes our way. When I ask for wisdom, I know that with any problem that I encounter that day, God has given me the ability and the strength to make the right choices.
- The formula for anyone to be at a *high risk* of developing an addiction is:
  Genetic vulnerability + Use of drug or alcohol + Poor coping skills to stress
- As a mother, I became overwhelmed dealing with my son and his addiction problems, and my other son diagnosed with schizoaffective disorder. I had to give the problems to God. I did this by pouring out all my grief, my pain, frustrations, and anger and released all these emotions and problems to the only one who can truly heal them.
  - When events looked bleak, I had to block my racing thoughts and say: *stop!* I have already given the problem to God and *started praising God* instead, knowing he can turn any situation around.

- ○ I refused to look at the circumstances because God works from the inside out. He changes the heart of a person before we can see the outward changes. So, when my son's addiction problems escalated, I continued to praise God. I had Bible verses to remind God of his promises (actually, he was reminding me—God already knows his promises.) But, I was claiming them and standing on his word for my son's life.
- ○ I had to take my eyes off my problems and focus on what God says. *Praising God* broke the bonds of addiction and mental health problems in my children.
- In recovery, everyone needs to develop ways to reduce stress that will help them become less susceptible to relapse.
  - ○ Daily prayer, time with God, releasing my feelings to Him gives me peace throughout the day. When the unexpected happens, I am prepared. God is in control, and the battle is His—instead of worrying, I am praising God.
  - ○ When I praise God, I am releasing God's power to work on the problem. When I worry about the problem, and beg God to do something, and keep begging—my lack of faith is blocking God from intervening.
  - ○ A Canaanite woman kept begging Jesus to heal her daughter, and Jesus kept walking, but when she showed Jesus her faith, Jesus granted her request.
  - ○ When we pray, we pray according to God's will. When we quote the scripture verse that applies to the situation—we are in the will of God. Then we *thank* Him for taking care of the problem(s).
  - ○ We don't beg. We are God's children and can boldly go to the throne of grace through Jesus Christ and make our requests known. Faith is demonstrated by believing God heard us and will take care of the problem.
  - ○ To further demonstrate our faith, we start praising God even more despite what we see, hear or feel, thanking God for taking care of the problem. When Praises go up, Blessings come down.

SURVIVAL TIP # 3

CHANGE WHAT'S NOT WORKING

Albert Einstein's definition of insanity: doing the same thing over and over again and expecting a different result.

In treating addiction, we need to stop doing the same thing over and over again with the expectation *this* time it will work when all the other times it did not. What makes *this* time any more special than all the other times? While trying to stop drug use, it is crazy to think—if we keep repeating the *same* process—that we will experience a different outcome. If it didn't work before, why should it work now—*if nothing* has changed? It is a waste of time, money, and effort to keep repeating what failed before.

Yet, this is exactly what many people did in trying to treat anyone with an addiction. For years, family members (me included) tried to help their children by having them go into multiple detoxification programs to get them off drugs. They continued doing this with every relapse in a never-ending cycle. Insurance did not cover the cost for these expensive treatment programs, making it a hardship to pay for all the treatments that only worked for a very short period of time. But families continued in the hope that this time, it will work. Parents often spent all their money on legal fees to keep their child from going to jail and paid for multiple treatment programs in a desperate attempt to get their child back to normal. Unfortunately, all their efforts to help their child did not change the ultimate outcome—relapse.

What many people didn't know (including the treatment providers) that unless something was done to control their cravings for the drugs—they would relapse. Short courses of treatment do *not* work. Most people had to find that out the hard way by spending hard-earned cash and see it all go down the drain by useless endeavors of drug detoxifications and short courses of treatment. Many of them had filed for bankruptcy, but it was worth it—if their child could recover.

Family members thought *if only they could get the drugs out of their system, they would return back to normal again.* I wish treatment for a substance use disorder (addiction) could be that easy—but it isn't. Like any disease, it doesn't go away by wishing it were gone. It still needs to be *treated.* Addiction damages the brain. Just like diabetes damages the pancreas along with other systems injured from the disease process.

What I am going to discuss will likely anger some people who are dealing with their child or partner's addiction. But without the truth, how can anyone be set free from misguided thoughts and actions? Unfortunately, there is no way I can sugarcoat the following information. So, don't stop reading or throw the book away. I want to help, but I can't help anyone if they don't listen to the truth.

The truth is: addiction not only affects the *thinking* of the person who has the addiction. It also affects the *family* member's *thinking.* A person with an addiction has this compulsive drive to take drugs—the family has this compulsive drive to *fix* and protect their loved one from the consequences of their drug use. This compulsive drive to *help* puts an enormous financial and emotional strain on the family resources and centers the focus on a person with an addiction while ignoring the needs of other members of the family. This is *not intentional.* It happens because we feel somehow responsible for our child's addiction. I know this seems crazy, but that doesn't keep us from feeling guilty in some way. Because of this guilt, we feel this compulsive drive to somehow fix the problem and do whatever we can to bring our child or partner back to normal again. Guilt keeps us from reaching out to others for help. The family will spend money they can't afford to have their child enter into one treatment facility and then another, and another, but they won't spend a dime to get help for themselves. Shame keeps us from telling other people our struggles, from seeing a counselor, telling our friends, family, priest, pastor, or minister.

Every time our child relapses with drug use, we become angry, disappointed, and depressed. Every time our child has been successful for a short while, we become happy and begin to think it's going to work this time. Our emotions become a roller coaster, dependent on the actions of one person (Co-dependent). We *suffer alone* in silence. Let us break the silence. We are *not* alone. Conservative estimates state that one in five families has a close relative that has an addiction problem. We *must* seek help and learn how to live again. Do not make our happiness contingent on our child's successes or failures. If we don't get help, resentments build, and when our child improves, bitterness spews out and undermines all our efforts to get them better. When we start living our own life, it will take the stress *off both of us*.

In this process of trying to *fix* our children, we end up enabling them to continue drug use. How can helping someone mean I am enabling them? It all stems from the feelings of guilt that make our actions irrational. How does avoiding the *consequences* of their drug use help them learn to make the right choices?

In our efforts to *protect,* we *keep* them from *learning*. We have to change our ways. I like the Parable in the Bible that talks about the Prodigal son. The son chose to take his inheritance from his father and leave and spent all his money on foolish things. When his money ran out, he ended up feeding the pigs. He had to eat what the pigs ate and slept where they slept. While cold and miserable in the mud, the son came to his senses. He knew servants in his father's house were treated better than he was and decided to return home. Never once in the story did the father seek out his son and offer him some food while he lived with the pigs or give him a blanket to make it more comfortable for him to live in the mud. But once his son came to his senses and headed back toward his father, the father ran and helped him.

We all learn by conditioned responses. If we are rewarded for a certain behavior, this encourages repetition of this action. If we are punished for a certain behavior, it discourages the repetition of this action. If we *reward bad* behavior, we will only get *more bad* behavior. So, when our loved one is in jail—don't bail them out. Let them experience the consequences of their choices. Don't give them money—they will spend it on drugs rather than food. We can have them do chores around the house and give them food or clothes but do not give them money in order to limit their access to acquiring drugs. Learn to *set* boundaries and *enforce* them. We are talking about acquiring survival skills to protect our children and ourselves.

When treating my patients who have a substance use disorder (addiction), I discovered a change in the family dynamics that seems counterintuitive to logic. At first, the enabler (a family member) tries to force their child or partner into treatment. They are very invested in helping them. But, when their child or partner starts to improve and makes great strides in their life, they encounter family resistance. How can the former enabler (family member) of a person with an addiction now become the barrier to their recovery? As the enabler, their *goal* was trying to *fix* their loved one's addiction. Their whole life revolved around this goal. Now their loved one is being treated for their drug use problem. They are getting better. They have stopped using drugs. They are working, paying their bills, and their relationships are improving. The former enabler should now be rejoicing, but instead, they are *complaining*. Here is a list of the most common complaints my patients hear from family members or partners on an almost daily basis.

- *You have no idea what hardships we endured.*
- *When are you going to get off those drugs?* Referring to the medications they take to treat their disease.
- *You are just trading one drug for another.* In reference to using Suboxone to treat their disease.
- *Why do you have to spend so much time going to all those meetings or counseling sessions?* I'm tired of bringing the kids to all their soccer, basketball, tennis, football practices, music lessons, ballet, etc. *Surely, missing a few meetings won't make a difference.*

Family members often nag and complain and then refuse to drive them to a recovery meeting when their car breaks down. Previously they would have done anything to get them into treatment. So, why is it when their loved one with an addiction is getting better, they are meeting so much resistance from the very people who tried to help them? I had a patient dragged in by his mother to get him into treatment for his opioid use disorder (addiction). In the beginning, she came to the office with her son every visit to make sure he didn't miss a single appointment. I could tell he was not very interested in getting help. Most of the time, he was high on drugs and indifferent to any suggestions made about going to counseling or group meetings. About a month later, he was arrested because he failed to appear in court on previous charges. He spent a week in jail. He was beaten fighting over his socks and shoes to keep them from being pulled off his feet, and he was miserable. He told himself, *he would do whatever it takes to keep from going back to jail.* When I saw him at his next appointment, he was a changed man. His father brought him to our group counseling meetings, and he attended every one. For almost a year, he was working, paying off his child support, and was doing great—until his father became ill and could no longer bring him to the weekly group meetings. My patient worked for his mother and lived in a trailer where she ran her business. She *refused* to bring him to the meetings. He lived out in the country, over fifteen miles away (one way), and at times he walked to the meetings. When the weather got colder, he couldn't walk that distance. His driver's license was taken away several years ago. Most of his money went toward child support. He lived on fifty dollars a month. He couldn't afford a cab ride and had no other means to attend. He relapsed because of a lack of family support.

It saddens my heart to see someone relapse. For a year, he had made great progress in his life and would have continued if he had adequate family support. The relapse could have been avoided—potential future death prevented—if only someone in the family drove him to a one-hour meeting once a week. For someone so concerned about her son getting off drugs, when he needed her the most—to drive him to a meeting, she *refused*. Unfortunately, I encounter this situation way too often.

Why is it when someone is getting better and they need the support the most, it is refused? Yet, when they are in active drug use and don't want any help, it's freely given? Why is it when they are moving forward in their life and doing better that family members start bringing up all the wrongs they did in the past? Constant complaining about all the expenses they incurred and hardships they endured. Family members pile on the guilt about all the mistakes they made in the past and don't focus on all the successes they are making in the present. Why is the enabler *punishing* their loved-one because they are getting *better*? Remember, when I discussed conditioned responses? When people are rewarded for a behavior, they are more likely to continue in this process, and when punished by constant harping, complaining, and fighting about their recovery, they are less likely to continue on this path. So, now the enabler is unintentionally blocking their loved one's recovery by making it more difficult to get better.

Some say *I would never act that way*. Yet, when I talk to my patients, they tell me their parents and partners constantly harp about when are they going to get off those drugs (medications to treat their disease)? Many times family members act like they are more knowledgeable about addiction than the treatment provider. In an effort to educate, I frequently offer friends and family meetings specifically geared to addressing any of their concerns about any of the treatments provided. I am lucky to have one family member attend. Those who have an addiction show up, but rarely does any of their family members or partners attend.

As a former enabler and complainer, I understand how family members or partners can get burned out trying to help a loved one who has no interest in getting better. All our emotional and financial resources are strained to the limit, and often feel *we can't take it anymore*. Unfortunately, we were putting all our efforts in the wrong basket. When a loved one is not interested in getting better, don't waste so much emotional energy, time, effort, or finances to help them in this stage. It will do them and us no good. When we try to help them, and they don't want the help, it becomes *exhausting,* and eventually, the family feels they have nothing left to give. So, when their loved one is in recovery and would benefit from family support, the family is so mentally, emotionally, spiritually, and financially drained, they decide to play their *tough-love card*: You *got yourself into this mess. Now, get yourself out of it*! (Don't we know they would have done it by now if they were able to do it on their own?)

We need to change our approach on how to help someone in *active* addiction. It is important for family members to keep communication channels open by *avoiding* angry outbursts, yelling, and ultimatums that drive them *away and prevents them* from asking for help when they really need it. To keep our emotions in check and be supportive is not an easy feat to achieve. We need to seek counseling on ways to handle our anger and frustrations, so we can help our child or partner when the right moment happens. We need to show genuine concern by loving and accepting them. We do this by talking to them so we can understand why they need the drugs so much and letting them know we are there to help when they are *ready* to change. *Anger* and *condemnation* push them away, but *love* and *acceptance* draw them in. We can only achieve this by getting help for ourselves. We need spiritual guidance, along with instructions on how to set healthy boundaries. We need to develop skills to shift the focus onto everyone in the family and not just the one who has the addiction problem.

Jesus said, "Take the beam out of our own eye before trying to take the sliver out of another." It means we need to fix *ourselves* before we can be effective in helping others. We need *help*. It still never fails to amaze me that family members will spend thousands of dollars to get their child in treatment but refuse to spend one dime to help them. It seems like they would rather watch a re-run of a television program they didn't like in the first place—than to truly learn how to help someone who needs their help.

It is important *not* to give up on them but we do need to avoid spending money on treatment programs that do not work. Most of the time, they will *need medication(s)* to *treat* their *intense cravings* that chronic drug use has created. Once they are in treatment, be aware that relapses happen and realize that *change* is a *process*. It takes time and can take many attempts before fully quitting.

Remember, when they are in *recovery* and wanting *help,* this is *when* the family needs to *provide* it—*not* when they are *actively* using and refuse to go into treatment. But it is still important to keep the lines of communication open. *Enabling* is helping them *avoid* the *consequences* of their behaviors when they have *no interest* in changing. In recovery—*Right now,* they need our support, our approval, and encouragement while they are making tremendous efforts to get better. Change is difficult—*don't make it any harder.*

In over thirty years of treating patients in my Internal Medicine practice, I have never heard anyone tell their family members to stop taking their heart, blood pressure, or diabetic medications. I have been asked if there was a cheaper alternative, but never to stop treatment entirely. Yet, many people find it acceptable to do this with someone who has an addiction. The consequences of stopping treatment can put them at a significantly increased risk of dying from an overdose the very *first* time they take a street drug. *Death* provides *no* second chances.

The enabler (family members) who becomes the barrier to treatment does not recognize their part in their loved one's relapse or death. They just grieve the loss of their loved one and wonder, *How could I have done things differently?* I don't want anyone to face the loss of a loved one due to a drug overdose or suicide. They are both preventable conditions.

To *avoid* a tragedy, we need to adjust our thinking and improve the following situations that I frequently encounter in treating my patients such as: *Stop complaining, Gain more knowledge about addiction, Avoid thinking they are cured, Addictive pathways never go away, and Recovery is a process.*

Stop Complaining

People in early recovery do *not* handle *any kind* of stress or criticism very well. They have a heightened stress response system caused by the changes in their brain. We need to *avoid* complaining and listing of hardships they had caused. They can never change what happened in the past and already feel deeply ashamed and guilty over their previous behaviors. They don't need any reminders. Piling on the guilt can easily lead them back to taking drugs to numb these painful feelings. We need to avoid saying,

> *"I spent all my money trying to get them help."*

- o But did we spend any time with them when they needed it most during recovery?
- • We need to understand they need *encouragement* rather than condemnation.

Gain more knowledge about addiction

We need to learn all there is about addiction. There are so many myths and conjectures, but we need answers so we can make intelligent decisions. Read books written or attend meetings that are given by trained addiction specialists. We have to understand what our loved one is experiencing so we can be better equipped to offer helpful advice and direction. We have to understand the majority of people with an opioid addiction need medication to control their intense cravings and preoccupation to use drugs. Without medication, very few people will succeed or remain in recovery. It is easy to get a person off drugs, but the changes in the brain make it extremely difficult to remain off them.

They struggle handling any kind of stress and get frustrated easily. Everything is an effort for them, and just adding one little complaint can throw them back to taking drugs again. This is why, while they are in treatment and are doing better, we need to stop complaining and stop telling them they are trading one drug for another. We don't tell that to people taking hypertensive *medications or those taking antidepressants.* Some of these medications can cause withdrawal symptoms when a person discontinues taking them. We don't consider people with hypertension or depression to be an addict. Yet, if anyone takes Suboxone and stops their medication and develop withdrawal symptoms—they are considered an addict?

To diagnose anyone with an addiction they need to have certain behaviors that affect their life. The following are the eleven criteria used to diagnose a person with a substance use problem (addiction)

1. *Hazardous Use*: have used substance that are dangerous to themself or others such as:
   a. An overdose, driving under the influence or blacked out.
2. *Social or interpersonal problems* related to drug use.
   a. Using substance has caused relationship problems or conflict with others.
3. *Neglected major roles* due to drug/alcohol use.
   a. Fail to meet responsibilities at work, school, or home because of drug use
4. *Withdrawal* caused from stopping the use of the substance(s)
5. *Tolerance*—the need to take more drugs to get the same effect.
6. *Use drugs* with increasing amounts or for longer periods of time than they intended
7. *Unable to control drug* use or quit:
   a. Tried to cut back or quit entirely, but they haven't been successful.
8. *Much time spent* using: A lot of time spent using or searching for the substance.
9. Physical or psychological problems related to use:
   a. Substance use causes physical health problems, such as liver damage or lung cancer, or psychological issues, such as depression or anxiety.
10. Activities given up to use
    a. Skipped activities or stopped doing activities they previously enjoyed in order to use the substance.
11. Craving: They have experienced cravings to use more drugs.

To diagnose anyone with an addiction they need to have certain behaviors that affect their life. If they only have tolerance and withdrawal from a drug and not the associated behaviors of addiction, they are *not* considered to have substance use disorder (addiction).

Avoid thinking we are cured

When family members and those who have addiction start thinking they are cured or has outgrown this phase in their life makes them susceptible for a relapse. They mistakenly think going to friends and relative homes and be exposed to other people who use drugs—won't affect them anymore. Since they have been doing so well, the family and those in recovery become lax in not telling friends and relatives to lock up all their medications before they arrive to avoid a slip-up. Everyone needs to know there is no *cure* for addiction. People can have their addiction in *remission* and no longer affects them—*for now.*

Even if they are doing well, they still need to keep avoiding or limiting exposure to any potential triggers or situations that will put them at risk. Just like an alcoholic has to accept that taking only one drink has the potential for the disease to take hold of their life again. This is no different for anyone in recovery. Even if twenty years have passed, they are still at risk for a relapse.

If anyone in recovery undergoes surgery and is given a narcotic pain reliever, the narcotic will reactivate the addictive pathways in their brain, and in a very short period of time, they are involved in full-blown addictive behavior. In some people, it can only take one pill to lead them down that dark road again.

Addictive pathways never go away

People forget, but the addictive brain pathways never do. Every time the right moment or opportunity presents itself, this addictive pathway is activated. Whether they take drugs or not depends on the coping skills they employ. If they haven't been attending meetings or practicing daily relaxation/stress reduction activities, they are at high risk for using drugs again. When they start believing they are cured, they are unaware of the *subconscious* processes in place that will lead them *back* to drug use. This is not due to a weak character, but is due to how the drugs have taken over the reward pathways in their brain.

The natural reward pathway is activated to increase pleasure for activities that promote the survival of the species, such as eating, sexual activity, and nurturing of children. Addictive *drugs stimulate* the reward pathway *more intensely* than the natural rewards can and make drug use become more important than eating or caring for their children. Anyone who has an addiction, the brain reward system has been *switched* to making drug use *more* important than any natural reward can ever achieve.

- These addictive (unconscious) drug survival pathway*s never* become extinguished and remain *dormant* for a long time. Lurking, just waiting for the right moment to become activated by starting the intense cravings for drugs all over again.

Recovery is a process.

People in recovery will have relapses. We have to understand that a relapse is *not* a failure. People in recovery need to *learn* what *caused* the *relapse* and plan a way to avoid the problem again. It is important to keep moving forward even if a slip happened and not give up. The old saying, *there are many ways to skin a cat.* Holds true for an addiction treatment. Just like there are many ways to treat diabetes or hypertension.

- In addiction treatment, there are very few people who can achieve success in recovery by *only* attending counseling and support groups.

The majority of people will need medication to treat their addiction. Just like people who have diabetes. Some diabetic patients can go on a strict diet, exercise daily and lose a hundred or more pounds and be successful in keeping their blood sugars in the normal range—providing their pancreas can still produce adequate amounts of insulin. Remember, over time, a disease will permanently damage the organ it's affecting. The majority of people with diabetes are unable to succeed with diet and exercise and need additional help to bring their blood sugars down. Most diabetics will need medications and dietary support for the rest of their life.

> o This is no different for anyone who has an addiction. They may need lifetime use of medication, counseling, and support groups to control their disease.

We need to stop condemning and stigmatizing people who have an addiction. This keeps them from seeking help or believing they can get better. The number of people I encounter who *feel* people with addiction chose to take drugs and they aren't getting any help from me—fills me with sorrow. Yet, many people who smoke cigarettes and develop lung, esophagus, bladder, and other types of cancers related to smoking are *not* denied our concern and help. They chose to smoke cigarettes but somehow, it is acceptable to treat them with encouragement and support, but not someone who has a substance use disorder (addiction).

Treating patients in my addiction practice, I have found ninety-eight percent of them started with a pain medication that was prescribed to them by their physician, dentist, or nurse practitioner due to an injury they sustained or procedure performed. They didn't choose to take drugs to get high—it was prescribed to them because they had a painful event. They didn't know the narcotic would affect their brain differently than other people's brains. The very first time they took the drug, many of them felt more relaxed, less depressed, less lonely, and had more energy. Others described they felt more confident and could handle any situation. The pain pill did *more* than reduce the pain. It made them feel normal. They didn't choose to become an addict. Their brain was already hardwired either by genes or environment to respond differently. The drugs activated the reward pathway in their brain, giving them pleasure and a desire to take more and more drugs. This wasn't a *choice*. It was an unfortunate *side effect* of the *medication* that has had *lasting consequences* in their life. They are as much of a victim to the problem as family and society are in dealing with it. It is important for us to give them compassion and understanding to those who are less fortunate than ourselves. Just because we can take a pain pill and leave it has nothing to do with our character or strength of will. It is all due to how our brain responds to stress and is primed by circumstances in our life. We have all had times we needed help from another person. Let us help one another and not judge because that person with an addiction could easily have been any of us *if* our circumstances and brain were wired differently.

SURVIVAL TIPS

- Anyone with an addiction who says I will try harder next time will never get better.
  - Addiction damages the brain, and trying harder doesn't work. They need help. Someone to guide them in this path toward recovery. When we rely on our own efforts, we are doomed to fail. We need God's power to change our nature and our desires. We need to ask God to change us. When we surrender our will and give it to God, that means we allow God to do whatever God needs to do to change our hearts and nature. No longer can we look at circumstances the same. In the past, I would complain and worry, but now I have confidence that no matter what comes my way, God is in command of my life. I continue to thank God for changing me even when I don't see any outward change in my behaviors or my circumstances. God works from the inside out. Man only looks at the outside appearances.
- For recovery to be effective, most people need medication to control their compulsive cravings and urge to use drugs. It takes a long time for the brain to improve from the damage

drugs had caused. They struggle with compulsive, out-of-control cravings and urges to use drugs. Medications curb these cravings and give their brain a chance to improve.

- o We have no problem with putting a cast on a broken leg to allow it to mend right. They need medications to help support them while their brain is trying to recover from all the damage drug use had caused.
- Both family members and anyone with an addiction can have irrational thinking. The whole family would benefit from counseling. I remember saying *my son has the problem. Why do I have to go to counseling?* Not recognizing I was as much of the problem as my son was with the drugs.
- We all learn by conditioned responses. If rewarded for a certain behavior, this encourages repetition of this action. If punished for a certain behavior, this discourages repetition of this action. Encouragement is more effective than punishment. God's love is what draws me closer and a desire to change. God's compassion and mercy for my sins need to extend toward others. To break the bonds that chain a person to a problem can only be broken by love. My patients know I care for them. I am there to help—not to judge them. I still hold them accountable for their choices and view the slip as a learning experience on what needs to change to become successful.
- People in recovery have a heightened stress response and do not handle even minor stress very well.
  - o I have to remind myself not to complain but look at and praise actions that are improving. Asking God for wisdom helps me see and praise the positives. My mind wants to default toward the negative, but by focusing on the positives, I get to see the beauty of God's plan for their restoration.

TODAY IS THE ONLY DAY THAT COUNTS

People in the early stages of recovery have a heightened stress response system. When they start focusing on the past and all the mistakes they made or all the abuse they had sustained, it only increases their anxiety and inability to cope. This is why they do not do well with conventional psychotherapy that focuses on the past. By stirring up all the trauma and anguish they had suffered, only creates more anxiety and inability to cope. This increases their desire to take drugs in order to instantaneously ease their pain.

Anyone in recovery needs to learn how to deal with *today* and not dwell on things that can't be changed. A therapist can guide them to learn how to assess their problems and the choices they make in order to avoid making the same mistakes again. We need to use those experiences as a *study guide* to learn how to change our thoughts and actions. We were never meant to keep spinning our wheels by reliving our painful memories. This keeps us stuck in the mud with no hope of changing.

In order to get better, we need to realize—*No one can undo the past.* When we accept this truth, we can now focus on what can be changed in order to move forward and allow us to let go of what can't be changed. The *if only I had done this, or not done that* can plague us. We have to accept, the past can't be transformed into something different. We've only got this moment in time that we have a modicum of control. The *now moment* is what needs to be focused on. So, let us *get rid* of all the *excuses*, the blaming and determine what can be done *now*.

First, realize that we are not alone. At times we may feel this way—isolated, embarrassed, ashamed, afraid, lost, overwhelmed, and confused about what direction to take or what to do next. Both the family members and anyone who has an addiction need to reach out to others for help. Realize our very nature wants to hide what is not acceptable, but *revealing* the truth to others causes a *healing* to take place. It provides a space to breathe again, to think instead of reacting and get help.

I find confessing our sins to one another and praying for each other is a powerful way to break the bonds of excuses that tie us to our mistakes. When we confess, we are honest in our response and become free because God has forgiven us. But when we make excuses, we are finding someone else or circumstance to blame and not take responsibility for our actions. *Just like God asked Adam and Eve, have you eaten from the tree that I commanded you not to eat from?* Their responses were an excuse. We always have an excuse when we mess up. I wonder if they had admitted their mistake and asked for forgiveness, would we be living in a different world today?

Addiction is not a moral failing or a reflection of our parenting. It is an adaption that has occurred in the brain due to the chronic use of opioids, alcohol, or other addictive substances. The adaption process is the way the brain attempts to maintain balance in our body.

As a physician, it never ceases to intrigue me how the body works to maintain balance. This process is called homeostasis. Our body will produce substances that cause our blood to clot and other substances that will cause our body to bleed. The careful balance of these opposing systems keeps us from bleeding to death or dying from blood clots. Our body releases substances that cause our blood sugar to go up, and other substances released to cause our blood sugar to go down.

This need to regulate and *maintain balance* also occurs in our brain. If we take an addictive drug long enough, the brain will try to bring the changes back into a more normal state (in balance). With continued drug use, over time, they will no longer get the same pleasure, pain relief, or energy they had before. This triggers the need to take more drugs and ultimately stronger medications for them to get the same benefits they had before. The more drugs they take, the more brain pathways, receptors are altered, leading to structural changes in their brain caused by chronic drug use. Dopamine is a chemical when released gives us pleasure. Chronic stimulation of the reward pathway by addictive substances causes their brain to counterbalance the drugs effects by reducing the number of dopamine receptors and increases the production of *chemicals* to reduce the amount of pain relief, energy, and pleasure the drugs previously had created. Over time, these changes start the cycle of developing addiction pathways in the brain. Forty to sixty percent of people who develop addiction have inherited the tendency, but the *other* forty percent can develop the problem just by prolonged exposure and the ensuing chemical and structural changes that occur in the brain over time.

Let me repeat: *no one* is immune. Once the changes occur, it takes a long time (or may never fully return to normal) for the brain to recover from the processes that created the changes in the first place. The younger they start taking an addictive drug, the more *difficult* it is for them to recover due to incomplete brain development. The part of the brain that make decisions and weighs the consequences of an action doesn't fully develop until around the age of twenty-five. The impulsive part of the brain is in control and explains why teenagers act before they think of the consequences. They can get involved in some dangerous and scary situations. The impulsive part of the brain functions like a person driving 100 miles an hour in a school zone and has no brakes.

The changes that occur in the brain caused by addiction bypasses the cognitive (thinking part of the brain) and activate the impulsive part of the brain, making them react rather than respond to a situation. This impulsive pathway seen in people with substance use disorder (addiction) can be activated with very little provocation. I had a patient who was drug-free for eight years and was doing great. He traveled with his wife to see his grandparents. When he went to use the bathroom, his grandfather had left his pain pills out on the sink counter.

He said, "*I don't know what happened. I had swallowed all the pills in the bottle with one big gulp BEFORE I even realized what I had done.*"

Now, this is how an impulsive reaction happens.

The *younger* anyone starts taking drugs, the less development of the cognitive control pathways (thinking of consequences and making a decision) and increases the development of the impulsive pathways. Research shows that when a fourteen-year-old and a thirty-year-old have used drugs for the same length of time that it takes twice as long for the fourteen-year-old to recover from addiction because their brain had never fully developed. Incomplete connections to the cognitive areas of the brain may become permanent. It can make that person to always struggle with impulsive actions and explains why it takes so much *longer* for a *younger* person to recover from addiction than an older person. Now it is easy to see why it *doesn't* make *any sense* to withhold treatment to an adolescent with addiction.

The standard of care at this time: No one can take *any medication* to control their compulsive drive for drug use until they reach the age of sixteen with parental consent or eighteen without it. I have many patients in my practice that started taking drugs as early as eight years of age. The only treatment provided them was counseling, but without medication to control their overwhelming compulsive desire to take more drugs, those treatments alone are usually ineffective. If only the medical profession and families would realize children, teenagers, and young adults need *more* aggressive treatment than less. We would have a lot better outcomes.

There is evidence that suggests drinking alcohol, smoking cigarettes, or vaping nicotine in children and teenagers leads to an increased risk for addiction to other substances. This is why it is so important not to have teenagers experimenting with addictive drugs. That includes cigarettes, vaping nicotine, smoking marijuana, and alcohol. It is hard to imagine that some of my patients started smoking at six years of age and then used other drugs when they were eight. They are now forty or fifty years of age, still struggling with their opioid, meth, cocaine, alcohol, and other addictions.

It is *important* to note: *no* addictive substance is completely safe at any age, but in children, it can destroy their future and lead them down the wrong path.

So, people in recovery need to focus on today. We can't change what happened before, but *now* things can be different. Boundaries need to be established and be written down. If they are broken, consequences of what will happen also need to be recorded. It works best if the parent and child agree on the boundaries and consequences *before* they are implemented. It will also be helpful to have a list of *rewards* if they do the right thing. A *reward* earned should *never* be taken away because of other bad behaviors. A child will think, *why even try; they will take the reward away anyway.* People respond to positive reinforcement (reward) better than they do to *repetitive* negative reinforcement (punishment). If everything is a negative reinforcement it loses its punch when a serious event happens, and they ignore it like all the other petty rules. So, the list for positive rewards should be at least twice as long as the list for negative consequences for behaviors.

Think of using rewards for instilling behaviors in our child that will make life easier for us, such as rewarding them if they wash the dishes, clean their room and make their bed. Whereas select punishment in areas that will affect our child's character, such as lying, cheating, or bullying. The old motto—pick our battles is important to follow by making the negative consequences be for the most important features we want to instill in our child. Don't make everything important and punishable. If our child doesn't pick up their clothes—don't use punishment consequences. The child will respond better with positive rewards. For example, if they pick up their clothes, they will get this_____ reward. If they do it every day for a week, they get an even bigger reward. If they don't do it—they get no reward. Stop nagging about petty stuff, but do focus on what is important. Such as our child telling us the truth. Even if it something we don't want to hear, we still need to praise them for telling us the truth. Because they didn't lie about the situation, the consequences may be reduced (but not eliminated) for their wrong behavior. Pick what else is important for our child to learn how to survive in society.

Some examples are *no*—stealing, cheating, bullying, and any other features that are important to our beliefs/faith and have these wrong behaviors be associated with the negative consequences.

Today, it is easy for a child to get caught up in the wrong crowd. Teenagers are very susceptible to peer pressure and the desire to *fit in or be popular*. It is important when a child is young to instill in them self-confidence and acceptance. When they do something right, they need to be praised for their efforts. A young child wants to please their parents and responds to praise. But if all they get is criticism and comparison to their siblings—this natural desire is squashed. Even in a child who is clumsy and breaks things. It is so important to praise them for their effort to bring their plate to the sink and consider changing the dishes to unbreakable material. Look for ways to help a child succeed and praise their efforts.

When a child is older, it is important to know where our child is and what they are doing. It is best to confirm the information with the other kid's parents. Confirmation helps people stay honest. This is *not snooping—this is being protective*. This is how a parent shows their love for their child by actively monitoring and observing their child. They won't like it, but neither do they like wearing seat belts— but it may save their life and their future. Stick to your plan and don't give in. It might be helpful to meet with other parents and create a network of working with each other. Letting each other know if one of the kids appears to display suspicious behavior that might indicate drug use. I once had a parent tell me that my child was taking drugs. At the time, I did not believe her. In retrospect, I wish at the time I was more receptive to this information. I wish I hadn't felt so defensive, but even with my denial, it still put me on high alert to check things out and later discovered she was right. Better to be proactive than wish something was done. Guilt eats at a person, and it is very difficult to shake.

When we do what needs to be done today, the future will take care of itself. So, save yourself and your child a lot of pain and suffering.

Get involved
    Stay involved
        Don't be ashamed about checking things out
            It may mean the difference between life and death
                Their future is at stake
                WE CAN DO IT.

SURVIVAL TIPS

- We are not meant to live in the past that can't be altered.
  - Guilt can lead to condemnation. We all make mistakes. As a Christian, confessing our sins free us from spiritual condemnation, but we are still responsible for the consequences of our actions. God promised Moses to go and take the Promised Land, but he listened to the unbeliever's fears and not to God's promise. Then God had Joshua instead of Moses lead His people to the land of milk and honey. The choices we make today affect what opportunities we will have tomorrow.
- Today is the only day we can change.
  - Learn to appreciate today. We can never go back. Gratitude and thankfulness can break any chain when we *praise God*.
- The younger anyone starts using drugs, the longer it takes to recover from them.
  - Our precious children need to be protected. By our diligence in monitoring and guiding our children, we need to know where our kids are and whom they are with. This is showing love in action. Ask God for wisdom and temper that wisdom with love. We need to praise our children, let them know they are special. *Never forget our words have power.* Pray for our children—not just to keep them safe, but pray for the qualities we want in their nature. The prayers for our child can be—*give my child a loving and teachable heart, to love God, to care for*

others, and a willingness to help. Whatever God lays on our heart—that is what we need to pray for.

○ When I first became pregnant, one of my patients came into the office and was overwrought with anxiety and stress caused by her son's destructive and cruel behavior, and he was ruining their lives. Nothing they did seemed to help him. In a moment of overwhelming distress, she wished that her son were never born. I remember praying to God that night for me to never have a child like that. The next morning I started with intense abdominal cramping and had lost the baby. Before I even tried to have another child, I prayed to God what traits I wanted in them. I wanted a tender, loving, kind, teachable heart and would become a person after God's own heart. It's never is too early to start praying for our kids.

• We need to create and enforce boundaries by making positive rewards at least twice as many as negative consequences for behaviors. Write them down, but let them know extenuating circumstances can modify the punishments and can be more or less depending on the situation.

○ I remember my kids were verbally fighting and yelling at each other. One of my sons went over to the paper hanging on the wall to see what his punishment would be for hitting his brother. Hmm, to run ten laps around our large backyard. He looked at his brother, then at the list, back at his brother, then the list. Rushing over to where his brother sat, he smacked him hard and headed toward the back door to start running when I called out—it's twenty for premeditated hitting.

SURVIVAL TIP # 5

RECOVERY IS MORE THAN STOPPING DRUG USE

Does treatment really work? If anyone had asked me that question ten years ago, the answer would be for only a small number of people. The reason for such dismal results was due to faulty beliefs and treatment goals. The conviction, addiction was all about taking drugs, and treatment was all about stopping drug use. Our deluded thinking led us into believing: If they could get the drugs out of their system, they would do fine and move on in their life. In the past, this was why detoxification units were so commonly used. Detox treatment was not cheap and insurance companies did *not* pay for them. Families would spend their life savings, retirement funds, and children's education funds to pay for treatments and even go into debt trying to help their child get off drugs.

They believed that once they got the drugs out of their loved one's system, they would be back to normal. Unfortunately, very few remained off drugs, and in a very short while, they kept returning to drug use. Medical care and families treated addiction like the common cold. Once the virus was out of their child's system, they would be back to their old selves again. Medical professionals, treatment facilities, and families all bought into this dream. Yet, nobody ever questioned how effective is this treatment? But families were desperate, and any glimmer of hope was worth the hardship.

Research shows treatment requires more than a short course of abstinence from drug use. Major changes in the brain have occurred due to chronic use of drugs. These changes did not come on overnight, and they certainly won't be gone quickly. Some people may never fully recover from these alterations. Just like people who have diabetes. Some diabetics (very few) can return to normal blood sugar control by losing a hundred or more pounds with diet, exercise, or surgery. With all those lifestyle changes, their blood sugars will go down as long as they continue exercising and watching their diet. But, once they stop exercising and dieting, their weight goes up along with their blood sugars. They were never cured of the disease. It was in remission as long as they continued to practice healthy living habits. Some people lost weight but still needed medications to control their blood sugar. Over time, prolonged high blood sugars damaged their pancreas to the point it could no longer make enough insulin to meet their bodies' needs. Just like some people with addiction may need lifetime medication to treat their disease. The chronic use of drugs damaged their brain to the point they can no longer control their disease without medication.

Practitioners, family, friends, and anyone who has a substance use disorder (addiction) needs to rethink their ideas about how long they should be on medication to treat their problem. Studies show that the longer they are in treatment, the better the outcome for the patient. Some of the changes in the brain caused by the chronic use of the drugs can take a long time to reset to a *new* normal. This *new* normal may never return the brain back to what it was *before* the onset of the addictive process.

Think of it this way, many athletes abuse their bodies by having multiple recurrent injuries, and over time, their bodies will never function like they did before all the injuries occurred. So, why would anyone think, when their brain has been bombarded with multiple insults by the drugs they used, expect their brain to function like it did before they ever took drugs?

Because of these chronic, long-lasting changes in the brain, I find it heartbreaking to hear a parent ask before I can even discuss the various treatment options,

"How long does my child have to stay in treatment?

My response is, *how long are you a mother/father to your child?"*

Addiction treatment is *not* a one-time fix. Too many changes and damage have occurred. The addictive thinking pathways will *never* go away. But that doesn't mean the addictive thinking can't be controlled or managed by forming new pathways that can counter the effects of the addictive ones.

Every person is unique, and their treatment has to be tailored to their individual needs and problems. Addiction is a journey of self-discovery, and along the way, their requirements change. After several years in recovery, many no longer have any cravings or desire to use drugs again. But they can easily fall into the trap of thinking they are cured and start hanging around the wrong people or places. This thinking, *I am cured* has led many people back to addictive behavior even after twenty years in recovery. A pastor in a nearby community was helping others that had an addiction problem. He helped a lot of people because of his personal experience in dealing with this problem. He did fine for many years until he had surgery and was prescribed a narcotic pain medication. The narcotic triggered an intense desire to use more drugs. Luckily, he recognized the addictive thoughts and cravings that could drive him back into active addictive behaviors and sought treatment before it destroyed all his work in helping other people.

Everyone has the potential to relapse no matter how long they have been in recovery. That addictive pathway is like a hidden bomb ready to detonate when:

- Anyone with a previous addiction to opioids takes a narcotic pain pill prescribed to them.
- When they experience any painful or stressful events.
- Once primed by stressful or painful events if they are around people actively using drugs or can get them some drugs can trigger a relapse.
- The impulsive need to immediately ease the intense anxiety and emotional pain they are experiencing—results in destruction of all the hard work they had accomplished.

A painful lesson learned. Anyone with an addiction (substance use disorder) has to be on high alert at *all times,* to monitor their *emotional* states and those they are around to avoid a relapse.

In the past, there was only one way to treat a person with addiction—abstinence. They were told to attend Alcoholic Anonymous (AA), Narcotic Anonymous (NA), or Celebrate Recovery (CR) meetings. A few got better, but the majority did not. Medical treatment at that time consisted of behavior modification therapy modalities such as:

- Cognitive Behavior Therapy (CBT)
- Dialectic Behavior Therapy (DBT)
- Motivational Enhancement Therapy (MET)
- Rational Emotive Behavior Therapy (REBT)

These therapy modalities were done trying to help them abstain from drug use, but they did not address their overwhelming compulsive drive for more drugs. Unfortunately, using these treatments alone was met with limited success. Think about it. How successful are we with treating anyone with hypertension or diabetes with just diet and exercise? Even if they went to see a dietician, weight watchers and joined a gym. A lot of the time, their success was never enough to avoid the use of medications to treat their condition. So, why would that be any different for those who have the disease of a substance use disorder (addiction)?

Why do all these support treatments have such limited success for the majority of people? Many times, those treatments do not consider the underlying problem and only focus on the superficial symptom of drug use. As a physician, I treated a lot of diabetic patients. If I only looked at the symptom of elevated blood sugar and tried to control it with all kinds of fad diets and failed to use all the other potential options needed for treatment, I would be facing a malpractice suit. I would miss preventing all the future complications they could develop caused by diabetes, such as:

- A brain that does not regulate hunger and satiety (the sensation of feeling full after a person eats).

- An abnormal incretin hormone that helps blood sugar control and improves satiety.
- Insulin-resistant fat and muscle cells causing elevated fatty acids and triglycerides that escalate atherosclerosis that can cause heart attacks, strokes, and poor circulation in the legs, and increases the risk for amputations.
- Micro-vascular damage in the eyes and kidneys that can lead to blindness and kidney failure.
- Damaged pancreas with a reduced beta-cell function that makes insulin.

If I failed to treat or not try to prevent any of the above complications in my patients, I would be sued. Yet, this is what many physicians have been doing to those who have the disease of addiction. They have only focused on one aspect of the disease (drug use) and ignored the other problems associated with the disease.

This crazy thinking that everything is back to normal is causing a lot of people to stop treatment way too early and end up relapsing. The problem with relapse, people die from an overdose and for those who survive find it difficult to return to treatment and thinks, *it didn't work last time, why should it work now*? Yet, it was working. They just needed to stay in treatment and not stop. The old saying, *if it ain't broke, don't try to fix it,* needs to be applied to treating addiction. If anyone is doing well, don't change it. When I first started practicing medicine, I had a patient with hypertension (HTN). Their blood pressure was fine, but I thought a newer medication would be a better option with fewer side effects. I changed their medication despite the fact they were tolerating it with no problems. What a mess. I quickly learned from that experience to never change an effective treatment unless the patient requests it.

What the treating physician and family don't realize that stopping treatment for a person with addiction puts them at incredibly high risk for overdosing and dying. The risk for dying is *higher* in those who have not been taking drugs for a while. Their body no longer has the same tolerance to the amount of opioids they used to take. When they take the same dose they used before—they stop breathing. When anyone consumes an opioid chronically, his or her body altered its metabolism and eliminated the drug from his or her system faster. It also changed how their brain would respond to the drug. These changes are what cause tolerance. When an individual has been off drugs for a while, this tolerance is lost. When they resume drug use, what was before a 'safe' dose to take is now a lethal one.

When anyone overdoses from an opioid and stops breathing, they will die unless:

- Someone does CPR.
- Narcan is administered to reverse the effects of the opioid.
- An ambulance is called while doing CPR, or Narcan has been given.

If the ambulance arrives late, no one gives them Narcan or does CPR, that person will die or develop severe permanent brain damage.

Short-term treatment for an addiction rarely succeeds. Yet, some medical care providers still promote, and family members blindly follow this advice. Unfortunately, this belief still persists and has caused too many people to relapse and die.

Let me repeat: Short courses of treatment *do not* work. Families have spent all their savings and retirement funds for detoxification treatment programs to get the drugs out of their loved one's system but found out the hard way—very few people could remain off drugs.

When treatment providers only focused on *abstinence* treatment without using any medication, most of the time, they *relapsed*. Unfortunately, many treatment providers and family members called them treatment failures. They were considered incurable and hopeless addicts who would rather get high than get help. This attitude only makes it harder for them to try and get better. Maybe, the practitioners should have considered the treatments they provided were inadequate and looked for other options. A lot of people who have an addiction have untreated underlying mental health and environmental conditions that can affect their recovery. Before a practitioner gives up on a patient, they need to explore *why* their treatment is not working.

- Do they have an underlying mental illness?
- Is their living environment, work environment conducive to recovery?
- Do they have adequate family and other support systems in place to help them in their recovery?
- The financial resources needed for medication and getting medical care, etcetera.

Recovery is more than stopping drug use. To be successful in treating their substance use disorder (addiction), we have to address the myriad complexities of the disease. There are *no* simple answers. Abstinence can be achieved easily. The problem is *sustaining* the abstinence and avoiding relapses. The most difficult time for any-one in recovery is the first two to three years in treatment. Family, treatment providers, and even the patient themselves have such high expectations. Yet, it is so difficult to achieve because:

- The low motivational state caused by the changes that have occurred in the brain reward system.
- The powerful stress hormones being released that cause heightened anxiousness, irritability, low frustration toler-ance, and angry outbursts.
- These changes can persist for a very long time.

Despite all the evidence, I am still stunned that family members keep wanting their child to get off the medication(s) that are help-ing them *before* any of the structural and hormonal changes in the brain and body have improved. I wish they could see how they are preparing their loved one to fail. I wonder why anyone would want to stop something that is working? Especially when they were so lost and miserable with no hope for improvement. Most of the time, a person with addiction knows they need the medication to get better. They had tried so many times on their own to quit and never could, *until now.* Their relationships with their children, spouse (partner) is improving. They have a job and are getting out of debt. Some are returning to school to train for a better job. Yet, despite all these improvements, they keep getting almost daily complaints from family members, wanting them to get off their medication. The family is acting like they are still taking drugs. Unfortunately, the family doesn't see Buprenorphine (Suboxone) as a medication to treat a disease and feels they are just trading one drug for another.

If they were trading one drug for the other, wouldn't they have the same *addictive* behaviors? Are they secretly spending money to pay for more drugs? Do they have relationship issues related to drug use, such as lying, no longer working, and stealing in order to buy more drugs? Do they have this overwhelming compulsive drive to take more and more drugs? If anyone is engaging in these behaviors while on treatment with Buprenorphine, then yes—they are trading one addiction for another. *But,* if they are working, stable in their family relationships, and has goals for their life, then Buprenorphine is a *medical treatment* for a well-managed *disease.*

To be diagnosed with a substance use disorder (addiction), they have to have three or more of the eleven criteria used to diagnose addiction. The criteria are based on two major behaviors, such *as a compulsive drive to take more and more drugs* and *negative consequences* from drug use. In essence, if it's affecting their life—they have an addiction problem. If they only have tolerance and withdrawal to the drug and have no other criteria, they do *not* have the diagnosis of addiction. There are many drugs that create tolerance and withdrawal symptoms, such as some blood pressure medications and antidepressants. Yet, we don't consider a person who takes them to be an addict.

For those in treatment with buprenorphine (Suboxone), as long as they don't have the associated *behaviors* to diagnose addiction, then their disease is considered in remission while on treatment. Just like anyone with hypertension whose blood pressure is under control. The negative effects of their disease are in remission as long as they *continue* taking their medications. Isn't that what treatment is all about for any disease? To reduce the negative effects the disease has on the body.

Functional MRI (fMRI) images show Medication-Assisted Treatment (MAT) improves brain function. FMRI measures blood flow to different parts of the brain. All cells in the body need fuel (brain cells use glucose) for energy, and when a part of the brain is activated (working), it causes an increase in blood flow to bring more nutrients to the area and lights up on the scan. Just like a marathon runner has increased blood flow to their muscles to meet the needs of the tissues that are doing the most work. The fMRI can tell what areas of the brain are activated and what parts are not. Functional MRI flow study was done to *compare* images of the brain in those:

- Who have never taken any addictive drugs.
- Who is actively using drugs.
- Who has been off drugs for different periods of time.
- Who is taking medication-assisted treatment (MAT) that consisted of either Buprenorphine or Methadone.

When they compared the images to those who never took any drugs, they found gradual improvement in blood flow the *longer* an individual was off drugs and in those who used MAT. The longer people were in treatment, the better the scans became. Those who continued using drugs showed worsening brain function.

Addiction is truly more than just taking drugs. It involves all the progressive changes, both structural and functional, to brain regions that involve:

- Reward and motivation
- Emotion regulation
- Inhibitory control pathways (the part that weighs the consequences and stops the action from happening)

All these pathways have been altered in the brain. So, it is understandable that treatment requires more than just stopping drug use.

It is important to realize there are reasons why anyone became addicted to drugs in the first place. They can inherit a susceptibility to drugs, but there are other factors that contribute to this process that we call addiction (substance use disorder). There are people who inherited the same risk for addiction but do not have the problem. It is now recognized that the genetic vulnerability *coupled* with how well they react to *stress* is one of the reasons why they started using drugs. Also, stress is a *big* factor for the cause of any future relapse(s).

Some people have a more intense reaction to stress than others. This can be genetically or environmentally induced. Children exposed to traumatic events change how they will respond to future events. Traumatic events that happen in *childhood* can cause *future* mental and physical problems during adulthood. These traumatic events that occur in childhood are called, Adverse Childhood Experiences (ACEs). The higher the ACEs, the more mental and physical problems they will develop as an adult. Some common Adverse Childhood Experiences (ACEs) faced by children are:

- Emotional or physical neglect
- Verbal abuse in the form of humiliation, fear of injury, or degrading them as a person
- Sexual abuse
- Living with a mentally ill or addicted family member
- Witnessing one's mother being abused

And other forms of traumatic separation, such as:

- Loss of a loved one
- Loss of a parent due to death or divorce
- Having a parent or loved one imprisoned.

Adverse Childhood Experiences affects an individual's developing brain and immune system, predisposing them to depression, cancer, heart problems, diabetes, or other chronic diseases *decades* later. Long *after* the traumatic events happened.

There is a questionnaire that can assess the severity of the ACEs a person has experienced to determine the likelihood they might develop future problems. Those who have a high ACEs score experience increased emotional distress, relationship problems, work performance problems, financial issues, and difficulty controlling anger. People with high ACEs scores, especially those involving physical or sexual abuse, have an increased incidence of developing depression. It has been shown that women with high ACEs scores experience more feelings of hopelessness and thoughts of suicide. Along with increased emotional distress, there is an increased incidence of nicotine, alcohol, and drug use. The higher the number of adverse events anyone experiences, the greater chance they have of developing addiction and suicide.

The adverse events people experienced, compounded with abusive relationships, have stunted their ability to develop adequate coping skills needed to handle overwhelming stress. Most of them never had good role models to learn effective coping skills from or been shown any attention that they are important. In the recovery process, it is necessary for them to learn how to love themselves in order to develop good self-esteem. Just getting off drugs doesn't prepare anyone how to live a healthy lifestyle, deal with disappointments, stress, relationship issues, and guilt that somehow they deserved their abuse or neglect.

If only I were a better kid, my parents could have loved me. If I gain all this weight, men wouldn't find me so attractive and feel compelled to molest me—as if it were her fault for their behavior. It is so important for people to learn how to *change* their *perspective* about themselves and their circumstances.

In order to see our self differently takes time. We need positive people to encourage us as part of our support group. Someone who shows genuine caring and encouragement can help them make changes in their life. As they make changes, they need the confidence of having someone they can count on—something they never had before. With consistent caring, they get the courage to move past the abuse and stop believing the lies told to them. We all have the ability to make a big difference in another person's life—make it a positive one.

SURVIVAL TIPS

- Recovery involves more than stopping drug use.
  - By understanding the struggles they undergo in recovery allows us a better chance to encourage them. Anyone in early recovery rarely hears a kind word. They hear a lot of, don't do this, or that, or complaints of past behaviors.
    - They are shocked when I say, *you made a mistake— we all do—let's learn from it. Where could we have changed the outcome?*
    - Berating them doesn't change what happened—it only makes them feel worse and want to use drugs to avoid these painful emotions.
    - Kindness makes a person want to improve, but releasing our anger and frustrations drive them away.
- Abstinence can be achieved easily. The problem is *sustaining* abstinence and avoiding relapses.
  - Get them into treatment. Many need medication to curb compulsive cravings.
  - No one will get better if other people in the house are using drugs. I had a patient living with her grandmother and was doing great in her recovery for a year. Her grandmother had a grandson move in the house since he had nowhere to stay. He was actively using drugs, and my patient relapsed. She continued to relapse until she moved out of that environment.
  - Who we are around has a powerful effect on all of us. I have to spend time talking to God throughout the day to keep my heart and mind focused on how God sees people. It is easy to get frustrated when they keep making the same poor choices, but God reminds me—He is the one who changes hearts and lives—not me.

- Addiction causes progressive pathway changes in the brain that involves: reward and motivation, emotion regulation, and inhibitory control.
  - All these alterations do not go away, but *new* pathways can be formed to counter the effects. This is part of the recovery process to learn how to combat the urges, control the emotional responses and gain the ability to avoid drug use.
- The longer they stay in treatment, the better the outcome.
  - There is a lot to learn and change. Just avoiding the wrong people and places can be challenging. How to analyze where they could have avoided a slip takes time and practice. Daily meditation to reduce their anxiety, stress, and emotional reactions can help them avoid taking a drug to calm down.
  - Changing our thoughts and the words we say about our circumstances and ourselves. So, when I replace my thoughts with what God says in the Bible about my circumstances, it renews my mind and changes my life. When I *think differently*, I *act differently* and make better choices.
  - Many people may need a lifetime of medication to treat their disease of addiction. God provides many ways to combat a problem and makes provisions for our needs. God provides resources for us to use. When the prophet Isaiah told Hezekiah he was going to die. Hezekiah prayed, and God told Isaiah to turn around and tell him, *take a lump of figs,* and they laid it *on the* boil, and he recovered. Just like God provided medications to treat illnesses in the past—He continues to provide them today.
  - God provides medications to treat people, and addiction is no different. Who are we to question His methods?

SURVIVAL TIP # 6:

ADDICTION IS MORE THAN TAKING DRUGS

Stopping drug use is easy compared to staying off drugs. Just getting off drugs doesn't cure the intense, compulsive desire to use them again. In order to comprehend the struggles they are experiencing, we need to understand all the changes that have occurred in their brain due to repeated drug exposure. When anyone first started taking drugs for pain or for recreation, they initially had control over their drug use. In susceptible individuals, when they take a narcotic pain pill regularly for a week—their brain starts to adapt and change how it responds to the narcotic pain medication. The development of tolerance is part of the process of neuro-adaption. They are unaware a change has happened in their brain until it is too late. A switch has occurred, and they no longer have the ability to stop using drugs. Their brain is like a computer infected with a virus. It no longer functions properly, and it has developed a *mind* of its own.

These changes come about as a result of repeated exposure to an addictive drug that constantly stimulates the *natural* reward pathway in the brain. This pathway is essential for survival and is activated when we eat, have sexual relations, and when we care for our children. If we experience no pleasure in doing activities that are necessary for our survival, we would no longer have any progeny to survive into the next generation.

Illicit drugs activate the brain's reward system in a stronger manner than the natural survival reward system does. For example, if eating food, having sexual relationships, and child nurturing stimulates the reward system 100 times more than scrubbing the floors, then taking alcohol or opioids stimulate the brain's survival reward system 150 to 300 times, and Methamphetamines stimulate the reward system up to 1,000 times more. Now we know why taking addictive drugs becomes more important than eating, having sex, or caring for their children. Their *reward pathway* has been *hijacked* by drug use, and the *normal* survival activities *no longer* have the same value as they had before.

Changes in the reward system cause the brain to *think* drug use is *essential* for *survival*. Because the brain 'thinks' they will die without the drugs, it has altered their brain pathways (neuro-adaption) to make sure they *never stop* using them. These pathway modifications make drug use change from a voluntary decision to an involuntary compulsion—no matter what—I can't survive without them drive. These changes make an individual to no longer have control over drug use. *Remember*, the brain thinks drugs are necessary to survive. This loss of control makes it impossible to stop taking just one pain pill or one drink.

In my group meetings, many of the participants would tell me when they finally got enough drugs to last for three days, they still ended up taking them all in one day. What they planned to do—never happened. Their brain had a different agenda. Every day became a repeat of the day before, constantly scouring for drugs with no end in sight.

Compulsive thoughts of taking drugs relentlessly bombard their mind until that was all they could think about. Acquiring more drugs or taking more drugs to the exclusion of everything else that was previously important, such as family, children, jobs, or even their self-respect, was lost. The addictive brain pathways will *never* lose their focus that drug use is *necessary for survival*. It doesn't matter how much harm it causes them. Acquiring and taking drugs will always have the *highest* priority over *everything* else in their life. This is not their choice. It doesn't matter if they were attacked trying to get drugs, raped, or even left for dead. Upon awakening, they will return back to the same place where they got the drugs before.

The repeated mistakes and encounters with the law are extremely frustrating to those who have never been addicted to drugs. They fail to understand—addicted people have *no control* over their behaviors. Now, it makes perfect sense why they *never* learn from:

- Their mistakes
- The injuries occurred while procuring drugs
- Their legal problems drug use has caused
- Why they keep making the same mistakes over and over again

Anyone else would have learned by now, and this is the perfect argument for why they continue. Their brain *won't* let them *stop.* Their brain sees *drugs* as the *only means to survive—even if it kills them.*

The body always tries to keep its systems in balance. This process is called homeostasis. If our body temperature drops, we shiver to increase muscle activity and generate more heat. If our body temperature goes up, we sweat to cool us down. Our body is constantly regulating our hormones and systems to keep it in balance.

When the reward pathway is being constantly stimulated, the body releases chemicals to offset the pleasure the drugs are producing. The more drugs they take, the *more chemicals* are released to *offset* its effects, leading them to develop an elevated brain reward system. Elevated brain reward means it takes a whole lot more drugs to give them any pleasure. Eventually, there comes a point they *no* longer feel any pleasure from taking drugs and only continues drug use to keep from experiencing the horrible withdrawal symptoms. Once people experience opioid withdrawal, they will do anything to keep from going through it again. The hot and cold chills, the shakes, the heart racing, the sweats, the intense abdominal cramping, nausea, diarrhea, and every muscle and bone in their body hurts. This is coupled with the mental anguish of intense anxiety and fear they are about to die. Some wish they were already dead to keep the pain away. Everyone with an opioid addiction knows what to expect if they can't get any drug(s). They will do *anything* to keep withdrawal from happening. The pleasure from drug use is gone, and there is only *misery* to be kept at bay.

Those who have an open mind and heart can see those in active addiction are suffering. They have tried multiple times to stop but couldn't because the changes in their brain won't let them. They are trapped. They have no way out of this endless cycle of acquiring and taking drugs. All the while, they are losing friends, family, jobs, and hope. Suicide is common among people who are addicted to drugs. Many people call it a drug overdose, but many of them are *successful* suicide attempts. They are exhausted from dealing with the repeated physical and mental withdrawal, which *intensifies* with every attempt to stop using drugs. Over time, exhausted with the whole process of getting drugs, many of them give up and want to end the torture their life has become. They want to end the misery of anxiety and fear that drives them to continue using drugs—long after the *drugs no longer* provide any *pleasure.*

In recovery, the reward system set point has been so altered that *no natural reward* can stimulate it. Everything is an *effort* because they feel no pleasure doing anything. Their brain is flooded with chemicals that increase their stress and anxiety levels, making them anxious, nervous, and irritable. Any criticism can lead to an angry outburst and a compulsive desire to take drugs. These changes in the brain reward system can last for years. Making it important for them to stay in recovery for more than four years and allow time for the brain to reset the reward pathway to a more normal setting.

When they have no control over their compulsive drive to take drugs, to be involved in support groups such as Celebrate Recovery, AA or NA are usually ineffective. Even those involved in behavior modification programs such as Cognitive Behavior Therapy (CBT), Rational Emotive Behavior Therapy (REBT), or Dialectic Behavior Therapy (DBT) still struggle without medication to curb this over-whelming compulsive drive to take drugs.

When I first started treating patients with medications to con-trol their obsessive need for drugs, I had difficulty finding a therapist willing to teach them how to develop coping skills to manage their anxiety. Most of the therapists no longer treated people with addiction because they found it to be ineffective. They always canceled their appointments or never returned for follow-up. Once I convinced them to try treating my patients who were on medication(s) to control their compulsive drive, they were surprised at how effective their therapies became and made such a difference in a person's life. The therapists discovered if anyone in early recovery was not on a medication to block their compulsive need for drugs, their therapy was ineffective.

Let me repeat: If the addicted person is not being treated with a *medication* to help curb/block this compulsive drive for drugs, they will relapse. This is no different with people who have hypertension, and a low sodium diet is no longer controlling their blood pressure, or a diabetic whose blood sugars are running high despite diet and exercise. *They all need medications to get their disease under control.* I wonder why this is such a difficult concept to grasp for family, treatment providers, and those who have a substance use disorder (addiction). We have no difficulty understanding that medications are needed to treat other diseases—if we want to avoid the complications from the disease. People who have a substance use disorder need medication (or several depending on the severity) to function properly to control their disease.

For family, friends, social workers, and treatment providers who recognize anyone with a substance use disorder has a disease and needs treatment. I wonder why they are all trying to get them off the very medication that is helping them? The treatment provider tries to wean them off their medication, and family members keep pushing them to stop taking their medication. This pressure by family and treatment providers creates turmoil in anyone receiving treatment. Instead of helping them, they are hindering their recovery. The family starts talking about how much money it costs for treatment, how much time they are wasting going to recovery support meetings, and how it takes them away from spending time with their family (mainly chauffeuring their kids from sports practices, music, or dance lessons). The constant complaining from family and friends piles on more and more guilt until they make a very *bad* decision and stops taking their medication to avoid all the nagging and fighting.

No surprise here what happens next. They relapse and will continue to relapse if they haven't developed good coping skills to deal with stress or had enough time off the drugs for their brain to heal sufficiently and allow them to make better choices.

In the thirty years of being an Internal Medicine physician, I have never heard family members tell their relatives who have hypertension, diabetes, or heart problems to stop their medications because they are doing better. The reason why they are doing better is because *their medication is working.* This is no different for people who are on medications for their disease of addiction. There is an old saying—*if it ain't broke—don't fix it.* If treatment is successful and the person is now steadily employed, relationships with family and friends are being restored, some are returning to school to get a better job, and they are happy. Why would anyone suggest they stop treatment and run the risk of returning to addictive behaviors and potentially dying from a drug overdose? The only person that should decide *to stop the medication is the person taking it.* It's their life on the line. If they want to get off treatment, I always suggest doing a slow taper and adjust their taper if any of their cravings return. It is important to give it time—about three to four months between each dose adjustment to allow them a chance to experience some painful and difficult situations to make sure they are stable before lowering their dose again. This gives them the opportunity to test their coping skills to determine if they would struggle or be successful. As a treatment provider, I would adjust their dose back up or down depending on how they did. If they start having any cravings, using dreams or any desire to return to drug use, I will increase the medication to their last previous dose where they had no symptoms of cravings. Every person is different, and it is important to tailor the treatment for each individual. Not everyone does well on the same blood pressure medications. As a physician, I need to find the right combo that works best for that person. Usually, most people do well with a combination of medication and several types of behavior modification treatments such as CBT, REBT, DBT, and support groups such as AA/NA Smart Recovery, Celebrate Recovery, and other programs geared to help support the person in the recovery process. There are some people who don't need counseling or support groups. They have a job they love, stable home environment and low stress in their life. As long as they remain stable in their recovery—I am Okay with it. The goal for treatment is geared the same way we treat other diseases. To make those with a disease have as near a normal life as possible—addiction is no exception.

People have to understand—there is *no* cure for Addiction. A disease can be in remission, but the addictive pathways and the learned behaviors will always be present, just waiting to be reactivated. People in recovery from opioid addiction need to avoid narcotic pain pills even after twenty years of abstinence. Their disease has the potential to reactivate quickly. *They can never forget that.* They can never go back to how they once were before they became addicted. An example: A person hasn't ridden a bike for over twenty years. At first, they are a bit wobbly when they start pedaling, but in a short while, they are riding like they never stopped. This is a learned response that our body has kept stored in our brain. Even if we are not conscious of its presence, when the situation is right, the memories will resurface.

Addiction is called the disease of *relapse*. The reasons for relapses are multiple and different for everyone. What we do know, people who have a good support system with their family and are engaged in some type of support program or behavioral modification program do better than those who have no support systems in place. The home environment is critical for anyone in recovery. It becomes almost impossible for an alcoholic in recovery to abstain from alcohol if everyone in the house drinks. The same is true for other causes of addiction. No one with a substance use disorder (addiction) should live in the same place if anyone in the house is using drugs. I have patients doing great in their recovery for several years until their boyfriend or girlfriend gets released from jail. They start using drugs again. Whenever I see anyone relapse after years of recovery, the first thing I ask, *is anyone using drugs in their home?*

For them to become successful in recovery, they need help in their journey toward wellness. In the next chapters, I will be discussing critical pieces of the puzzle to help them become overcomers rather than victims of this disease.

SURVIVAL TIPS

- Getting off drugs is easy compared to staying off drugs.
  - Even a Christian can struggle with addiction. Addiction's processes, wants and needs are in direct opposition to God's desire for their life. God wants to set us free. Addiction wants a person to become a slave to drug use. We have to remember as a Christian, God's nature lives inside of us and will battle our fleshly needs—if we allow God's Holy Spirit to change us. When I give my problems to God and ask Him to change me—it permits God the freedom to work within me. God gives us free will, and we have to ask and surrender to his plan and not ours.
  - Surrendering my problem(s) to God to bring the right people, circumstances and do whatever is needed to bring about a change. This is a very scary moment—do whatever needs to be done to become all that God has in store for me. I prayed that to God and He revealed to me the ugliness of my sins and how it affected everyone around me. The mental torment and anguish that was inside me became unbearable. I cried out to God to either *change me* or *take me home*. I couldn't take it anymore. From this experience I learned a valuable lesson to never give God an ultimatum. That night I had such intense abdominal pain that I couldn't even stand and crawled an inch at a time to the next room and weakly called out for help. Somehow my sister heard me and brought me to the hospital. During all this pain, I could hear voices—so many voices that I could not distinguish any individual words, but I understood the message of earnest pleading as a part of me hovered

74

above looking at me writhing in pain. Somehow, I was on the operating table, and they put an IV in my arm, and I remember saying, *let your will be done* just before I lost consciousness. I had finally *fully* surrendered my life to God. All those voices were the angels pleading to God for my life. God had to employ extreme measures to change my heart of stone to one of flesh. I had built a fortress to keep other people out from hurting me—but the fortress I had created kept me locked inside. God had to destroy that protective shield and expose all my pain in order for me to become healed. Miracles happen in a snap, but emotional healing takes time.

- Most addicted people need medications to curb their compulsive drive for drugs, or they will relapse. Medications are needed to help with this problem. I have people tell me, as a Christian, I shouldn't need to take something. Didn't God create the resources to make the medications? We have no problem wearing glasses, hearing aids, or clothing. Why should medications be any different?
  - Taking Buprenorphine (Suboxone) is *not* trading one addiction for another. It works by curbing the compulsive drive to take more drugs and has been shown to improve brain function.
- Family members should avoid complaining about how long their loved one needs to remain in treatment. People in early recovery do not *tolerate* any type of stress. Their system is hyper-reactive and can lead to explosive words and actions and the desire to use drugs to calm down. Criticism does not help them and only makes things worse.
  - Focus on praising them for their efforts. Any word of encouragement has more power to help them change than any criticism could ever accomplish.
- People in recovery need to have their home environment free from drugs in order for them to become successful.
  - The people we associate with—we will become.

RECOVERY IS A LIFETIME PROCESS

To become successful in recovery, everyone needs to develop ways to slow down the impulsive-reactive responses the addiction processes create in the brain. A way to understand how the impulsive part of the brain works is by looking at how the brain is structurally organized.

Survival instincts are located deep in the primitive part of the brain, where it's essential to move quickly and impulsively without thinking about it. Otherwise, we would be dead before our feet decide to run. The impulsive/survival area in our brain is located next to the memory center, emotional center, and motor center. Clustered next to each other, these structures allow our brain to make lightning-quick connections with each other. The impulsive thoughts and actions are influenced by previous painful memories and emotions and not by logic. When we encounter a situation:

- The hippocampus quickly remembers past experiences.
- The Amygdala houses the emotional fear response that can causes us to fight, flight, or freeze response by either fighting, running away, or making us unable to move or make a decision.
- The motor cortex becomes primed and ready to react to any threat needed for survival.

This very necessary survival mechanism has now been taken over by drug use. The brain remembers (hippocampus) previous very painful withdrawal symptoms. This kicks in the emotional center (amygdala) with intense anxiety, irritability, and fear. These two mechanisms then will drive them to seek out drugs (motor cortex). By repeated exposure to even the *thought* of going into withdrawal puts them into an emotional tailspin of *panic*. When anyone with an opioid addiction stops taking any opioid drugs, they experience intense physical and mental withdrawal symptoms. The more times they try to stop or think about stopping, the brain worsens the dread and intensifies the discomfort they are feeling before they are actually in full-blown withdrawal. The brain has a way *of magnifying* their discomfort and fear response, and it can carry over into any area of their life that causes even minor stress. This *hyper stress response* can become a habitual *autonomic reaction to any stressful event* by causing:

- Intense physical symptoms of heart pounding, profuse sweating, and shaking of hands.
- Coupled with the mind racing, repetitive thoughts of, *I got to take something, anything to calm down. I can't stand feeling this way.* These thoughts further intensify their anxiety that leads to a panic episode.
  - These thoughts keep driving home the message: All this can go away with one pill, one snort, or injection.

Now it becomes clearer why people in recovery need to learn how to cope with stress and deal with urges. Addiction has this compulsive, impulsive drive for *instant* relief of *stress and anxiety* that leads them to make poor decisions and relapses. For those in recovery, they have to learn ways to create barriers to delay the impulsive part of their brain from acting out, thereby giving them enough time for the thinking part of their brain to kick in.

In order to slow down this impulsive—got—to—have—it—now responses requires learning coping strategies on how to slow down the impulsive reaction from happening and giving time for the information to reach the frontal cortex (thinking part of the brain), which is located far away from the survival primitive parts of the brain. Coping mechanisms help put a pause—a moment—to allow time—for the brain—to think things through rather than instinctually reacts. Some of the ways to slow down this impulsive action are:

- Have them delete all the phone numbers of people they previously used or obtained drugs from, making it more difficult to acquire any drugs.
- Give their partner the keys to their car, so they have to walk to obtain any drugs. When they start walking to their friend or dealer's place, it gives them time for the information to be processed in the thinking part of their brain. By slowing the impulsive reaction and putting an interval, a pause, between the impulse and the action allows them to consider their actions.
  - They now have a choice to make. Do I stop, turn around and go back home? Or, do I keep walking toward my drug dealer's house? Now, it becomes a conscious decision rather than an automatic impulsive reaction to handle the problem.
- Any way they can slow down the impulsive reaction by *delaying* the action, gives them a chance to make better choices on how to handle their problems.
  - Have a friend or loved one lock up their medication in a safe and don't give them the combination to keep them from compulsively taking more than prescribed.
  - Put a camera over their front door, so they can see who is there to avoid answering it when the wrong person shows up.
  - When they go to family celebrations, give their partner a code word to use when triggered with a compulsive urge or thoughts to use. That word means *we got to leave now!* No delay, no thanking the hostess for inviting them—they need to go now with no stops in between.

To help people cope with difficult life situations and avoid a relapse, they need to practice *daily* stress reduction techniques such as:

- Mindful Breathing exercises where they only focus on their breath. They breathe in to the count of five, hold to a count of four, and then out to the count of seven while only focusing on their breathing. They can use different ratios on how long to breathe in, hold, and out—this ratio is how I do it for myself. If a thought intrudes, they redirect their mind to counting their breath by breathing in—hold—and then out. By only focusing on their breathing, it gives them a chance for their mind to rest and become free from all their worries and problems. Just like our body needs rest—so does our mind.
- Safe place visualization first involves Mindful Breathing to relax, and then they focus on a place where they felt happy and safe. The more specific the *details,* the more real it becomes.
  - My safe place is sitting at an old metal kitchen table with pink cracked plastic seats listening to my mom sing, *old Suzanna, don't you cry for me* in her Italian accent while stirring a pot of spaghetti sauce on the stove. The aroma of baked bread filled the air and made my mouth water in anticipation of eating my favorite meal.
- Mind-body relaxation exercises calms their mind and eases the tension in their bodies.
  - Yoga involves focused breathing combined with stretching different muscle groups in their body.
    - I remember the first time I did a yoga class; I had never felt so relaxed that my body felt like a limp noodle. For three days, I kept saying, I can't believe how relaxed I feel.
  - There are other mind-body relaxation programs that can achieve the same benefits.

When we practice *daily* relaxation methods, by continuous repetition, we develop a *learned* state of relaxation. This learned behavior creates *fast* tracts in our brain that I like to call super-highways. It allows information to be processed quickly and automatically to achieve the desired effect. A tennis player, through repeated practice for years, has developed an effective swing that always hits the ball in the 'sweet spot' of the strings giving the right pop and spin as it hits the mark on the court. They did not achieve this with one practice. It required time and effort, but once achieved, it becomes a rapid automatic response they no longer have to think about. The brain had formed a special pathway (super-highway) to quickly transmit information from one area to another. So, when a stressful event happens, and we start our mindful breathing exercises, it transmits the relaxation impulse via the super-highway-express for us to quickly calm down and reduce the emotional, impulsive actions from happening.

They have to learn how to recognize their emotional state *before* engaging in any conflict and find ways to reduce their reactions. A trained therapist, clinician, or anyone experienced in teaching them the coping skills needed to reduce their stress. They need the discipline to practice them daily in order to reset and lower their anxiety threshold. Trying to shortcut this practice puts them at risk for future relapses and can easily derail all their efforts to get better.

The following diagram is a visual of how the survival instincts are clustered together, and the thinking of the consequences of the action is located far away.

Close Associations between survival (Reward) with Emotion, Memory and Motor cortex.

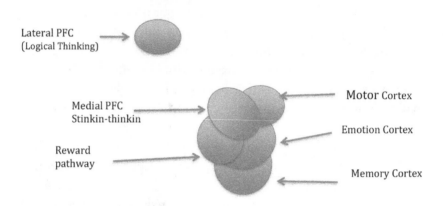

The lateral Prefrontal Cortex (PFC) processes and weighs the consequences of an action (Logical thinking) and is located far away from the impulsive survival mechanism.

The medial PFC is close to the reward and survival areas of the brain, where our thinking is influenced by emotion, memory, and the need for instant reward. It is the part of the brain that gives excuses (wrong thinking)—what AA calls our Stinkin-thinkin thoughts and ideas.

The medial PFC (Stinkin-thinkin) thoughts can be subtle or more obvious. Some *obvious* examples of Stinkin-thinkin are:

- It's okay to have just one drink despite the fact they could never stop at just one.
- I want it *now*. Without considering whether they can afford a new car.

- There's nothing wrong with visiting my cousins. So, what if they use a little weed and some meth. I don't go there very often.
- I got a promotion at work. Time to celebrate. There's nothing wrong with taking something extra to make it even more special.

Stinkin-thinkin *always* gives a person bad advice because it's based on their emotions, impulsive need, and desire to have it done *now* and not consider the consequences of their actions. A person struggling with addiction has *two* different areas in their brain competing to put thoughts into their mind. It is like having an angel on one side of their head and the devil on the other.

One thought is based on immediate gratification and emotional needs, and the other thought is based on the assessment of the problem and what would be the best course of action. They are in a tuga-war, each wanting to control them. Unfortunately, emotion always seems to trump logic *unless* they find ways to delay the action. They need to allow time to process the situation and weigh the consequences to determine the right course of action. Instead of jumping off a cliff and seconds later realize that wasn't such a good choice when they crash into the ground.

The longer anyone is in Recovery, the more vigilant they need to be in recognizing their Stinkin-thinkin thoughts. Now, the Stinkin-thinkin has become very cunning and sly. *Remember*, addiction always has a hidden agenda and wants to bring them back to drug use. These thoughts are less obvious and can be subtle like:

- Everything is going great, and I don't need to go to any more meetings.
- I already know how to do the relaxation techniques, so I don't need to practice them anymore.
- Since I no longer have any cravings I am cured of the problem.

If they start listening to these Stinkin-thinkin thoughts, it will slowly lead them back to addictive behaviors.

Part of the recovery process is recognizing their Stinkin-thinkin thoughts that want to undermine all their efforts to get better. They can't do this on their own. They need help. Cognitive Behavior Therapy (CBT) and Dialectical Behavior Therapy (DBT) are treatments used to delay impulsive reactions. Individuals learn how their circumstances affect their thoughts that influence their feelings and cause them to relapse. Using CBT and DBT help them learn how to analyze their impulsive reactions and find ways to reduce their stress in order to make better choices. For every slip or relapse, they need to learn how to assess where they could have changed the outcome.

I have them use an index card. On one side, they write down the circumstances of the situation (what happened):

- Who are they with?
- What thoughts did they have?

- What were they feeling?
- What happened?
- On the other side, they will write what they are going to do differently.

Most people struggle with this final step. They need guidance on how to figure out what went wrong.

When I ask them, "What will they do differently?"

I typically get a shrug, or they'll say, "*I'll try harder next time.*"

I respond with, "You already tried hard. Why will next time be any different than this time?"

For them to learn how to break down their impulsive action to use drugs. They have to learn how their *thoughts* affect their *feelings* that lead to their use of drugs. So, I start asking questions to determine how to change the outcome.

- Where were you located?
  - They could be at home, a friend or relatives house, at a theater, a concert, etcetera
- What were you doing?
  - Listening to music, at a party, home alone, getting off work…etcetera
- Who were you with?
  - Family members, co-workers, strangers, old hang-out buddies…etcetera
- What thoughts were you thinking?
  - It's been a long time since I have been around other adults.
  - Nothing to do.
  - Tired of work, work, work, and no play. Want to have some fun for a change
  - No one will know
- What were you feeling?
  - Feeling depressed, lonely, bored, angry, upset, disappointed, or hurt.
- Finally, what happened?

It can be difficult for some people to recognize how their emotions can trigger a relapse. Any strong emotion can cause a lot of distress for them and can trigger an anxiety reaction that makes them want to take drugs to calm down. A common situation I encounter in people who slip and use drugs is seeing an old friend. When they slip up and used drugs, this is the process I employ to help my patients learn how to analyze what happened. This information will be used to generate a plan on how they can avoid making the same mistake again.

Shelly came to her appointment in an extremely good mood. She talked about how an old friend called and made plans to get together and catch up. Before I could open my mouth.

She interrupted, "*I know what you're going to say, but she doesn't use drugs anymore. So, I figure there's nothing to worry about. We're going out to eat. It's no big deal.*"

When she returned for her appointment, she shuffled through the door with her head down.

"How did the visit go with your friend?"

"*You already know I messed up.*"

"What happened?"

"*I'm such an idiot. Instead of going out, we decided to head over to her house and make dinner. She invited some friends over. After we ate, someone pulled out a pipe, and we all took several hits.*"

"Where could you have prevented the slip? When she invited all her friends over?"

"*No, I shouldn't have gone over to her house.*"

"How about when your friend called and said let's get together. Could you have avoided taking drugs then?"

"*If I didn't go out with her, I would not have slipped. But...just hearing her voice made me feel so happy and excited about connecting with an old friend.*"

"How are you going to avoid a slip the next time an old friend calls?"

"*I don't know.*"

"How did she contact you this time?"

"*First on Facebook, then called me on the phone.*"

"Do you think there's a connection?"

She nodded. *"I have to change my phone number and delete my Facebook account."*

"When will you do that?"

"Today."

The process of breaking down the events starts at the moment of relapse and for us to work backward. Looking to find in the sequence of events where they could have been able to avoid a relapse. We do this process with every slip. Over time, they come into the office already with a plan on what they will do differently.

I had a patient tell me she had to sever all contact with her family. She knew how to manipulate them into giving her some of their pain pills. Even when she had told them to never give them to her again. She still found ways of coercing them into giving her another pill. She knows what to say, how to act to get her own way. She can't trust them to say no, and she can't trust herself not to twists things until they relent and give her one of their pills. She has to avoid them.

Part of recovery is *discovering our triggers* and how to *avoid* them. Since the impulsive part of the brain is activated by drug use, the ability to *control* this response is usually ineffective. The memory part of the brain remembers previous drug use with his or her friend (even if the friend claims to be off drugs—cravings are triggered by being around anyone they *ever* took drugs with). The cravings are *not* consciously recognized. It is like priming a pump. When the right moment happens, they are hit with an overwhelming urge to use drugs. The *subconscious* part of the brain processes all the information and only allows a very small portion of the information to reach the conscious part of the brain. Think of it as a computer. All the activity is happening in the processor, and we only see the screen.

What a lot of people don't know the *subconscious* brain can be brainwashed. At one time, movie theaters would put one picture of popcorn and soda in the movie. Just one screen, and no one could see this one screen because of the speed it flashed by, *but* the sales for popcorn and soda escalated. This practice was later deemed illegal to do. But, it does show how powerful subliminal messages (ones a person is not consciously aware of) can control the behavior of people. These subliminal messages can occur while watching a program and seeing a person drinking or taking drugs. Suddenly they have an intense craving for a beer or a pain pill. Smelling a certain perfume can trigger a sudden need to take something because it was the same scent that another woman wore while using drugs. They could walk down the street and suddenly get hit with an unexpected urge because the road looked similar to the one where they had previously got drugs. These hidden *subconscious* cues can create intense cravings for no apparent reason and, for the unprepared, can lead to relapse.

How can a person cope with the unexpected?

Although, initially, it can be difficult to deal with the common causes for relapse such as, avoiding people they used drugs with, or going to places where they used drugs, or being around needles or other paraphernalia associated with drug use. Once they change their friends and no longer associates with anyone who uses drugs, it becomes easier to avoid a slip.

But, those *crazy urges can still hit* at unexpected moments, even years into recovery—maybe anytime in their life because of the unconscious associations the brain has made. I had several of my patients, after more than five years in recovery; tell me they had a using dream. Their brain got triggered, and they can't figure out why. That's why if anyone is in recovery, starts thinking, I am cured and begins to hang around those who use drugs—they are setting themselves up for failure. They may do fine for a while until a painful event happens. When we are at the wrong place, at the wrong time (in emotional or physical pain), the addictive brain pathways kick in with unexpected torrential forceful cravings. How they handle these thoughts will determine if they relapse or resist the urge. If they haven't been practicing stress management on a daily basis or staying in meetings to be prepared for unexpected urges, they will more likely fail rather than succeed in their efforts.

A lot of times, they become successful in avoiding their *drug of choice* but end up becoming addicted to other substances. They didn't realize that *all* addictive drugs work in similar areas of the brain. So, now they are addicted to two or more drugs instead of just the one they thought they had a problem with. I see this commonly with marijuana. Patients will tell me they aren't addicted to the drug and just use it to relax.

I say, "If you aren't addicted, then stop using it."

Unexpectedly they discover they can't. We can't rely on a drug to help us *relax*, have fun or deal with a stressful situation. We have to learn how to relax by *developing skills* (coping mechanisms) to successfully navigate all of life's ups and downs.

People in recovery feel like they are living in a minefield loaded with bombs that can explode at any minute. People, places, things, and everywhere I go, a memory resurfaces that:

- Triggers a craving
- That causes an urge
- And then a reaction by taking a drug. (What the brain wants is what the brain gets).

Television shows, grocery stores, gas stations, certain streets, smells, even certain towns, people you know, family, old girlfriends, current girlfriends, anger, frustration, anxiety, disappointments, loneliness, and celebrations. All can trigger a relapse. Where can a person go to escape it all? *They Can't.*

They have to learn coping skills to delay the impulsive responses and find ways to relieve their tension and stress. It becomes a lifetime effort to constantly be aware of how they feel and alert to any potential problems while practicing a daily routine to reduce stress. All this takes time but is worth the effort to regain their lives back again.

Anyone in recovery has a choice to make: *Do I control my own life, or will I let drugs destroy it for me?*

SURVIVAL TIPS

- Stressful events can trigger the addictive brain pathways undermining our desire to stay 'clean.'
  - We have no control over what Life throws at us, but we do have control over how we will respond to it. Asking

God to give us wisdom and guidance on how to *avoid* problems is a lot less stressful than becoming stuck in one.

- A lot of times, we need an attitude adjustment. If God permitted a problem to happen, then there is something I need to learn from it.
- Problems can become opportunities for us to excel. When Goliath mocked the army of Israel, King Saul had promised great wealth and marriage to his daughter to anyone who would kill Goliath a giant of a man. David a mere shepherd boy heard this and volunteered to kill Goliath. This one act turned his life of obscurity to obtaining great wealth and marriage to the King's daughter.
- Never despise small beginnings.
  - Most importantly, My Heavenly Father, give me the faith to believe, the willingness and desire to start, and Your strength and power to do all that I have been called to do.
  - I believe, but God, help me with my unbelief.
- Discovering our triggers help us make plans to avoid them.
  - Avoiding a weakness is easier than resisting one. If I avoid going into the bakery, I won't end up sampling all the goodies.
- Stinkin-thinkin is emotional thinking that triggers addictive thinking.
  - There is nothing wrong with our emotions *except* if we allow them to make our decisions. Our emotions can blind us to the truth. We have to examine the evidence and not make assumptions. Our assumptions increase our emotional pain and can lead us into making rash decisions.
  - Never go to bed angry because it will grow and fester through the night.
  - Just because I feel a certain way doesn't mean I know what is really happening.

- We need to develop coping skills to delay the impulsive—got—to—have—it—now response.
  - Patience is one of the fruits of the Spirit. It is an area I struggle with by wanting God to act quickly and do something. I am looking for an outward sign, but God is changing me from the inside out. I have to keep reminding myself, let God do His work and stop hindering Him. *Faith* is what moves God. I have to stop complaining, which shows my unbelief, and start *praising* him instead.
- Recovery requires a daily routine of stress reduction exercises that are needed to produce *new* learned behaviors that will combat these impulsive addictive pathways.
  - Time alone with God, focusing on what He says in the bible is a wonderful way to reduce my stress. When I stop focusing on my problems and focus on God, miraculous events can happen. When Peter stepped out of the boat and walked on water, he did fine as long as he kept looking at Jesus. But when the wind blew and distracted him, he started to sink.

SURVIVAL TIP # 8

WHY CAN'T I BEAT THIS ON MY OWN?

Without help, anyone with substance abuse (addiction) can't get better by their own efforts. The changes the drugs have made to their brain pathways have altered the way they *think*. Their thinking is influenced more by emotional reaction and less by logical reasoning. A husband gets into a fight with his wife and goes out and gets drunk or takes some drugs, thinking *I'm getting back at her*. Not realizing the only person he is really hurting is himself. To recognize impulsive, emotional thinking requires a lot of training and effort to stop the action from happening. In AA, they call this abnormal reasoning as Stinkin-thinkin. Stinkin-thinkin takes many different forms. The longer they are in recovery, the more subtle and *sneaky* this abnormal thought process is to detect. In recovery, they need constant vigilance to detect this Stinkin-thinkin. It has only *one* ultimate goal—to start drug use again.

I had a patient in recovery for over two years. An old friend from his childhood contacted him on Facebook, and they decided to meet. When he came in for his appointment, he was extremely excited about seeing his old friend. I know this may seem strange, but whenever I see anyone in the first three years of recovery become very excited about anything—I am on *high alert* that something else is going on. I am suspicious because people in early recovery have an elevated brain reward system that makes *everything difficult and joyless*. They feel like they are just existing and nothing is pleasurable. So when they become excited about something, I know there is a *hidden agenda* that they are *not recognizing*. My patient assured me his friend never took any drugs before in the past or is currently taking any.

When I saw him in a follow-up appointment and asked, "How did your visit go with your old friend?"

With his head bowed, he mumbled, "*I never saw him.*"

On the way to see his friend, he forgot his friend lived near his previous drug dealer's home. He ended up going there instead. Even though he didn't remember this detail, when he planned on meeting his friend, the *subconscious* part of his brain did not forget and saw it as an excellent opportunity for him to return to drug use. This was the *real reason*—the hidden agenda for the excitement. In recovery, people have to always be on alert. They can't learn all the pitfalls they encounter without help and need instruction and the discipline needed to avoid all the mind-fields around them—just waiting for the right opportunity to derail their efforts.

Trying harder doesn't work. Can we tell our pancreas to try harder and produce more insulin, or change the color of our skin? Addiction has damaged their brain. The addictive process changes have *altered their thinking and motivation* areas of their brain. For anyone to recover from the assault drugs had done to their brain requires multiple people to help them. They can't do it alone, and willpower, by itself, does *not* work. Recovery is a long-term process for anyone with an addiction and for their family dealing with the problem.

The family's expectations are, *this time, they will do better, or this treatment program will turn my child around.* So, every time their child relapses, more anger, disappointment, and frustrations build into an ever-growing pit of despair, discovering a person they thought they knew, believed, and trusted become someone they can't believe or trust anymore. To know that a person we love—loves the drugs more than their children, our relationship, or their job. Wounded more than if their loved one just stabbed them in the heart, they grieve in silence and suffer alone in their misery. How can anyone move past this devastation, this loss? As much as this hurts, do *not* take the blame. It's not due to who we are or how we look. It has nothing to do with us and has everything to do with the *changes* the drugs had caused by *altering their reward and motivation pathways*. So, flush those guilty thoughts and negative feelings of inadequacies down the toilet, where they belong and no longer accept that we had done something wrong and are responsible for what has happened.

Do *not hold* onto these negative emotions, it will destroy our relationship with our loved ones. When our child or partner was in active addiction, it stirred up a hornet's nest of frustrations, heart-aches, and anger from previous transgressions when they promised they'd do better next time and didn't. Resentments grew inside us, along with our grief in seeing all our hopes and dreams for our child or partner destroyed by drug or alcohol use. To hold onto all these turbulent thoughts, heartaches and worries keeps us stuck in the past by re-experiencing all their previous transgressions. Bitterness fills our heart and boils over into our words and actions, causing more anger and distance in the relationship. So, while the family members are trapped in the past with all this anguish, their loved one is now embarking on a new journey of self-discovery and moving forward in their life. We feel left behind, stuck with all these painful memories and betrayals. How can anyone move past all this devastation?

Family members would all benefit from mental, physical, and spiritual healing. So, they can all move forward in unity instead of letting bitterness divide them by rehashing the past. Forgiveness is the only way for us to let go of all the pain and resentments. Forgiveness is a *decision* not to let the past dictate our thoughts, feelings, and actions anymore. Forgiveness does not mean what the other person had done was right. They decided to let go of the emotional pain and no longer allow un-forgiveness to affect their life anymore. Withholding forgiveness is like hitting our arm with a sledgehammer every day and expecting it to hurt the other person. We are only hurting ourselves. Un-forgiveness keeps the family members tethered to the past and gives them an excuse for why they never achieved any of their own goals. They now become a *victim* to all the pain, misery, and angst they suffered trying to get their loved one off drugs by putting their life on hold, while trying to get them better.

Until we move past the pain, we can't change and begin to grow again. *Pain* changes us. It can make us bitter and judgmental or become more compassionate and forgiving. The only difference between a victim and an overcomer is the *attitude* they have about the circumstances. One feels devastated by the circumstances, and the other sees it as an opportunity to grow and learn from the experience. Life is all about *attitude*. What attitudes or thoughts we have determines the outcome in our life. Let all the past wrongs go. Don't let those negative thoughts and feelings keep us stuck in the past and block us from our future—It's not worth it.

Remember:

- Forgiveness allows us to let go and move forward in our life.
- Unforgiveness ties us to the past and gives us an excuse to stay stuck and not move forward.

It's not surprising, people in active addiction or in early recovery, the divorce rate is twenty percent higher than the national average. They have more than a sixty percent chance the relationship will fail. This is more likely a conservative estimate since the majority of people do a *no-fault* divorce. Nobody wants to admit their partner has an addiction or have others become beware of a problem they have kept hidden for years.

When people are in active addiction and refuse to acknowledge, they have a problem or want any help—this is the time to step back. We *still* need to keep communication lines open but not spend a lot of financial and emotional energy. Let them live their life and suffer from whatever consequences their behaviors bring while the other family members move on and live their own life. This may seem harsh, but the old saying, *we can lead a horse to water, but we can't make them drink*, applies here. Trying to *make* someone do something they don't want only creates more resistance and conflict. Better to find ways for them to discover their own motivation and desire to change.

What we do need to do is engage in non-judgmental conversations and show them empathy. Watching them gobbling down the food, we inquire; *it must be really hard to find where to get your next meal or a place to stay. I would never be able to do this. I bet it's pretty rough—how are you coping?* Take their hand to let them know you care and wait for them to respond. So easy for us to tell our loved ones what to do, but we have to *wait* and let them speak. After they talk, empathize how we would feel in the grips of a *disease that takes away our free will* to change. Before they leave, give them a hug, and tell them, *"I love you, and I'm praying for you. When you are ready, I'm here to help you find a way to get better."*

I had a patient in recovery for about six months, and he came to the office upset about his ex-wife remarrying.

He kept complaining, *"How could she do this to him since he was getting better?"*

He felt betrayed, angry, and justified for feeling this way because she didn't wait for him. I asked, "How long have you been divorced?"

"Ten years."

I had to hold back a gasp when he said ten years. On further questioning, he didn't start seeking help for his addiction until he heard that she was dating another man regularly. Sometimes, getting on with our own life propels another person to do something about their life. I'm not suggesting a time frame for how long a person should wait for their addicted partner or child to get better. But I do feel that everyone needs to fulfill his or her full potential—with or without the other person. When we give up on our dreams, ambitions, and opportunities, resentment grows. Don't put our life on hold while *waiting* for another person to get better. They may never change—but we can.

The choices that have been made in the past can't be undone. The, *if only* I had done this, or not done that, can plague us and build into bitterness. These thoughts only bind us to a *past* that can't be changed, and the preoccupation makes us *ignore* the present that can be altered. For anyone who has an addiction problem and their families, they both need to learn how they can move on in their lives and shed the guilt and the shame. We would all benefit from finding a new path that can heal us. So, we all can move forward in unity instead of letting bitterness divide us by rehashing the past.

I developed the *Freedom Plan* as a guide to help people take back their life. Setting them free from all the bitterness and negative emotions seething inside them and to keep the poison from spewing out of their mouths that will destroy all their efforts to help their loved one get better. The ultimate freedom fighter is Jesus Christ, who has broken the chains that sin has caused in our life and set us free to have a new relationship with our Heavenly Father. When we become spiritually free, we become a new creation no longer bound to the past, and all things (potentials and possibilities) become new. The Freedom Plan I developed is based on the principles that God wants us to employ in our life to *break free* from *any oppression* we have. The Freedom Plan helps us move forward and break the chains that bind us.

Let us all become free when we start the process of learning the Freedom Plan that involves, *Forgiveness, Learn from the past, Acceptance, Change our behaviors, Change our thinking, Stop the excuses, Stop procrastinating. Life is a journey. Set boundaries, and Live in the moment.*

FORGIVENESS

Forgiveness is the foundation we need to move forward. To forgive other people and ourselves is the first step needed, to let go of the pain and start severing the ties to the past.

- Forgiveness is not saying what the other person did was right or saying, what we did was justified. Forgiveness allows us to let go and release all our negative emotions and feelings about past wrongs or mistakes. Forgiveness grants us the ability to move forward in our life, not shackled by the guilt, the missed opportunities, and loss.
  - When we ask God for mercy and to forgive us of our sins, God wants us to extend that same mercy and forgiveness toward others.

- We have to accept that all the wrong choices we made can't be undone, no matter how much we wish it were different. The old saying, *don't cry over spilt milk*, applies here.
- If we spend so much time looking at the past, feeling guilty over things that can't be changed, we *lose* the *opportunity* to make a difference today.
  - *Remember,* for those of us in Christ, that God can turn any wrong into right when we believe and trust in him when it's according to his will.

LEARN FROM THE PAST

We have to learn from the past so we don't keep repeating the same mistakes. Don't let our emotions, anger, and hurts *cloud* the benefits we can gain from the experience and become a better person because of it.

- We can learn from the past, but we were *never meant to dwell* there.
  - To spend all our time and energy praying, crying, and wishing the past were different. Trying to undo something that can't be altered is a waste of time and energy. It keeps us stuck and unable to move forward in our life.
- The Serenity prayer written by Reinhold Niebuhr can apply to everyone who wants to move forward in his or her life.

The Serenity Prayer

God, grant me the serenity to accept the things
    I cannot change.
The courage to change the things I can,
    And the wisdom to know the difference.
Living one day at a time,
Enjoying one moment at a time..."

ACCEPTANCE

When we finally accept that the past is the past—it can set us free. We can't undo what has already happened. No amount of wishing, praying, or wallowing in misery can ever change what has already happened. We have to let go of the blaming and the excuses and stop wasting so much of our emotional energy on things that can't be undone and miss out on what we can change. When we focus on our past mistakes, it keeps us stuck to the poor choices we made or situations that happened, and we will never learn from the situation because our emotions are blinding us to the truth. We need to *let go* and move on. We need to stop judging and harboring un-forgiveness in our hearts. It is destroying us. Acceptance allows us to no longer be bound by the mistakes we had made in the past and gives us an opportunity to learn and grow from the experience. When we have gone through a difficult and painful experience, we formed a bridge that can connect us to other people by having more understanding and compassion for those who are stuck in this same problem.

- We need acceptance so we can grow and move forward.
  - If we stop growing, we are dying. Living in the past is a form of dying to our hopes and dreams. We live in lost memories of regrets rather than actions and fail to jump at all the opportunities right in front of us.

CHANGE OUR BEHAVIORS

We need to stop the endless cycle of repeating the same action and expect a different result. First, we have to recognize what we have been doing doesn't work.

- The saying, *if it ain't broke, don't fix it* applies in reverse— *if it ain't working, then change it.* Continuing in behaviors that lead to adverse consequences and think, *this time it'll*

work is crazy. We can never grow by doing the same thing over and over and over again and expect a different result.
- o Just like an old record player with its needle stuck in the same groove, it will never finish the song.
- Time to do something different. To achieve our goals, we need a plan on how to break down a problem into small pieces that we can do today.
  - o Analyze what areas had a partial response and what areas were ineffective and *rework* the plan.
  - o Gradually we chip away the obstacles until our masterpiece has been created when we reach our goal.
- No one does anything important perfectly the first time they try.
  - o It takes practice, patience, and careful *evaluation* of the *outcome* to get on the right track.

CHANGE OUR THINKING

We have to change the way we think in order to change our outcome. What we think—we will do. So, in order to *change the action*, we need to first *change the thought.*

- Everyone has the *power* to change with God's help through the renewing of our minds.
  - o When we replace what we think with what God says, our mind starts to default to the Word of God as we apply His truths in our lives.
- Reactive Emotive Behavior Therapy (REBT) says *if* I change my thoughts, I can change my feelings and my actions. So, *today* I decide to do things differently.
  - o Maybe get professional or spiritual guidance, read books to learn more about addiction, go to family support groups, and spend time in the Word of God.
- Do whatever it takes to learn, grow and change. Sometimes in order for our loved ones to change, it may require us to change first.

- Changing the way we think gives us a new perspective on events. When we start analyzing *our* wrong thoughts that kept us stuck in the past gives us an opportunity to develop a new way of thinking.

STOP THE EXCUSES

When we *stop* making excuses for why we failed and blaming others or our circumstances, it breaks the emotional ties that hinder us from moving forward.

- We can *easily* provide all the reasons—why we can't change.
  - Now, we need to discover all the reasons—why we can change.
- We are in the driver's seat of our destination and our future. We choose to
  - Become a victim to this problem or an overcomer.
  - Become helpless and unable to change because of multiple excuses, or climb out of the pit and make changes in our life toward a better future.
  - Live with regrets or achieve the desires of our hearts.
- To achieve our destiny, we cannot allow any excuses to keep us from reaching our goals and to live a fulfilling life.

STOP PROSCRATING

We have a destiny to fulfill, and we only have one life to live. Don't put off what can be done today by planning on doing it tomorrow. Tomorrow may never come.

- Time is ticking. We need to do it now...not later. Get moving.
  - Stop thinking about the problem.
  - Start thinking about the solution.
  - *Set it in motion.*
- Do it *today*.

- The only way to achieve anything important in our life is to have a *plan*,
  - The ability to break down the problem into small steps that we can do today.
  - Small steps will lead to bigger steps, and eventually, we will reach our goal.
- We need to start living our life again is the only way to keep the bitterness out of our relationships.
- NO one else is meant to walk my life but me.

LIFE IS A JOURNEY

Our time on earth is limited—make the most of it. We need to have a vision and not become sidetracked in activities that don't lead us toward our goal. One way of keeping us focused on our goal is by taking a picture of the goal we want to achieve. It can be a picture of a doctor or a house we want to build. Whatever that goal is, we need to have the picture placed where we can see it every day, maybe even multiple times a day. We can tape it on our mirror, refrigerator, and calendar or download it on our computer or phone screen.

- We need a daily reminder of what direction our path needs to follow in order to achieve our goals.
  - This constant awareness of the goal allows us to direct our thoughts.
  - We no longer look at the situations we encounter as problems but as opportunities to figure out what needs to be done today to move me closer to that goal.
- We all need a vision of what we want to achieve.
  - But without a plan and the steps needed to accomplish it. The vision turns into a hopeless dream instead of a goal to pursue.

SETTING BOUNDARIES

Boundaries are like a protective shield that keeps us from becoming distracted. Boundaries are like putting a fence up to keep people from throwing their trash into our yard. Boundaries are a way to keep us from becoming emotionally drained and protect us against unreasonable demands from interfering in achieving our destiny.

- o This is not being selfish. This is *self-care (preservation)*.
- Boundaries are standards that we won't let ourselves or other people cross.
  - o Boundaries are needed to put *order* in our life.
  - o We have to prioritize what is most important, or we will accomplish nothing of importance. Think of our life's priorities as putting sand, pebbles, and rocks in a jar. The larger the item, the more important feature we need to accomplish.
  - o If we fill the jar with sand, there will be no room for rocks or pebbles.
- Boundaries help other people know what to expect and reduce our stress and conflict.
  - o When we stay resolute in our standards, we will experience a lot less strife and drains on our emotional energy.
- If we are flexible with our standards, then everyone will try to push the boundaries and drain our emotional energy.
  - o When we say no to our child, and the child starts fussing and crying. When we yield to our child's demands and give them what he or she wants—we just taught our child a very valuable lesson. The *rules don't apply to them.* As long as they cry and fuss long enough, they will get whatever they want. The child's thinking, *I want therefore I deserve to have,* can carry over into other areas of their life.
  - o When a parent sets boundaries and enforces them, their child would fuss for a while but learns quickly, it makes

no difference and quits, and the next time, their child will fuss less and less. Eventually, by repeated reinforcement of the boundaries, they will not fuss at all because they have learned *no* means NO.

- For anyone who is a wishy-washy boundary enforcer—*now* is the time to change and be firm. It's never too late to change.

- No longer will we tolerate disrespect. For years, my sister endured her father-in-law's constant belittling of her, his son, and their child. Finally, she had enough of his verbal abuse. Instead of having her father-in-law come to her home for the holidays, she brought dinner to his house. Whenever the father-in-law started his insults, they would leave. I don't think the father-in-law ever made the connection that his behavior was causing them to leave early, but it certainly helped them not to hear all the criticisms he so freely dished out.
  - We need to protect our mind from the words we hear to keep us from starting to believe them.
  - When we allow little things to invade our mind they will grow and begin to affect our whole life.

- Boundaries are needed to:
  - Protect us so we can focus on achieving the goals God has placed in our hearts.
  - Keep our life sane and free us from *unreasonable* demands, criticisms, and expectations.
  - Keep us from becoming overwhelmed and exhausted in helping others that we don't have any time or energy for our family or for ourselves.

- Even Jesus used boundaries when He would go off by Himself to spend time with His father. This was His time to become restored from the demands of the day. No one else went with Him.

- *Remember:* Boundaries allow us to concentrate on what is most important for us to accomplish.
  - So, our life's jar becomes filled with the most valuable and crucial things God wants us to accomplish and not have our life wasted on petty, insignificant sand.
- We can't achieve this great plan God has for us if we allow all our physical and emotional energy to become drained by others who already have the time, ability, and resources to do it themselves.
  - We are not helping them, but we are enabling them not to learn from their mistakes.
- We need time to spend on ourselves—this is not being self-ish. This is self-care by knowing our limitations and not allowing unreasonable demands and expectations to derail our future, our destiny, and our life.

LIVE IN THE MOMENT

We only have today, yesterday is gone, and the future is not guaranteed. We only have this moment in time we can change.

> *Today* is the day to make a decision that I will not live my life reflecting on the past and wishing things were different or living in a fantasy future that may never happen.
> *Today* I deal with my problems.
> *Today* I decide what direction I will go.
> *Today* I will take new steps to start on the road toward my destiny.

I need to stay aware of what is happening around me. This moment can never be changed once it passes.

- The motto in recovery is to live one day at a time. This is true for everyone.
  - Too often, we let mistakes or hurts or circumstances freeze us from moving forward and keep us from learn-

ing and growing from the event. One way of letting go of the past is to accept, we are all human, and things happen. Instead of struggling against something that can't be changed, acceptance allows us to see reality for what it is and move on.

- The now moment is where all our efforts need to be focused on. Plan…but be flexible to changes that occur and continue to move forward. Enjoy every day, every moment, as a gift to start again. A new day is a new opportunity, a chance to make a difference.

Let us get off the merry-go-round of repeating the same things over and over again and expecting by some miracle a different outcome will happen. *Learn* from past *mistakes* and make a *new* plan. If that one fails, then evaluate what did work and what didn't and make another plan and another until we find the one that does work. Start living our life again. Start in the areas that have been neglected and enjoy the journey. Don't allow feelings of guilt to keep us from discovering purpose and joy in life.

SURVIVAL TIPS

- In early recovery, the changes in the brain reward system make everything joyless and difficult to do.
  - This low motivation state is something they cannot control. We can help by having them do simple tasks that can be accomplished quickly. Complex projects will rarely get completed, but it does cause a strain in our relationships and increases their frustrations and anxiety that can lead to a relapse.
  - Praise their efforts. Don't complain they didn't do enough. When we focus on the positives, it will encourage them to do more.

- Trying harder to get off drugs does not work unless they change their plan.
  - We can only improve when we analyze what and where things went wrong and make a plan on how to avoid it in the future.
  - Pray and ask God for wisdom, guidance, and direction. A lot of people need to see an addiction counselor who can guide them in how to make a plan and adjust it as needed.
- The only way to move forward in life is to let go of the hurt, anger, and frustrations.
  - Forgiveness is a conscientious decision not to let the past dictate our thoughts, feelings, or actions.
  - I have found for me to fully forgive, I need God to heal my heart. So, when the same circumstances happen, it no longer hurts inside and allows me to respond with compassion instead of bitterness. With God's healing, there is no residual festering pain because he has already taken it away.
- Boundaries are necessary to keep us sane.
  - I pray for what God wants me to accomplish in my life. Other people will always try to distract me, but I have to remain focused on my goal. I can be flexible but never lose sight.
  - Set a routine and follow it.
- The difference between a victim and an overcomer is the attitude we have about our circumstances.
  - Learn from the past, but we were never meant to dwell there. Ask God for wisdom every day. Ask Him to show us the path to follow and open our spiritual eyes to the truth, and not become blinded by what we see.
- If it ain't working, then change it.
  - The only way to get better is to figure out what went wrong.
  - Everyone's walk with God is different. Ask our Heavenly Father to give us a teachable and understanding heart.

I want to learn everything that God wants to teach me the first time around and not have to go through all those painful experiences a second, third, or more times until I eventually get the message.

○ Thank you, Lord Jesus, for hearing me and answering my prayers, and helping *me learn* my lessons the first time around.

THE TRUTH WILL SET US FREE

What is truth? When we see or hear a person or an event, the sensory information is *filtered* through the *subconscious* part of our brain and tells us what is happening. This *subconscious* processing is *different* for every person. The filter is based on our individual life experiences, social and cultural norms that have been ingrained in all of us. We are *not* aware this *filtering* is occurring. We just know, what we are seeing, hearing, or thinking is the truth, and there can be no other explanation. I am right—you are wrong has caused all kinds of conflicts in our personal and global relationships. In our processing of events, is it really the truth or *our interpretation* of the events?

Our *unconscious distorted* thinking makes it difficult to treat someone with a substance use disorder (addiction). A lot of times, they had distorted thinking long before developing addiction, and it became a major culprit why they got addicted to drugs in the first place. If these distorted thinking patterns are not recognized and corrected, it will lead them back to drug use. Distorted thinking is deeply seated in our brain, our personality and is *manifested* by:

- How we cope with change.
- Deal with stressful events.
- How we live our life.

How do we recognize if we have distorted thinking? To determine if our thinking is distorted is by figuring out if the thought is rational or irrational.

- *Rational thoughts* are the truth and *not* our interpretation of it.
  - ○ Our previous emotional pain does not color a rational thought. It helps us deal with relationships in a way that *promotes* cooperation and unity.
  - ○ It allows us to view circumstances in a way that helps us grow through the process and become a better person rather than get stuck in the past with all our emotional baggage.
- *Irrational thoughts*, if looked closely at them, are *not* the truth.
  - ○ A lot of them don't make any sense and can cause conflicts in our relationships.
  - ○ Distorted thinking occurs because painful *feelings emerge* that modifies our perception of the situation.
  - ○ Our distorted thinking leads to anger and disputes that affect everyone around us.

Distorted thinking isolates us in our pain, and the feelings intensify. We will never find a way out of our problems if we continue in our distorted thinking. If we don't *change* the way we *think*: We will be stuck in patterns that create pain and discord. It takes practice and awareness to know:

- Not all we think is right.
- Not all we see is true.
- Not all we hear is correct.

With our distorted thinking, we have blinders on, and it becomes impossible to see what cannot be seen. When we recognize our distorted thinking, the blinders come off. We can now clearly understand what the problem is because the distortions have been removed. In the Bible, Jesus mentioned these distortions when he said; *take the beam out of your own eye before taking the speck out of another.*

Some of these cognitive distortions may have been present in our life since childhood. These *deep-seated beliefs* and *thought* patterns are hard to recognize and eliminate—but not impossible to achieve.

Common distorted thinking patterns will be grouped into categories. Some of the thinking errors can fit into multiple categories. I am concentrating on the thinking patterns I have encountered in my patients with a substance use disorder and even some I discovered in my own personal life that has caused me problems.

The distorted thinking categories are:

- Thoughts that isolate us.
- Thoughts that keep us stuck.
- Thoughts that are emotion based and cause problems in our relationships.

THINKING PATTERNS—ISOLATE US

Cognitive distortion thinking patterns that isolate us are *Denial, Hostility, Aggressive behavior, False self, Blaming, Shame, and Negative thinking.*

Denial

Denial keeps us from knowing the truth. If we don't recognize we have a problem, how can we correct it? Denial keeps us from changing and locks us into making poor choices, and leads to negative outcomes.

- Nothing works because we keep trying to fix other people and not look in the mirror.

- Anger and hostility build because we feel everyone else is wrong and we are right.

An example of denial: Someone took his stash, and he had to find more drugs before going to work. He lost another job because he never got to work on time, again. He comes home and has a fight with his wife. She threatens to leave. He can't see how drug use is destroying his life because he thinks, *drugs have nothing to do with this. The boss never liked me and that's why he lost his job. Nobody else follows his stupid rules, but I'm the one that got fired.*

- When confronted about his drug use, he says, "*I'm not as bad as Joey. I only snort heroin and not inject it—now he has a problem.*"

Aggression and Hostility

When we use aggression or hostility toward other people, it's used to prevent them from confronting us about our problems. We can scare or threaten others by our words or actions, by intimidating other people and force them to submit to what we want.

- An example: "*Stop nagging, or I'm leaving, and who is going to support you and the kids?*"
- This tactic is used, so they don't have to listen to what the other person has to say and thereby *ignore* the need to change.

Blaming

When we hold other people or circumstances responsible for our pain or actions that give us an excuse not to change or be accountable for what happened.

- We are *not helpless,* and blaming another, it deprives us of the power to change. If we blame another person, then we are not at fault or have to take any responsibility to change.

- Blaming is finding excuses why we act a certain way. One of my patients explained why he couldn't stop drinking.
  - *"If my wife didn't nag so much, I wouldn't have to drink so much."*
- Blaming is used to garner sympathy from others.
  - We don't see how the sympathy is keeping us stuck in the muck.
    - The only reason why I never got my high school diploma was because Sheila accused me of stealing her book report when I did most of the work. Sheila is the reason why I can't get a decent job.
- Blaming can also be used in reverse, making us feel responsible for another person's behavior or actions.
  - One of my patients said to me, *"If I was prettier, my husband wouldn't be having so many affairs."*
    - This thinking will never correct the problem. Trying to become prettier will not change an unfaithful mate. She accepted the blame, and that gives him a green light to do whatever he wants with no accountability for his actions.
- The only way to *correct* a problem is to *deal* with it and no longer take ownership for another person's actions.
- No one can control the behavior of another person. *We can only control our responses.*

Rationalization

- When we make excuses to explain our behaviors. They are justifying why they do these things to make it more acceptable to other people and to themselves.
  - The only way I can sleep, ease the pain, or function is to take more drugs.
- Use their helplessness to manipulate others to feel sorry and provide for their needs.
  - *"I can't get out of bed because I'm in such horrible pain. That's why my husband does all the cleaning, cooking, and laundry after he gets off work every night."*

- Unfortunately, I hear this next excuse way too often.
  - *"The only reason why I take most of my husband's pain pills is because I have a lot more pain than he does."*
  - It keeps a person and other people from knowing the truth. They have an addiction to pain pills and need help.

The False Self

The false self is created because the real-self actions are unacceptable to them. They create this image of themselves. What they want to be, rather than who they really are.

- They are nice to people, say and do the right things because this is what a good person does. But, their words or actions do not reflect what they really feel, think or want to do.
- The false self-image blinds them into believing they are this perfect person, while inside, they are seething with resentments, hurts, and anger. Because these negative feelings are unacceptable, they stuff them into an ever-growing box.
  - Eventually, they have to take drugs to cope with their frustrations and their stress for not being this perfect person they visualize themselves to be. Rather than discover their true self and learn to deal with their feelings and put boundaries in their life.
- A lot of *people pleasers* have a false image of themselves. They are always willing to help, even at the expense of the time they need for themselves or for their family.
  - All their efforts stem from a desire to gain other people's love, acceptance, and respect. Unfortunately, that rarely happens. But, that doesn't stop them from trying even harder.
  - Sometimes *people-pleasers* try to avoid conflict by doing whatever another person wants to keep from having a

fight. On the surface, they appear amicable and agreeable, but on the inside, they are boiling with anger.

- The false self can see other people through distorted lenses and can unconsciously project their bad traits onto everyone around them while they paint themselves as perfect.
   - An example: Since childhood, Keith could always find ways to get some cash by bulling other kids to give him their lunch money. As an adult, he stole over fifty thousand dollars from his grandmother's bank account. He felt wrongly accused because he earned that money by doing small errands around the house. Keith feels everyone is trying to cheat him, and that is why he refuses to help anyone in need, unless there is something in it for him. He projects his selfish behaviors onto other people while thinking he is an honest and helpful person.

Shame and deep guilt

Shame and guilt keep us from connecting with other people by feeling unworthy or feel others are judging us. Shame leads to negative thinking that can lead to negative results.

- Shame keeps a person stuck by not trying to get better.
- Their low self-esteem keeps them from applying for a promotion, deserving a respectful partner, or seizing an opportunity. They don't feel like they warrant anything better. They think if they punish themselves harshly for previous wrongs, it demonstrates their remorse for their actions and will somehow atone for their past mistakes.
- By only accepting the past is gone and can't be changed will allow them to move forward.
- We only have the power to change is today.
   - Letting go is the only way to move forward.
- Surrender is a word that many people think is bad. They see it as giving up, but in reality, it is *letting go* of the prob-

lem and not allowing it to affect them anymore. It releases the guilt that binds and smothers their life.

  o Surrender can cut straight to the truth and tell us: There is *nothing* we can do to *change* the *past*.
  o The past is meant to be a tool to_*learn* from but we were never meant to live there.

- Relinquishing the anchors that drag us down and become free from the guilt that only keeps us from achieving our goals and dreams. Lost dreams have their own anguish.

Negative thinking

Negative thinking is *fear*-based. They think about what they *don't* want rather than what they *do* want (positive thinking). Negative thinking leads to negative *feelings* that generate more negative *outcomes*. Some common irrational beliefs that lead to negative thinking are:

- Low self-esteem creates low expectations that lead to a dismal life caused by all the lost opportunities and poor choices they make.
- Negative emotions can lead to depression and anxiety.
- Negative thinking can make us fear the future and make us afraid to even try because we have no control over the outcome.
- Shame from the past makes us feel unworthy of a better life.

Demanding and commanding

When we put expectations and judgments on others by saying: They should or must do this, or have to do that. Even when other people *don't know our* rules, we still place unrealistic expectations on them and on our self, to perform a certain way.

- When these demands are not met, we become hurt, frustrated, and angry. Then rage takes over, making this small *meaningless event* turn into a nuclear explosion because they should have known better!

- These feelings become so intense and uncomfortable that it makes them want to take something to calm down and make these sensations go away.
  - My boss *shouldn't* have talked to me that way. My nerves skyrocketed, and that's why I had to drink a bottle of whiskey to calm down.
  - I *must* make a million dollars by thirty, or I am a total failure. My birthday is next month. I don't know how I can ever face anyone again.
  - To be happy and have people look up to me, I *must* have the most recent phone, car, or clothes to wear.

Over-generalizations

These are all or nothing thinking that has no room for other options. Words such as Only, Always, and Never represent this thinking pattern.

- I *always* mess things up.
- I *never* get any lucky breaks.
- *The only* way I can get relief is by taking a handful of pills.

Frustration intolerance

We get upset easily, and that gives us an excuse to give up or to give in. Words such as: *I can't stand, I can't handle, or I can't deal* are used as excuses to give in or stop trying.

- I *can't stand* your constant complaining.
- I *can't handle* working at this new job.
- I *can't deal* with my kid's tantrums. It's a lot easier to just give them what they want.

Awfulizations—

When we use words to express extremes and provide excuses for our behavior. Words such as horrible, awful, worst thing ever, and adjectives ending with est. (meanest, dumbest, laziest, cruelest, stupidest).

- My boss is so *awful* by expecting me to arrive on time. He is so mean, and that's the only reason why I have to take a few drinks before coming to work to tolerate his pettiness.
- You won't believe *how horrible* my co-worker was, and that's why I slapped her stupid smug face.
- My husband is the *cheapest* person ever, that's why I spent all our savings on this brand new fur coat.

Negative self-talk

When we see the worse in a situation that always brings about poor choices that lead to a negative outcome that convinces the person their negative thoughts were right in the first place (a form of self-sabotage).

- I always pick the wrong men, and they end up leaving me.
  - By thinking all men will leave her, Abby justified why having an affair would be a good idea. When her partner left her because of the affair. It reinforced her belief that she can only pick the wrong men.
- Nothing will work out, so I might as well not even try. Negative thinking is keeping them stuck in a bad situation and won't allow them to look for possible answers because they won't work anyway.

THINKING DISTORTIONS—THAT KEEPS US STUCK

Cognitive distortions that keep us from moving forward in our life are, *Helpless thinking, Un-forgiveness, Excuses/rationalizing, Minimizing, and Victim mentality.*

Helpless thinking

When anyone feels helpless, they don't even try to get better, and it keeps them stuck in their problem. As an explanation for their behavior, some people will say,

- *"I'm an addict, what can I say."*
- There are a lot of treatments available that are effective, but if they feel they are helpless, no treatment will work for them because they won't even try to get better.
- Some people use helpless thinking in order to garner sympathy and support by manipulating others into helping them.
  - I had a family bring in their mother for me to treat her severe heart problem. She told me she has had over twelve heart attacks and can't do anything. She handed me a boxful of medications she takes a day that her previous doctor had prescribed. I did a thorough evaluation and multiple tests were done on her heart and I found nothing wrong. She insisted she has severe heart problems, so I referred her to a cardiologist who confirmed my assessment. She still demanded I prescribe her heart medications, and when I refused, she decided to see someone else. Her family told me for years, she has them do everything for her while she sits in bed all day. She displays a classic example of a person who thinks they are helpless and demands others to see her that way, too.

Un-forgiveness

When we hold onto past hurts, it keeps us stuck in the past by reflecting on all the wrongs that had happened to them.

They use past problems as an excuse not to move forward in their life. The un-forgiveness binds them to a past that can't be changed.

- If it weren't for aunt Betty getting sick twenty years ago and my parents helping her, I would be a millionaire by now instead of working as a clerk in a grocery store. I could have used all that money to start my own business. My parents should have thought of me instead of her. They have let me down big time. That's my money they wasted, and I'll never forgive them. They have ruined my life.
- Life can only be lived in the moment—not yesterday. Change can only happen today.

Excuses

We use excuses to tell others why we can't change. The excuses cause them to *remain stuck* in their situation.

- *"I would quit smoking if only my partner would quit."*
- *"I never reached my goal because nobody would help me."*
- Excuses are used to elicit sympathy by having a pity-party and whine about why they can't do something.
- All the excuses do is blind us from the truth. They need to ditch the excuses in order to make a plan to change their circumstances.

Minimizing

When we make a situation or problem appear to be less than what it really is. By not recognizing the seriousness of the situation, we never feel the need to change.

- *"Yes, I drink and get drunk, but not as often as Henry does. Now he is a true alcoholic."*
- *"I only took a couple hundred from the till. They make plenty of money and I need it more than they do.*
  - *I can't understand, what's the big deal? Everyone else does it. I'm just the one that got caught."*

Victim Mentality

When they feel unjustly mistreated by people or circumstances and that life is unfair. They use the past as an excuse for why they can't keep a job, go to school, or get any breaks in life. The list goes on.

- Wanting people to feel sorry for them, they exaggerate the negatives in their life and discount the positives.
  - *I always fail.*
    - Do they really? They did pass first grade.
  - *Nothing ever works for me.*
    - Did they even try?
- When tragedy strikes, they can become the victim and never move past their situation, *or* they can learn from it and move on with their life. Victim mentality keeps them stuck, and they will never accomplish the desires of their heart.

EMOTIONAL THINKING—RELATIONSHIP PROBLEMS

Cognitive distortions due to emotional thinking that cause problems in our relationships are: *Jumping to conclusions, Catastrophizing, Black and white thinking, Labeling self or others, Taking feelings too seriously, and the 'Shoulds.'*

Jumping to conclusions

When we make an *assumption* about a situation or a person *without any evidence* to support it. This can be seen commonly in people who think they know the future and what other people are thinking. Some examples are:

- Fortune telling is having the belief that we know what will happen in the future. It restricts our options and keeps us from dealing with the present.
  - *"There is no way I will ever get that job, so there is no reason for me to even try and apply."*
  - *"I might as well stay home, nobody will ever ask me out for a date."*
- Mind reading happens when we think we know what other people are thinking or feeling. We also know why other people act a certain way without any evidence to support it.
  - Shelly goes to work, and the boss walks by without saying hi. She knows the boss is upset with her work, and she's going to get fired. All day her anxiety builds until anger takes over. That's why she stormed into her boss's office and gave her boss a piece of her mind and stomped out yelling, "*I quit!*"

Catastrophizing

When we magnify a problem, it amplifies our anxiety by automatically imagining the worst possible outcome to any situation. Their mind will race with all kinds of unsupported ideas and fears, causing their anxiety level to escalate, making it even more difficult to deal with the situation.

- I had a patient constantly worrying and in a state of panic, thinking her husband might be seriously injured or dead if he was even one minute late coming home.
- I had a farmer worry and predicted disaster every time it rained. He automatically thought his crops would get flooded and have nothing left to harvest.

Black and White thinking

When we evaluate everything in extremes as either all good or all bad with nothing in between.

- These expectations cause tremendous anxiety and can lead to depression because we can't see the *good* in any circumstance that isn't what we expected.
  - If I don't land this one special job, I am a total failure.
  - If I don't get this promotion at work, I might as well quit.
  - If I'm not married by age twenty, I'll be alone for the rest of my life.

Labeling

When we use negative labels to describe others or ourselves. The label limits us from reaching our full potential and also affects our relationships.

  - *"I'm such a screw-up. I can't even kill myself and do it right."*
  - *"I'm such a loser, that's why my wife left me."*
  - *'She is such a bitch for refusing to go out with me."*
  - *"My boss is an idiot, a mouse has more brains than he does."*

Taking our feelings too seriously

What we *feel right now* in the *moment* we *assume* will be a true reflection of our future some examples are:

- My date didn't show up. *"I just know that he is with someone prettier, and I'll be an old maid for the rest of my life."*
- *"I just lost the account. I know I'll never get another one."*

The "Shoulds" thinking

When we judge others and ourselves, that can leads to a lot of guilt, anger, and distress. The should's have a long list of *unbreakable rules* that everyone must follow. If we break our own rules, we are overwhelmed with guilt because we hadn't lived up to our own expectations.

- These rules are rarely told to other people.
- We *assume* others should *know* they are breaking the rules and shouldn't be acting or doing things this way (even if they don't know what they are), and we become angry or resentful. They *should* have known what they did was unacceptable, which causes conflict in our relationships.
  - *Jimmy should have known that I had a bad weekend. He should've been more understanding why I didn't do the project and take the blame for not completing it. Now I'm in trouble with the boss.*

HEALTHY RATIONAL THINKING

Just like it is important to recognize irrational thinking patterns, it is equally important to know what are healthy rational thinking patterns. *Healthy Rational Thinking* does not allow *emotional* thinking to mislead us into making poor choices.

- We step back and *examine the evidence* of an event and *not* jump to conclusions or assumptions.
  - So when her boss walks by and doesn't say hello. She thinks her boss maybe has a lot of his mind or has a personal problem. She asks questions to gain a better understanding of the situation and inquires if there is anything she can do to help?
- Healthy rational thinking gives us the ability to think in a more positive way and not allow past painful experiences or emotions to cloud a situation.
- So, how can anyone plagued with irrational thoughts acquire more healthy rational ways of thinking?
  - To recognize irrational thoughts, we have to question, *is this really true?*
  - What *evidence* is there that shows this thought is accurate?
  - Only by stepping back and evaluating the information can we determine if the thought is rational or not.
- Shelly came home upset because she failed her chemistry test.
  - She screamed, "*I'm a total failure.*"
  - Shelly had passed her other tests, so that doesn't make her a total failure. Just because she failed one test doesn't make the rest of her life a failure. This form of exaggeration and labeling is causing her extreme emotional distress and blinding her to other possible solutions. She feels helpless and is going to give up on her dream to become a nurse because of one failed test.
    - What she needs to do is examine why she failed the test so the next time she won't.
- Her *irrational* thinking is limiting her ability to focus on the *true problem* and how to fix it.

HEALTHY HABITS

Healthy habits promote healthy behaviors that reduce stress and misunderstanding. We achieve healthy habits by learning to *Set boundaries, Become more assertive, Forgive quickly, Use coping positive thoughts, Reduce anxiety, Take care of mind, body, and spirit, Let go of expectations.*

Learn to set boundaries

Boundaries help us have less stress in our life. It keeps us from becoming overwhelmed by too many demands and obligations.

- It allows other people to know what to expect and not waste their time trying to change it.
  o "Hey Mom, can you come over and clean my house and take care of the baby for me today?'
  o "No, I got a lot of work to do today."
  o "Okay, I'll call my sitter."

Learn to become assertive

We express our desires and needs in a way that doesn't make the other person feel threatened. How can anyone know if they did something that hurt us if we don't tell them? We don't yell or accuse them, but we need to explain *why* it hurt us so we can promote a bridge for better understanding.

> o *"I know I over-reacted when I screamed when you tracked mud all over the floor. I just spent over three hours on my hands and knees scrubbing it clean. Is there some way we can figure out how to avoid this from happening again?"*

Learn how to forgive

The quicker we ask for forgiveness the moment something happens, the easier it is to do.

- Do not let the mistake fester. The longer we wait, the worse it becomes. Don't go to bed angry. The longer the delay, the harder it is to forgive or to ask for forgiveness.
  - I believe that is why it says in the Bible if we have something against our neighbor go to them and make it right before giving a gift to God.
  - God does not want us to judge others, or we will be judged by the same standards we judge others.
- Forgiveness is necessary for anyone to move forward in their life and not become stuck in the past. The way we forgive others will be the same measure that God will use with us.

Learn coping thoughts (positive self-talk)

When we say positive phrases, it allows us to get through difficult situations and move forward in a positive and effective way. When we say positive words and hear those words—it can reframe the way we think about a situation or a person.

- Some of my favorite coping thoughts are:
  - This, too, shall pass.
  - I have been through a lot worse and came out fine.
  - Stop looking at the problem and start looking to God for the solution.

Learn ways to reduce anxiety

We need to find ways to reduce anxiety and practice doing an activity every day to reduce stress. Take a walk and focus on everything around us and not on the problems plaguing our minds. Listen to the bird's chirp, the wind rustling the tree leaves, look at the color of the grass and flowers.

- Focusing on the present gives us a sense of peace and tranquility, allowing our mind a moment of rest.
- Just like our bodies need to rest—so does our mind.
- There are other forms of mindfulness (living in the moment) such as:
  ○ Meditations that focus on our breathing.
  ○ Mind-body connection activities such as doing yoga, Qi-gong, and Tae Chi that center our thoughts on our movements and breathing.
- When we have a lot of anxiety, using distraction techniques is effective by diverting our attention from our problems by doing other tasks. We can watch a funny movie. Laughter can lift our mood and release a lot of tension. Do not watch any violent movies, they can actually increase our stress response and make things worse.
- Our brain can only *fully* concentrate on one thing at a time. We can do a pleasant activity or start a new hobby by learning how to sew, knit, paint by numbers kit or develop a new skill. A lot of women in my addiction group enjoy using metallic colored pencils to do adult coloring books and found it helped reduce their stress. I had another woman start stenciling shirts and made it into a full-time business. We never know where a hobby can lead to a successful business.
- Other ways to give our mind a rest is to turn off the television, cell phones, and the Internet and spend an hour, four hours, or even a day spending time with friends and family, but not with anyone who uses drugs. We can plan a mini trip like driving to a town about one or two hours away and explore the area, try eating at a local restaurant or even stay the night. Do something new and break the monotony of our lives.

- Music can be a great stress reliever, but for some people, it can grate on their nerves. So, invest in headphones to avoid fights with other members of the family who don't like the same music. Reading a book can be informative or just entertaining—a much-needed distraction when we have had a very stressful day.
  - Ideally, plan on making at least one break throughout the day to lower our stress level that will help us have less drama in our relationship with others and with ourselves.
- When we keep stress at a high level all the time, it becomes toxic to our body and affects our immune system.
  - These changes can lead to serious health problems that increase our risk for diabetes, strokes, heart attacks, and cancers.

Taking care of our mind, body, and spirit

When we take care of all our needs, it allows us to function at top performance. When we have a consistent routine of eating, sleeping, and awakening the same time every day, it optimizes how our body functions and enables us to perform at our best.

- Our body has fine-tuned coordinated hormones to be released at precise moments.
- When we eat at irregular times, it doesn't change the timing when these hormones are being released making us feel sluggish, tired, or not alert.

Let go of our expectations

When we accept where we are in the moment allows us to move from judging and tolerating people to understanding and growth. No longer will we spend any emotional energy on things (un-forgiveness, judging, and criticizing) that are destructive to ourselves and toward others.

- Our mind can now explore new avenues and ventures and frees our inner spirit to move toward acceptance and loving others as we learn to love ourselves.
  - We need to have our body, mind, and spirit functioning at peak performance in order for us to live a fulfilling life.

SURVIVAL TIPS

- Everything in our life is filtered through our subconscious mind.
  - The truth (The Word of God) is like a two-edged sword that cuts through our deep misguided thoughts and attitudes of our heart.
  - We all have blinders on. God's word and His Holy Spirit that lives within us can reveal our true thoughts and motives. Allowing us to move past the lies we have lived with and become free of our prejudices that have caused so much misunderstanding and hatred in our lives.
- People with addiction have *unconscious* distorted thinking that affects how they cope with change and stressful events.
  - Change is difficult for most people. To trade what is comfortable and familiar to venture into unknown territory makes us not want to move in the new direction that God is leading us. We have a lot of excuses to stay, but our destiny is at stake, and ultimately, our happiness will be, too.
  - Distorted thinking isolates us and creates problems in our relationships. Our beliefs keep us from seeing a situation from a different perspective and block our ability to connect with others who think or act differently than we do. It can keep us from evolving into a person God wants us to become.
  - If we don't change the way we think, we will be stuck in patterns that create pain and discord.

- We need to learn *not* to box people into our own way of thinking and expectations by believing our way is the only way to think or act.
  - We are the standard that others should follow and make others feel guilty when they don't meet our expectations.
- Not all we think, see or hear is correct. Let God's word open our hearts and mind.
  - A prayer, I pray: God, give me a teachable heart and one of understanding. Heal me, God, so that I can be a healer to others who are lost and in pain. Guide me onto the right path. God, let your love and grace touch everyone I encounter to change their despair into hope, lost into found, and free them from anything holding them back into your loving arms and find love, peace, and hope.

SURVIVAL TIP # 10

WITHOUT HONESTY, NO ONE GETS BETTER

In the previous chapter, I had mentioned how we delude ourselves by the defense mechanisms (blaming, rationalizing, denial, etc.) we create to deal with changes or stressful events. Sometimes, the very thing we used to *protect us* from pain is actually what keeps us from *dealing* with the problem. When a difficult situation happens, many people will magnify their problems to the point that it looks un-surmountable. These exaggerations are defense mechanisms used as an excuse why we never tried to improve or achieve our dreams. If we don't confront our defenses with the truth, we only make matters worse. We complain, groan and moan about our problems and try to elicit sympathy from others. If other people agree with our assessment or difficulties, then that makes it more acceptable for us to quit or not even try to change. We can turn any small problem into a major production to garner sympathy. The sympathy can become as potent as any addictive drug and keep us stuck in a miserable life of our own making. The only way to break free is to recognize the *excuses* are the problem, and they got to *go*. They are hindering our future.

In recovery, it's *essential* for us to be honest with ourselves and with others. Without *honesty*, there is no other way to get past the denials and defenses we have built around us. The excuses have to go—so the *power of truth* can open our minds to all kinds of possibilities. The excuses are the *lies* we tell ourselves. The lies hold us back and lead us down a path of un-fulfillment and misery. There is a part in us that already knows what we lost. We all grieve in different ways:

- Some of us will settle for what we have and spread our misery around to all the people we encounter.
- Some give excuses as a Band-Aid to cover their loss. All the while, the wound is festering and getting worse but is ignored because the Band-Aid of excuses is covering the expanding crater that is developing inside them. The deep pit of frustration, anger, bitterness, sadness, and hopelessness grows. To deal with this pain, people will:
  - Take drugs to ease the ever-growing pit of despair.
  - Some have lost hope and see no end in sight, and become severely depressed, and eventually they commit suicide as a permanent solution to their problems.

All this misery is caused by not discovering one simple truth: The *Power of Today* and what *God* can do for us. Today is the day we can change and decide to follow a new path. We will no longer let past circumstances or experiences hamper us from achieving our goals. To move forward, we have to let go of previous hurts, discouragements, and abuse in order to see the opportunities that are right in front of us. Only in the present can we change into a new direction. Only with clear vision, not clouded by discouragements caused by previous mistakes and failures, can we find a path that is right in front of us and take a step forward. It is the small steps (choices and actions) we do daily that multiplies and builds momentum towards the destiny that is inside of us.

Many people inquire, *how do I know what my destiny is?* Our destiny is revealed by what naturally comes easy for us to do, and we enjoy doing it. God is a loving God. He instilled in each of us unique abilities and talents that we need to *use* in order to fulfill our destiny. He would not want us to accomplish something we hate for the simple reason—we probably wouldn't do it. God wants to reward and encourage us in our journey with him and give us joy in the works he calls us to do. He loves a cheerful heart. Our destiny is prebuilt in us with all the tools necessary to fulfill it. God has already eliminated all the excuses, and we need to step out in faith and believe that God will bring the right people and opportunities as we go forward toward that goal. Don't get distracted—that's why the apostle Paul talked about forgetting those things that are behind and reaching forward to those things that are ahead, keeping our eyes focused on the prize. Jesus came to heal the sick. He wants us to reach out and heal others by the talents and desires he has placed in all of us to fulfill our destiny of God's plans for our life. As a Christian our destiny has always been meant to reach those who need God's grace in their life and to set them free.

When my car breaks down, I have no ability, interest, or pleasure trying to fix it. This is not my destiny. In third grade, I was seated in the back row next to the encyclopedias. I was very near-sighted and couldn't see what the teacher wrote on the chalkboard, so I read the encyclopedias instead. The first book I picked up to read described all kinds of rare diseases and it started my fascination with how the body worked, revealing the natural talent that God had given me. We all need to follow what we enjoy doing and let that become our guide to the destiny that God wants us to accomplish.

When we are fulfilled, we bring happiness to others. The purpose of living isn't how much money we accumulate or how many things we own. It's the connection we have with one another and helping them to reach their goals. I am so grateful to all the people that God brought into my life that helped me achieve my goals. When we reach the end of our life, we get a sense of fulfillment from the people we love and who love us. The people we helped and those that helped us give us joy. The satisfaction in knowing that the life we lived made a positive difference in helping others.

The truth will set us free will only be accomplished by being honest. We need to strip away the excuses and start changing. I tell my patients who have a substance use disorder (addiction) that the lies stop here. The stories (lies) we tell ourselves and to others will have to *go* in order to get better. Of course, when I *first* see a new patient, they will agree to anything I say because they are in the middle of withdrawal and are miserable. They would do anything, say anything, and agree to anything in order to get relief. So, it becomes a process of stripping away the excuses. Teaching them how to get to the bottom of their problems, learn how to deal with the pain and disappointments. So, they can *learn* from their mistakes and move forward.

Whether it's a plant or animal, if it stops growing, it's in the process of dying. Even water, if it's not moving, will become stagnant and not fit for consumption. The universe revolves around change. Change is inevitable and part of living. Yet, why do people resist it? It all depends on the attitude of a person experiencing it. If we have a negative view of the world, then change will be regarded as something to avoid. But if the change is seen as an opportunity to grow and learn from the experience, then change can be exciting, challenging, and motivating. Change stretches us, makes us more resilient, and helps us become a better person. As long as we don't get mired in un-forgiveness, blaming others, or situations that keep us from learning. Change is necessary, or we will become stagnant—no help to anybody and become a burden and not a blessing. When we become a victim the excuses keep us stuck but when we become an overcomer we inspire others to do the same.

Change is uncomfortable and, at times, painful. Sometimes it strips away our comforts, our belief's or image of our self and gets to the true essence of our being. Change is progress even when it doesn't look like it. I had a patient dragged in by his mother to get help for her son's addiction. He was clearly high on drugs and wasn't interested in getting better. Later, he got arrested and spent a week in jail. He got beat up, fighting over his shoes and socks. When I saw him on his next visit, he was a changed man. *He would do anything to keep from going back to jail.* It was a miserable experience, but it lit a fire in him to change. Not all things are what they appear. Nobody wants to be incarcerated, but for him, it was a blessing in disguise that turned his life around in a new direction.

Change puts a new perspective on events. When we struggle through painful experiences, it changes our assessment of the situation. We can decide whether to get bogged down in misery or gain more understanding and compassion for others. Because of our experiences, we have become equipped with this *unique* ability that God wants us to use in drawing people to him.

- *Caution*: For those in early recovery (less than two years), they are at high risk for relapse if they are around others who are actively using drugs. They need time for their brain to heal and have stable changes in their personal life (stable relationships and job) to be effective in helping another person with addiction and not put their own recovery at risk for a relapse. They should never try to help one of their previous drug-using buddies because the memories of previous drug use triggers an unconscious process that primes them for a relapse. They have to be aware they are at high risk for relapse when a painful event happens, such as a breakup with a partner or loss of a job, and being around the wrong people (those using drugs or can easily get them drugs). So, for anyone who is having a lot of stress in their life—this is *not* the time to be involved in helping another person with addiction because of their increased risk for relapse. When they are vulnerable, they have to step back and not be around anyone actively using drugs.

People are more than the labels others have given them. A person is not an addict. This is one of the things I do not like about AA/NA. They have a lot of wonderful features, but I cringe every time I hear people introduce themselves by saying, "My name is Joey, and I'm an addict or alcoholic." I understand why AA has them do this, so they never forget they have this problem. But having a problem does *not* determine who they are. Just like people who have cancer or hypertension, we don't make their illness become their identity and tells us who they are. They are more valuable and important than any label anyone can give them.

We need to shed the skin of labels that puts people in a box. We need to explore who we really are and to break free of all those labels and put them in the incinerator and burn them to a crisp. No longer will we allow them to keep us from achieving the impossible.

Honesty involves becoming vulnerable about our needs and fears. We have to be aware of what we are feeling in order to communicate it to others. It's important we don't make cruel statements to others and then say, *"I'm telling it how it is."* We are not being honest. It's the anger being expressed under the guise of honesty. Our *hidden* motives are difficult to understand and correct for the simple reason they are not readily recognized. *Important:* We need to learn to fix ourselves before we venture into trying to fix another person. Even the Bible mentions, take the beam out of our own eye before trying to take the speck out of another. So much of what we feel, think, and say comes from information that our brain has filtered to *fit* into *our* values and ideals. It is not the complete unadulterated truth. The information we receive has been marred by previous painful events, attitudes, or beliefs and has been processed and packaged to fit into our own unique belief system.

So, how can we fix something that we don't know is a problem? It is like having a brain surgeon do surgery with their eyes closed. Honesty has a way of opening our eyes and is the most powerful tool for anyone who has an addiction. They need to recognize:

- *I cannot do this on my own.*
- They are *powerless* to see their "Stinkin-thinkin" addictive thought processes influence their choices and hinder them from knowing the truth.
- The impulsive and emotional parts of the brain are influencing their thought processes and create the addictive 'Stinkin-thinkin.'
  - *I got to have it now, regardless of the consequences.*
- This emotional response is *powerful* and *very deceptive.* It takes someone trained in recognizing addictive thought processes, either by life experiences (a sponsor) or education (addiction counselor), to reveal the truth and find ways to combat its message.

The ability to say, *"I need help"* is essential for anyone in recovery. Honesty is needed to admit, they are powerless against this disease that has hi-jacked their brain. The honesty to evaluate what caused them to slip and have a relapse. They need guidance from experienced people to lead them on a different path and to help them become free from drug use. The addicted person cannot learn from the experience without assistance. It is crucial for those in recovery to attend meetings or meet with an addiction counselor. We go to meetings, not to be condemned for past mistakes, but to learn how to prevent *future ones*. We do this by analyzing how the slip/relapse happened and making a plan on how to avoid it in the future.

I had a patient relapse because she attended a friend's funeral caused by an overdose from drugs. She had known this person for over fifteen years and felt it was disrespectful (Stinkin-thinkin) not to attend the funeral. When she arrived, her old drug-using friends were all there, and at the funeral, they all got high on heroin.

I asked, "What was she going to do the next time a friend of hers dies from an overdose?"

She said, "*I got to go, otherwise I'm not showing them my respect.*"

"Did you show respect by getting high on drugs?"

She nodded her head no.

"Is there some other way you can show respect without affecting your recovery?"

We discussed different options, but many of them had risks for relapse. Until she decided to go to the gravesite a week later after everyone had left and pay her respects then. We now have a plan that has a better chance at success. If the plan doesn't work, then we will explore what went wrong and keep the parts that did work while we construct a new plan. The way to *success* is paved with many *wrong turns*, but eventually, we will discover a new path to follow that will lead us to fulfill our full potential.

It is difficult for family members to separate their emotions to be effective in allowing an addictive person to find their own motivations to assist them in the recovery process. It's easier to tell them what to do or not do, but this *does not* lead to long-lasting results. Only when they are involved in the decision-making process are they more likely to learn and grow from the experience.

In this learning process, we have to let go of the excuses. It is easy to blame others for why we messed up. Only by being honest with ourselves and accept our *limitations and our mistakes* can we learn to navigate around our problems.

If we have diabetes and love to eat donuts, then it is foolish for us to think we can go into a donut shop and not sample or buy any. We know we can't resist them and the wisest course of action is to avoid the shop. This is no different for anyone who has an addiction. They have to avoid the people they took drugs with and not go to the places where they previously purchased drugs to avoid messing up their recovery. The problem comes when they have been in recovery for three months, a year, or even twenty years. Because they no longer have any cravings, they begin to think, addiction can no longer affect them anymore, and they start hanging around people actively using drugs. Many of them will relapse.

A patient of mine was in recovery and drug-free for over six months. Her family was having a 4th of July picnic. She planned on attending. I suggested this was not a good idea, but she went anyway. She thought, *since she no longer had any cravings and was doing great in her recovery, that she had this addiction problem whipped (Stinkin-thinkin).* When she arrived and smelled the aromatic scent of marijuana and other drugs floating in the air—a sudden intense urge hit her. She didn't anticipate this would happen. Instead of leaving immediately, the Stinkin-thinkin part of her brain kicked in with the idea, *what's wrong with taking one puff—one snort—one shot? I've been good and deserve a reward for all that hard work. Nobody will ever know it happened.* She relapsed. When we start feeling we have *control* over our addiction, it becomes a *set-up* for a *mess-up*. In order to justify our mistake, we blame others for the relapse. I had one of my patients' constantly blaming his partner for why he keeps relapsing.

"She makes me so angry by her constant nit-picking."

I said something that completely flabbergasted him. "Have you ever considered, you may be purposefully doing things to annoy her in order to get into a fight, so that gives you an excuse to take drugs?"

He opened his mouth in astonishment, cleared his throat a couple of times, and then slowly nodded his head in agreement.

When we blame another person or situation, it gives us an excuse for why we don't have to change our behaviors. We got to stop playing the blame game and start pointing our finger back at ourselves.

The Stinkin-thinkin part of the brain is very devious. It always has a *hidden agenda* with the *ultimate goal*—for them to *resume drug use*. If getting into a fight leads to drug use, then it will create more situations to stir up trouble to get them back on drugs. Anyone who has a history of addiction needs to be on high alert and diligently assess, *what is really happening?*

Important to know: Whenever there was an *excuse* for a relapse—there was a *hidden agenda* behind the situation. It can take a long time for people in recovery to reach this level of self-evaluation and discovery. It takes a trained person to assist them in this process.

Excuses prevent us from changing, and if we keep doing the same thing over and over again, we will keep getting the same old results. We have to take a new path. We cannot keep going down the same one as before. We need to take a *different route* to get to a *different destination*.

SURVIVAL TIPS

- Honesty to yourself first and then to others.
  - Admit we are powerless over this addiction, and we need help.
  - When we surrender to God and let go of our excuses and defensive thinking, we open our hearts and minds to change and move toward a new path.
- Accepting our limitations.
  - When we recognize our weaknesses, we become strong when we rely on God's strength and wisdom.
  - Avoiding a problem we struggle with is easier than trying to fix it after we relapse.

- ○ Every time we slip up and take drugs, it becomes easier to mess up again.
- Learn from our mistakes.
  - ○ God allows us to make mistakes. He doesn't cause us to make them but will use mistakes as a means to change us. All things work together for good to those who love God and to those who are called according to His purpose.
  - ○ For all things to work together for good, we need to learn from it and allow the problem to change us in order to fulfill God's purpose in our life.
- *Change directions to avoid wrong situations.* There is nothing wrong with running away from temptation. Just like Joseph tore his robe to escape the clutches of temptation from Potiphar's wife.
  - ○ Success is guaranteed when we avoid a bad situation, but resistance requires the ability to say no. We have to be *consistently* strong mentally and spiritually to say no to temptation.
- As Christians, our responsibility is not to change us but to maintain our connection with God, who changes our nature and desires. We need to use the tools He brings along our path to get better. These tools can be recovery meetings, therapy or family counseling, practice daily stress reduction and avoidance of triggers, and asking for wisdom to detect any Stinkin-thinkin thoughts.
- Protect our recovery by knowing:

> We are not invincible.
> > But we can be overcomers.
> > > Through Christ Jesus our Lord and Savior
> > > > Who has already overcome the world.

MANY ROADS LEAD TO ADDICTION

It's important for everyone to know: What our potential risk factors are for developing addiction. Just like we should know what risks factors we have for developing diabetes or a heart attack. To be aware of our potential risk can help us avoid the problem or reduce its severity. When we know that we have risk factor(s) for developing addiction, we need to become more diligent in restricting the use of any narcotic medication prescribed to treat any painful procedure or condition. Knowing our personal risk corresponds to the saying, *an ounce of prevention is worth more than a pound of cure.* Avoiding a problem is better than spending years or a lifetime dealing with the changes in the brain caused by addiction.

Common known risk factors for developing an addiction are: *Addiction can be inherited, Adverse childhood experiences, Attitudes, Behaviors, Mental problems, Untreated ADD/ADHD, and Type and route of addictive drugs used.*

Addiction can be inherited

Anyone with a family history of addiction can inherit the susceptibility to develop addiction. The closer the genetic association, the higher the risk. If they have a mother, father, sister, brother, or child with an addiction, they have a greater risk than if their relatives were their uncles, aunts, or grandparents with addiction.

145

- Anyone in the family, who is currently struggling with addiction or *had* the problem in the past, increases their risk.
- Most people are aware of the increased risk associated with having an opioid, alcohol, benzodiazepines, marijuana, cocaine, or methamphetamine addiction.
  - But many people forget *nicotine* use also increases the risk of developing any type of addiction.
  - In 2019, the number of people in the United States who smoked cigarettes was fourteen out of every one hundred adults, that were eighteen years of age or older. More than thirty-four million people in the United States were addicted to cigarettes.
    - These statistics did not include the number of people who vaped nicotine, chewed tobacco, or for anyone younger than eighteen who used any nicotine products. No wonder we have so many people struggling with addiction in our society.
- *Important* to repeat: If any family member, that includes grandparents, uncles, and aunts, ever had or have (past or present) an addiction to any addictive drug such as alcohol, opioids, cocaine, benzodiazepines, methamphetamines, marijuana, and *nicotine,* it puts other family members at an increased risk for developing a substance use disorder (addiction).
- Increased risk makes us susceptible to *any* of the above addictions—not just the ones their relatives had.
- When I evaluate a patient's family history to determine if they might develop a problem with a narcotic, I ask, "Does anyone in the family have a history of alcohol or other drug problems?"
  - Most of the time, they say "no."
  - Then I ask again, "Did anyone *ever* have a problem in the past?"

- o Then I hear about their alcoholic father or mother, who doesn't drink now, or others who used to smoke but don't smoke now.
- o It doesn't matter if a relative isn't addicted to something right at this moment. If they *ever* had a problem, it still makes other family members susceptible to becoming addicted to the same or other types of drugs.
- I have seen prescribers write a prescription for a narcotic pain pill, give it to a patient after they had surgery or a dental extraction without consulting about the patient's family history of addiction, or knowingly give the prescription to a patient who had a previous addiction to opioids in the past.
  - o The prescriber *wrongly* assumes since it has been one, two, five, ten, or twenty years had elapsed that it won't be a problem for them to take it now.
- Ignoring their patient's risk has led many people back into active addiction again.

Adverse childhood experiences (ACEs)

Traumatic events a child experiences increase their risk for developing an addiction. These adverse events they experienced before the age of eighteen can consist of but not limited to: Verbal, physical, sexual abuse, or traumatic separation.

- Also, any emotional and physical abandonment a child experiences can increase the risk for addiction such as:
  - o Having one or both parents incarcerated
  - o Divorce
  - o Death of a parent
- Issues of not having enough food to eat.
- Not have a trusted person to care for them.
  - o Living with an alcoholic or other drug-related relative(s).

- Develop emotional trauma when they experience any event that threatens their safety.
  ○ When they see their parents fight verbally or physically.
  ○ If they have been hit or verbally abused by people they trust, such as family members, relatives, friends, teachers, club leaders, or church members.
- All these adverse events will increase their risk as an adult to develop diabetes, cancers, mental problems, chronic pain, and drug addiction.
- One of the *biggest* concerns these adverse events have is that it not only affects their health later on, but can also affect the health of their progeny due to epigenetics. Epigenetics is how the environment can change what proteins their body will produce and what ones will be blocked by adding or subtracting compounds to the histones that change the shape and function of our DNA.
  ○ These structural changes are passed onto future generations.
  ○ The alteration of the proteins produced affects the regulation of their immune system, making them more susceptible to cancer(s) and to diseases such as diabetes, heart attacks, and addiction. It also changes how they will cope with stressful events and increases their risk for developing mental health problems.
  ○ So the adverse events that happened to our Great grandfather can affect us now on how we deal with either physical or emotional stress and can make us more susceptible to developing an addiction.
- The higher the ACEs score—the higher the risk for developing an addiction.

Attitudes

The people we are around and spend the most time with can make us more or less susceptible to developing an addiction. If family members are actively using drugs, then their children will more likely take drugs. They will start using drugs at a younger age and can permanently affect their brain development. Drug use hinders the connection between the impulsive parts of the brain to the logical—this is not a good idea part of the brain.

- College students who drink never think they drink too much.
  - Because all their friends are drinking as much as they are.
- If advertisements make drug use look very attractive, this will skyrocket the number of people taking drugs and increase the community's acceptance of drug use. In Colorado, they have pictures of ice cream, cookies, candy plastered on door fronts that have marijuana in them. All these pictures are geared to appeal to young people and increase their desire to use drugs.
- Many states are making marijuana legal.
  - We are now seeing a record-breaking number of teens and young adults using marijuana. Once marijuana became legal, people's (mainly kids) *perception* of the drug makes them think it is safe to take.
  - Most people are unaware of all the risks associated with marijuana use.
    - Marijuana causes delayed motor reactions and, when coupled with alcohol use, causes significantly increased motor vehicle accidents.
    - Increases the number of people getting schizophrenia and other mental health disorders that are overwhelming mental hospital admissions.
    - Memory is reduced, and a reduction in a person's IQ and can cause a low motivation state.
    - If anyone uses marijuana daily, they are likely addicted to this drug.
    - Pregnant women using marijuana have now shown problems with social development occur in their children starting around the age of six. The more

women who use marijuana while pregnant will reveal even more future problems in their offspring.

Risk-taking behaviors

If anyone craves adventure—the more dangerous the event, the more exciting it is for him or her. The thrill of engaging in risky behaviors increases their susceptibility to developing an addiction.

- Driving at excessively high speeds, climbing steep, treacherous mountain cliffs, jumping off a mountainside to the water below.
- Doing anything to experience that adrenalin rush and dopamine surge is what makes them more susceptible to experiment with drugs.
- They are willing to try anything that exposes them to taking dangerous and highly addictive drugs.

Mental problems

Mental problems can make people with this condition more susceptible to drug use. The mental problems can range from anxiety problems, depression, attention deficit disorders (ADD/ADHD), bipolar and anger issues.

- Many people with mental health issues use drugs to regulate their negative emotional states. People who have *untreated* ADD (Attention Deficit Disorder or ADHD (Attention Deficit Hyperactive Disorder) are at an increased risk for developing a methamphetamine addiction. Many people who have ADD/ADHD state that methamphetamine calms them down and helps them focus. Whereas most people who don't have ADD/ADHD when they take methamphetamine, it hypes them up, gives them lots of energy and can make them feel jittery with a racing heart, and problems with sleeping. Some people taking methamphet-amine become paranoid and can have schizophrenia-like psychosis, violent behavior, increase in suicides, significant heart problems, and an increased incidence of strokes. Methamphetamine can damage the brain's cellular mem-branes and is neurotoxic, and cause significant changes in how the brain functions. With chronic use, people can develop problems with attention and memory.

- People who have bipolar depression and schizophrenia find taking opioids can help reduce some of their symptoms associated with untreated mental health problems. Initially, opioids can help reduce some of their anxiety, lessen their racing mental thoughts and help them sleep.
  o It does not fully treat their condition, but it allows them to function a little better. But the effects of the opioid lessens as tolerance develops and drives an escalating need to take more and stronger opioids to get some relief for their mental illness.
- The benefit of opioids or other drugs does *not* outweigh the risk for developing addiction and all the health prob-lems associated with drug use, such as:
  o Increased risk in developing infections such as HIV, hepatitis C, and sepsis that can damage their heart valves requiring heart surgery.
  o They can stop breathing and risk permanent brain dam-age or death.
- Prolonged use of opioids over time worsens depression and isolation and increases the potential risk for suicide or death.

Untreated ADD/ADHD

ADD and ADHD are caused by their inability to control their impulsivity and increase their risk for addiction at an early age.

People with this condition will overreact to any problem rather than pause and respond to what is the best way to deal with the situation.

- o It is extremely difficult for them to stop and think. This always gets them into trouble.
- o This impulsiveness leads them to experiment with drugs and not think about any of the consequences associated with drinking or drugging while driving under the influence or doing any other risky activities.

The type of drugs and the route

Any drug that quickly stimulates the release of Dopamine in high amounts increases an individual's susceptibility to becoming addicted to that drug. Any addictive drug that reaches the brain the fastest are more addictive than those that take time to stimulate the brain receptors.

- • This is why IV drugs are more addictive than taking the same drug by mouth.
- • Be aware that any drug that affects the natural reward system in the brain can make a person susceptible to developing an addiction.
  - o The brain provides pleasure as a reward for behaviors that promote survival.
  - o The natural reward system is the pleasure center of the brain and can be altered by drug use.
- • Addictive drugs *hi-jack* this natural reward system by stimulating the reward system more intensely than the normal survival rewards can. If the natural rewards stimulate the brain 100 times more than normal activates, then addictive drugs hit the reward center at 150, 300, and even 1,000 times stronger
  - o Chronic drug use has caused the brain reward system to become altered and changes their perception of what is needed to survive.

- o Drugs hi-jacked the reward center and make having sex, eating food, or caring for their children to *be less* important than taking drugs.
- o Drug use is now viewed as necessary for *survival,* just like water is for anyone lost in the desert with only a few drops left in their canteen.
- People in active addiction will do *anything* to get drugs. These addictive alterations in their brain drive a compulsive need to take more and more drugs. It dissolves away any of their previous values, hopes, and dreams. Drug use becomes even more important than life itself.

Be aware: Addiction is a no-respecter of age, religion, economic class, ethnic group, sexual orientation, success, celebrity status, physicians, therapists, politicians, judges, or even law enforcement.

- Addiction has the potential to happen to anyone.
- Even if no one in their family ever had any addiction issues.
  - o The prolonged use of addictive drugs (some say as short as five to seven days changes can occur) alters the way the brain responds to the drug(s) and has the potential to start anyone down the destructive road of addiction.
- *Remember*: No one is immune.

SURVIVAL TIPS

- Addiction can be inherited.
  - o We don't have to develop the problem if we avoid or limit the amount of drugs, alcohol or nicotine that can trigger it.
  - o Learning stress reduction techniques help reduce our anxiety and stress response system and can help people become less susceptible to addiction.
  - o Important to know our family history to determine if we are at risk for addiction.

- Adverse Childhood Experiences (ACE's) can increase their risk for developing mental, physical, and addiction problems.
  - When we release all the pain and suffering to God and ask him to free us so we can forgive—healing starts taking place.
  - We can't change what happened to us in the past, but for those who are a Christian with God's grace, they can become healed and freed from the pain by allowing The Holy Spirit that lives inside to guide them to a new path.
  - Stress hormones are toxic to our system. When we rest in God's peace and surrender all our heartaches to him, and use the tools he has blessed us with (daily relaxation skills)—our system will reset to a lower and lower anxiety response.
    - Read John 14:27 (Verse is in the endnotes) and claim that peace to be in our life.
- Mental illnesses such as depression, ADD, Bipolar, and strong emotions such as anger and rage increases their risk for addiction.
  - Important to treat any mental illness. Studies show, if the mental health problem is not treated at the same time as the addiction, they won't do well in either treatment.
- Addiction is no respecter of age, occupation, or economic class.
- No one is immune.
  - Addiction could happen to any one of us if it wasn't for the grace of God. Let us care for those lost to this disease and encourage them. It's remarkable how powerful a kind word can be.

SURVIVAL TIP # 12

WORDS WE SAY HAVE POWER

The words we hear, what we say to others, and to ourselves have power. When we repeatedly hear the same message over and over—we start to believe it's true. Repetition amplifies the information and becomes a form of brainwashing that breeds the adoption of the belief—then fighting for that belief. We will argue a point, not for understanding or effective communication, but to prove—I am right, and everyone else is wrong.

In order to change, we have to modify the words we say to ourselves and *not believe* all that we hear from other people. If we want to transform our lives, we can no longer call our self, *stupid, worthless, can't get any breaks, a horrible mother, father, sister, brother, or child.* We need to start saying the things *we want to become.* When we repeatedly say positive things about ourselves, we gradually begin to believe them. *With God's help, I am capable of doing a great job. I am a great parent. I learn quickly and make wise choices.* Positive or negative word choices shape our *subconscious mind*—the part we are not aware of. These words have such a powerful effect on our lives. The subconscious mind is where *all* information is filtered. It sifts through the millions and trillions of bits of information and only allows a minuscule amount to drip into our consciousness. The subconscious filter *changes* how we interpret the information the brain is processing. Depending on how the filter has been programmed to respond, it can let positive or negative ideas and motives seep into our consciousness and awareness. The *programming* comes from the words *we say* about ourselves and the words *we hear* others say about us.

Let me repeat. We are *unaware* this filtering of information is occurring. We just feel or think a certain way, not realizing we can *change* our life circumstances by *changing* the *filter* in our subconscious mind. At some point in our life, we will get into a difficult situation. When that part *deep* inside tells us—*I can do this*, confirms the filter has been programmed to think positive. We start looking for opportunities to change our circumstances and ways to accomplish what we previously thought was impossible to achieve. When we *start believing*—we *start doing* the very things we keep hearing and hearing over and over again.

We have to speak the words out loud so we can hear them. Just thinking the thoughts is not as powerful as saying them. In the Bible, it talks about how faith *comes* about by hearing and hearing the word of God. In the past, I always wondered why hearing was repeated. Why was it so significant? It took over five years for God to reveal to me the significance of why the word hearing was repeated twice. It was so simple that I wondered why it took me so long to understand its significance. The *repetition* of the words we *hear* gets down into our *hearts*. We need to repeatedly say, so we can repeatedly hear the words in order to get the message into our subconscious mind. *Words* have such a powerful effect on influencing our *thoughts, feelings,* and *actions*.

People we spend the most time with influence our thoughts and the words we say about our self and to others. This changes our filter. Our filter can become *corrupted*. That's why we need to set *boundaries* to protect our *subconscious processing*. When we are surrounded by negativity, it becomes contagious, like a virus that can spread from one person to another and then infects the entire group. It is hard to think positively when all we hear is negative. It seeps into the *subconscious* part of the mind that ultimately *directs the decisions* we make by influencing the conscious mind's attitudes, thoughts, and beliefs. We can be kind to a negative person, but we cannot spend a lot of time with them. Their negative words will eventually become our thoughts and words.

I find it exciting when science finally catches up with what the Bible has already said several thousand years ago. The apostle Paul wrote to the Philippians for them to think about what is noble; whatever is right, pure, lovely, and admirable, if anything, is excellent or praiseworthy. Telling everyone who wants to *change their life*, they have to *change their thoughts and words.*

One of the first steps in recovery is the need to change what they say about themselves. No longer can they call themselves, *I am an addict—I am hopeless—helpless—worthless.* Joel Osteen wrote the book, *The Power of I Am.* (Osteen, 2015). The message he brings can make a huge difference in how to approach life. Our life is *changed* by the *words* we say about it.

If a person says there is no way I can succeed. These words have a way of magnifying their distressful emotions and intensify their anxiety.

If we say, *I have concerns about the situation, and I need to evaluate it further*, it lowers our emotional response and allows us a chance to consider other possible solutions to the problem. We are not letting our emotions overtake our ability to consider potential alternatives to find a solution to the problem.

The brain reacts to highly stressful events by activating the *Fight, Flight, or Freeze* reaction. Our stress response system was used in the past to keep us from getting killed. Rarely do we encounter a bear attacking us. But we do encounter the boss yelling or co-workers complaining about us. The survival stress response is *unable* to distinguish between life-threatening events and everyday irritations and disagreements. Adrenalin is released and surges through our body, preparing us to either fight or run away. Once it's triggered, it releases *everything* it has to keep a person alive. Our heart pounds, and blood rushes to our skeletal muscles, preparing for action, at the expense of less blood flowing to the higher cortical areas of our brain (logical thinking areas) and other body organs. Cortisol is released that increases our blood sugar in the blood to provide energy for our muscles to either run or fight. Once the stress response system is triggered it becomes an *all-or-nothing* response, with no shades of gray response. Our life depends on this rapid release and spontaneous actions to avoid death. This instinctive response is *not* consciously mediated.

Today the *Fight, Flight, or Freeze* mode is still present and is activated when we encounter stressful events. We have learned different ways of showing this response because it is not socially acceptable to hit or kill each other when we disagree with them, but these modifications still have all the chemicals and hormones roaring through our veins. We have adapted our behaviors to a more *socially* acceptable manner to deal with this response (but not necessarily a more healthy way to deal with the situation).

In the *Freeze* response, people isolate themselves and numb their emotional or physical pain by taking drugs or alcohol to alleviate their discomfort. They feel paralyzed by the stress and are incapable of choosing a response. An example of the *Freeze* reaction: A deer stays stuck in the middle of the road and stares at the headlights of the car that is just about to hit them. Rather than get off the road— the deer stays rooted to the ground and doesn't move. We, too, can get stuck in our circumstances by the words we use that ensnare us.

The excuses mount:

> *I can't do that.*
> *I don't have the education.*
> *I don't have the right connections.*

All these excuses and many more prevent us from dealing with the situation. All the excuses do is to keep us from moving forward in our life. We become frozen in the problem and unable to move past it. In order to change the outcome of our life, we need to change the words we say. *I may not have the education right now, but I am going to start by taking one class at a time until I achieve my goal.*

In the *Fight* response, we react with anger and lash out verbally or physically. We intimidate other people by criticizing or speaking in a condescending way. The *Fight* response can be a positive response if we can engage the logical part of our brain.

Examples of redirecting our *Fight* responses are:

- Defending our rights
- Setting boundaries
- Protecting our self if physically attacked.

The positive *Fight* response does *not* come naturally. The logical part of the brain has to consider the pros and cons of a situation. It takes time to respond rather than to react in a split-second. If our emotions are engaged, it becomes extremely difficult to control our responses when we are angry or upset. Emotional reactions are impulsive and bypass the logical part of the brain. It takes skill training and practice to learn how to delay the impulsive reaction and allow us time to logically assess the situation to make better choices that promote a more effective outcome.

In the *Flight* mode, a person will try to avoid *any* situation that might be stressful. They will leave the room, hang up the phone mid-conversation, impulsively break up a relationship or quit a job without thinking through the situation—rather than confront the problem. This *Flight* response can be manifested in a people pleaser response. In order to avoid conflict, the people-pleaser will do anything the other person demands, even if it's unreasonable or detrimental to them, in order to maintain peace and for other people to like them. A people-pleaser keeps their emotions locked inside with no outlet for them to express their growing ever-expanding resentments and anguish that leads them to take drugs to numb their pain or, worse yet, suicide to avoid the conflict permanently.

The stress response system is located in the primitive areas of the brain in close proximity to the reward, memory, emotion, and motor circuits. Whereas the reasoning areas of the brain are located further away. The primitive areas of the brain are all geared to keep us alive. In a life or death situation, we have no time to think of the pros and cons of a situation. We would be dead, long before deciding what to do. Survival is impulsive and reactive without reasoning or consideration. This system was needed when real danger was present and required an immediate response, but we rarely encounter these types of situations. Currently our stress response system is like dropping a nuclear bomb to kill a mosquito. It gets us into trouble all the time—saying the wrong words or doing the wrong things. When our whole system is in survival mode, we are primed to react in a split-second, not allowing any time to consider other options—due to less blood flow to the logical areas of our mind. Trying to reason with anyone in survival mode will be ineffective. Our *only* focus is survival, and we can't see the whole picture. We can only respond by running away (flight), ignore the situation (freeze), or physically or verbally attack (fight).

To control these primitive responses, we need to change the way we *describe* an event, so we can change the way we *react* to it. The words we *say* are the words we *will do*. What we believe about ourselves pushes us towards the destiny that our *words* direct us to go. Just like a steering wheel in a car directs our path, so do the words we speak. We can change our destiny by simply changing the words we say about ourselves and to any circumstances we encounter. If we say, *this is the end of me.* So it will be. If we say *this is an opportunity to learn and grow from it.* Then we will learn and grow from it. Everyone is in the driver-seat of his or her own life. What we say about any situation will determine the outcome.

Words affect:

- How we cope with different situations.
- How we feel about our self and others.
- What we will do.
- How we react or respond in a negative or positive way.

Debbie Tieke, the author of *The Art of Invitation* (2021), has written a program that focuses on improving the relationships we have with each other. One way to reduce conflict in a relationship is learning to pause before speaking. Our *first* thought is impulsive and usually a negative one. Taking time for the second thought to emerge leads to less conflict in relating to other people. *Be aware,* our first thought is automatic and is based on our emotional instinctive reaction rather than a logical evaluation of our circumstances. The first thought *colors* the present situation with our *previous* painful events and has us overreact in an unreasonable manner. What makes the situation worse, our emotions blind us from the truth, and we can only *see* our point of view. Emotion trumps logic. Only by pausing and consider what really happened, without attaching any emotional baggage to the situation, can anyone learn to discern the truth.

Part of my job as a treatment provider is to instill value in a person. If anyone feels worthless, they won't even try to get better because they don't feel like they deserve a loving relationship, a good job, or being happy and fulfilled. In order to change their mindset, I actively look for positive things they have done and praise them to elevate their self-esteem. I do not make things up, but I do find one item they did right to give them encouragement to take another step, and with each step, they gradually gain confidence in themselves.

I had a patient in an abusive relationship and had extremely low self-esteem. Her abuser constantly belittled her ability to take care of herself by reminding her, *she was stupid, could never get a job or make it on her own.*

When I asked, "Why is she staying in the relationship?"

She said, "*She could never leave him because she was weak and helpless.*"

I told her, "She is full of courage."

She looked at me, shocked because all her friends and family confirmed she was a weak person by staying with him.

Not certain she heard me right, she asked, "*Wh... What did you say?*"

"It takes a lot of courage to stay in an abusive relationship and deal with the unknown—not knowing what could happen next. We just need to learn how to direct this courage into finding a way out."

That was the day we made a plan—small steps—to get free. It took over two years, but she is now free. She has her own apartment, a job, and she and her kids are happy. Part of recovery is instilling hope and confidence in them. In her previous situation, she had never heard any words of encouragement, but every time she came to my office, I made a point of finding something positive to say. We do have the power to change our lives and those around us, by the words we say.

Change starts with one small step—then another—then another. It's not an overnight process. Whoever told them, go to this treatment facility, and they will be back to normal in a week, a month, a year is filling them with false hope. Change is slow, and it takes time—time to do it right.

Another one of my patients recently told me *I had saved his life.*

He talked about how he was on the brink of killing himself— and I was his last shot to get better. He already had a plan to kill himself later that week. Addiction had taken away his life. He was sixty years old and felt his life was over. He had lost so many opportunities to play in a band or do computer programming and felt he was too old to start over.

I shocked him when he heard me say, "*That's a bunch of rubbish. As long as you are breathing, you still have a purpose to fulfill.*"

He still had his skill as a musician and was encouraged to pursue his love of music. I scheduled him to see an addiction counselor while I treated his opioid addiction. He left the office with a renewed sense of hope—a chance for a brighter future. Since then, every day is better than the last one. He started a band and is in a steady relationship. His life is restored. Every time he comes into the office, he has a big grin on his face and glows with happiness. It lifts my spirit every time I see him. Although he tries to credit me for saving his life, I know the real truth. God has answered my prayers and brings people to my practice that God wants to heal.

At first, my patient did not believe in any God.

I gave him one challenge. "*Ask God to reveal himself to you.*" God is never afraid to reveal the truth of his existence, his mercy, and love for us, but a person has to ask.

Since then, over the years, he has come to believe by saying, "*It doesn't make any sense not to believe. How can random events create life, let alone humans?*"

If anyone opens their mind and asks God to reveal Himself to them—He will. God loves to show His mercy and love to anyone who asks.

The words we say have the power to restore or to destroy. When we use words to encourage another, we are restoring them. When we complain and criticize, this discourages and destroys them from achieving their dreams and future. It takes a strong person to overcome these negative words. It is important for all of us not to criticize anyone in recovery about their previous behaviors. They cannot change the past. The old saying, *don't cry over spilt milk* applies here. When previous mistakes are brought up repeatedly (remember the power of our words), they start to believe:

- They can't get better.
- Lost their confidence to try.
- Then end up taking drugs again.

Many of my patients tell me, when their family keeps bringing up the past, all they want to do is use drugs again to dull the pain. They know they did wrong and already blame themselves. We don't have to keep reminding them. The guilt and shame are so great; it already is difficult to move forward. As a Christian, it should be easier to move past this condemnation—but for many, it isn't. We know that God has made us a new creation and has put his nature inside us. We know when we confess our sins that God forgives us and remembers them no more. But the problem is—we remember them. As Christians, God convicts us of our sin, so we can turn away and become free by confessing our inability to change and ask God to change our desires and our heart. But Condemnation—the shame—does not come from God. Condemnation will never change us or make us free, and it will only destroy us. So, the only way to become released from condemnation is to fight the thoughts and feelings with what the Bible says about us. I am a new creation. The old is gone—the new is here. When an old thought emerges, I replace it with: *I have already asked God for forgiveness, and God remembers it no more.* It is like a file on our computer has been permanently deleted and can never be retrieved again.

It is only through *acceptance*—we can't change the past, and we only have the power to change this moment in time. Making better choices gives us the courage to reach out and pursue our dreams. *Today is the only day we can change.* God is the ultimate chain-breaker and wants His truth found in the word of God (The Bible) to set us free.

As family members, we have to learn how to forgive. We have to let go of the past wrongs. I have heard family members say, *I have forgiven them.* If they have forgiven them, why do they keep bringing up their previous mistakes? Every time their loved one is getting better—why is there the need to keep reminding them of the past? Obviously, family members, along with those in recovery, need to seek help, whether to see a counselor, a Pastor, a Priest, or talk to God in order for the whole family to heal. God, in His ultimate wisdom, knows the only way to become released from condemnation is forgiveness of our sins—for the wrongs we have done. When we confess our mistakes to God and to others and ask for forgiveness. We are no longer bound to the past and are free to pursue the future. God remembers our sins—no more. So, stop repeatedly confessing past mistakes to God because He doesn't know what we are talking about. When God forgives—*He forgets*—it ever happened.

If something is not working, then we *all* need to do *something* different. Family members need to realize they are unintentionally *destroying* the one that they want to help by the words they say. Our words have *power.* If we keep saying the wrong words, then we need to figure out what is wrong with *me* that need *healing?* It is only through healing can we completely forgive.

When an area in our life no longer hurts, then we no longer feel the need to lash out toward those that had caused the pain. Healing takes time. We can't put a Band-Aid over it and think it's healed. This is our denial system—a Band-Aid over the problem. The problem still exists, but since it's covered, we think it no longer affects us. Yet, all the while, the wound is festering and getting worse, seeping into more and more of our life, destroying relationships, opportunities and happiness.

Sometimes our denial system is so strong that we fail to recognize we have a problem. Many times I hear family members tell me the following messages:

- Why do I need counseling? They are the one who has the addiction.
- I am the victim here.
- Why do people want to focus on me when they were the ones who wronged me?
- I tried everything to get them better, and this is the gratitude I get.

Judging, Blaming and becoming the Victim keep us from *healing*. Healing causes us to let go and not let the pain of rejection and helplessness keep us from rejoicing when our loved one is getting better. The poison that we had inside us is gone, and our words are filled with encouragement and not bitterness. Healing is part of forgiveness. Full forgiveness cannot happen until the pain inside of us is gone.

Ultimately, it all comes down to us. If I am happy with my life and how others respond to me—keep doing the same thing. But, if I am not happy with how things have worked out for me or my loved ones, then I have to do things differently. *Awareness* that all is not right is the only way we can change. If we live with blinders on—we can never see the light of truth in front of us. *Important* for us to know: We can't *change* what we don't *see*. This requires a lot of soul searching, praying (this worked for me), or seeing a counselor to guide us in this path of self-discovery and awareness.

Painful events have the power to *wake us up*. Pain is like an alarm clock—that startles us from the slumber of our lives. Pain awakens us into awareness by telling our mind—Mission Control— We have a *problem*—shocking us out of our everyday routine. We got to do something different. We can embrace the pain and learn from it. Or, we can let our denial system kick in and become the Victim by creating a deep pit of pain, suffering and poison to spew out from our mouth onto everyone we encounter. The victim will justify every action—even horrendous actions, by blaming others for their behaviors and never learn from it. To grow and change is part of life. Only by letting go of all the excuses (remember our words have power) and move forward can we break the chains that held us back and stunted us for so long. The universe is growing and always changing—we need to change, too. A part of us dies every time we decide to become the victim. To stop growing is a form of dying until all our dreams are gone.

In treating my patients, I won't let them see themselves as a victim and give me excuses. I instill in them, they are responsible for their own actions or choices. The choices they make today influence the number of choices they will have for tomorrow. If they make a mistake and used drugs, I don't want to hear them say to me, *I'm sorry*. This means nothing to me. It is an excuse to get out of being accountable for their behavior. I would rather have them tell me what happened and what they plan to do differently the next time they encounter the same problem. When someone tells me they will do better next time. They are *not* learning from the experience. Addiction has a way of undermining their desire to stay off drugs. So, saying, *I will do better next time* never works. It is easy to say I'm sorry, or will do better, than spend the time needed to analyze what happened in order to avoid it from occurring again. They need to figure out where they could have been able to say no.

An example: Danny found a brochure in the mail that his favorite band will be coming to town. He loves music and wants to go. He has been off drugs for a year and feels he needs to reward himself with a good time (Stinkin-thinkin). He decides to bring a buddy with him who has never taken any drugs and will help him stay *clean*. I let him know it was a bad idea and explained why. To be in the same environment where he previously took drugs will be a huge trigger. He gave me this elaborate scheme (full of Stinkin-thinkin ideas) on how he can avoid a relapse. I let him know it was still a bad idea. He went anyway and got separated in the crowd from his friend and relapsed by shooting up heroin.

In an effort to understand where in the process he could have said *no*, we worked backward. It wasn't until he reached the point of throwing away the flyer to his favorite band coming to town is where he would have been able to say no.

I will try harder, I will do better next time—will never work. We have to come up with a new plan by analyzing the situation and trying something *new*. Doing the same thing over and over again and expecting a different response is crazy. So, when an old addicted friend calls and says lets get together—we have to work on a plan on how to avoid this slip in the future. Some have changed their phone numbers, others have moved. They have to do whatever it takes to keep from making the same mistakes over and over again if they ever want to get their life back on track.

When anyone says: *I can do this—my mistakes don't define my value as a person*, they are learning the power of using positive words to transform their life. They no longer see a poor choice as a reflection of who they are as a person, but as a learning experience to grow and make better choices in the future. For every action, there is a consequence in response to that action. It is a simple principle of physics—for every action there is a reaction.

Remember, our attitude can make a huge difference in our life. We can't change what has happened to us. But, we can change our attitude and the words we say to either move us forward *or* keep us stuck in the past. We are in the ballpark, and the ball is in our court. We can decide our destiny, the path we want to follow.

- I get to choose to have a good day or a bad day.
- I can choose to be happy or sad.
- I can choose to be angry or at peace.
- It all comes down to choices and the words we say.

Words, Words, Words are so *powerful*, but so many people think of them as insignificant. If only we realized the full power behind the words we say—we would learn to speak more carefully.

SURVIVAL TIPS

- God, in His ultimate wisdom, knows the only way to become released from condemnation is forgiveness of our sins—the wrongs we have done. When we confess our mistakes to God and to others and ask for forgiveness, we are no longer bound to the past and become free to pursue the future. God remembers our sins—*no more*. So, stop repeatedly confessing *past* mistakes to God because He doesn't know what we are talking about. When God forgives—*He forgets* they ever happened.

- By following the apostle Paul's recommendations he made to the Philippians for us to guard our mind and heart by thinking of things that are noble, right, pure, and praiseworthy…will renew our mind and change the filter in our subconscious mind to become positive.
  - A positive mindset allows us to see any obstacle as an opportunity.

- In order to change our thoughts and beliefs, we have to change the words we hear and say about ourselves.
  - Learn what God says about us. David talked about how God had perfectly and wonderfully made him. All of us are perfect in God's eyes. He was the one who created us.
  - For the longest time, I struggled with why God had created me the way he did. I was born blind in my right eye. As a child, I was happy and friendly, but once I became aware of my damaged eye, I withdrew into my protective fortress where nobody could hurt me anymore. I had to keep proclaiming, God has perfectly and wonderfully made me in order to break the chains that encased my heart. God has a purpose for everything.

- Don't let our similarities keep us from appreciating our uniqueness.

- When we declare with our mouth, "Jesus is our Lord," and believe in our heart that God raised him from the dead. We will be saved. For it is with our heart that we believe and is justified, and it is with *our mouth* that we profess our faith and are saved.

- When we become a child of God, we can boldly go to our heavenly father and ask for forgiveness and know that God has heard us.
- *Stop* holding onto past sins that bind us in condemnation when we have already been forgiven. Sin is doing anything that will cause harm to us and to others. When we ask for forgiveness, we also need to ask for God's Grace to do what I cannot change on my own.

- Condemnation comes from the law. The Ten Commandments were meant to show we could *never* achieve God's standards.
  - We all fall short in trying to follow them. In our attempts to follow them, we fail every time.
  - We lose hope and *draw away* from God.
  - Condemnation will never bring us closer to God.
- When Jesus died on the cross for our sins, God formed a New Covenant that I like to call the Divine switch. Jesus took our sins, so we could receive His righteousness. Jesus took our punishment for our sins so we could receive God's Mercy and Grace.
- As a Christian, God sees us in Christ—Holy and without blemish.
- Conviction comes from our Heavenly Father who knows what we are doing is not good for us and wants us to stop and turn to Him.
  - Sin hurts us, and conviction is God's way of drawing us closer to Him. When we sin, we know what we had done was wrong, and we need God's help to change. Applying the word of God found in the Bible and let God's words renew our mind, change our heart, and our desires are how to break free from the bondage of sin.
  - When we give our problems to God, He will walk by our side and never forsake us.

- ○ Remember, God always knows what's best for us. He knows our full potential because he created us.
- ○ Everyone is uniquely special to God—that's why no one has the same fingerprints.
- When we keep hearing the words over and over again. The repetition ingrains its message into our subconscious and slowly seeps into our conscious thoughts, and we begin to believe it.
- Depending on the message we keep hearing—it can be for our betterment or determent.

The choice is yours.
What are *you* going to be?

BE AWARE: STINKIN-THINKIN NEVER GOES AWAY

Those Darn Thoughts Can Trip A Person Up in *any* Stage of Recovery.

Treatment involves learning how to avoid falling victim to "Stinkin-thinkin." Chronic drug use has changed the brain circuitry and affects a person for a very long time. Some people relapse after more than twenty years of recovery, making some speculate it could even last a lifetime. AA calls the circuit changes caused by addiction Stinkin-thinkin to explain the *abnormal thought* processes that *lead them back* to drug or alcohol use. Abnormal thinking patterns remain dormant for a long period of time. Stinkin-thinkin is like a lion stalking its prey, waiting for the right moment to pounce and attack.

The addictive processes work in the *subconscious* level of their mind. Anyone in recovery is *unaware* of this abnormal addictive thinking and its ultimate agenda. They think life is good. Finally, free from the addiction that has held them hostage and taken so much of their life, pursuing drug use. Those in recovery must *never* forget the Stinkin-thinkin pathways are very patient, just waiting for the right opportunity to derail and destroy all their efforts toward recovery.

I had a patient in recovery for six years, and his marriage had survived his addiction years. Since he no longer has any cravings or thoughts of using drugs, he stopped attending any of the meetings or seeing a counselor. He felt free from the noose that was around his neck, choking the life out of him. Life is good until he answered his wife's phone, and the message went to voice mail. He clicked on the message and learned his wife was having an affair with another man. Rage, anger, and hurt overwhelmed his mind. Bile rose into his throat as he threw the phone into the wall. He couldn't handle the pain, the grief, and the sorrow. He tried calling some friends, but no one answered their phone. He was all alone in his misery, with no one to comfort him. He had to get away to think. He drove as fast and as far away as he could to escape the pain. Tears blurred his vision, and when he slowed down, he discovered he was back in his old neighborhood, where he previously took drugs. A craving hit so intensely that it shook him. Wild thoughts flooded his mind (Stinkin-thinkin thoughts), *just one time to ease the pain from the betrayal. No one will know—just a little dab of something to calm down. Anything, so I don't have to go through this alone. Only one time,* the voice inside his head got louder and louder—as his anxiety spun out of control, *no one is going to know.*

What he didn't realize, the *pain* caused his unconscious addictive pathways to become activated and automatically drove him back to a place where he used drugs in the past. Setting him up to be in the wrong place, at the wrong time, when his emotions were overtaking his reasoning. Once he was primed by the wrong place and the wrong time, an intense craving hit him with such force that it would have taken an army battalion to keep him from using drugs again.

In the unprepared person, these *hidden dormant* addiction-thinking pathways are lurking for the right opportunity to:

- Trigger an intense emotional reaction.
- That creates anxiety and an unexpected, overwhelming craving.
- That leads them to relapse.

When the unprepared person experiences an intense emotional reaction, they usually give into this unexpected and intense urge. The only way to combat the unexpected is to be *prepared*. Everyone in recovery needs to learn the early warning signs that can alert him or her that danger is ahead. Just like we have road signs that alert us to a problem, such as a detour ahead. But they need to be paying attention to the road to see them. People in recovery can't ignore the early warning signs that danger is ahead and to be careful. If they don't pay attention to these signs, it can lead to disaster.

As time lapses, many people begin to think they are *cured.* They have had success in refusing drug use, been around old friends, and hadn't used any drugs. They start to think *they have outgrown this problem.* Some alcoholics who have been in recovery for years have learned how to avoid drinking when they visit with their previous drinking buddies. They know what to expect and had years of practice at refusal skills. Because of their successes, they begin to think they are immune or cured of this problem. They do well for a while *until* a painful emotional event happens. The death of a loved one, the loss of a job, or a divorce will set this dormant pathway off quicker than being struck by a lightning bolt. When emotionally painful events occur, their stress response system kicks into *overdrive.* All kinds of hormones and chemicals surge through their system, making their heart pound, skin sweat and their hands shake and have trouble breathing. If they can't get anything to calm down, their fears escalate, and their reaction becomes more intense, making it even harder to stay away from taking something to calm down. The repetitive thought, *I got to take something* keeps repeating itself with, *just one drink or hit to calm down. All you need is just one,* and they will quickly find out that one is never enough.

Many people in recovery find *emotion* misleads them more than helps them. I have a twenty-year-old woman involved with an older man. After dating for over two years, they decide to live together. Life was great until she noticed, whenever she wanted to have sex, her partner kept making excuses that he was tired or not feeling well. Rather than discuss the situation with him, her Stinkin-thinkin kicked in. She was convinced he was having an affair with another woman, and he no longer found her to be attractive. Her mind raced back to all the other men she had in her life and how they all left her for another woman. She became so upset that she ended up using drugs again. The drugs couldn't calm the hurt, anger, and turmoil she felt inside until she finally confronted him. He had been diagnosed with low testosterone and was too embarrassed to tell her about his problem. She suffered from all this emotional angst that had nothing to do with reality. Her emotional pain caused by memories of previous boyfriends jilting her and her assumptions caused her to relapse.

In all the years treating my patients with addiction, I have found several situations that have caused many of them to slip up. I've had several discussions in my group addiction meetings on: What circumstances did they encounter that led them to relapse? I've collected all this information to help others recognize some common causes for relapses. I call this list, Early Relapse Warning Signs and Symptoms—to bring awareness to any potential problems ahead if they *continue* on this path.

I put these early relapse warning signs into five general categories. Some of them can overlap into more than one category. The categories I discovered that affected them the most were: Emotions, Attitudes, Control issues, Relationships, and Life problems.

EMOTION

Emotions can *distort* reality. These distortions can cause problems for anyone in recovery and have to be recognized and treated. Some of these problems are: *Depression, Boredom, Lonely, Lack of joy, Strong emotion, Hold feelings inside, People pleasing, Inferior thinking, Superior thinking, Overreacting to stressful events, Compulsive/impulsive behaviors, Thrill seekers, Need to Celebrate, Negative emotions.*

Depression

Depression can give people an array of symptoms in varying degrees. For men the symptoms are subtle and can be more difficult to diagnose. To be diagnosed with depression, they need to have the symptoms persist for at least two weeks. Some of the common symptoms involve:

- Increased or decrease in sleep
- Appetite changes
- Energy level with either tired all the time or not able to sleep
- Decreased concentration
- Decreased interest in daily activities and relationships.
- Feelings of worthlessness or guilt.
- Thoughts of suicide or history of previous suicide attempts.
- In men they can become irritable, angry or despondent and increase their use of alcohol or drugs to treat their symptoms. They can also have violent behavior.

Some experts say depression is anger directed inward, causing symptoms of lack of interest to do anything. This low motivational state keeps them *stuck* in their circumstances. The less they do, the harder it becomes motivated to do anything.

- Everything becomes a chore. They start telling themselves and everyone around them, they need help.
  - They have their spouse, and children cook and clean, bring them a glass of water, do the laundry while they stay in bed.
- They need medication to treat their condition.
  - Pandering to every need will not get them better. It only reinforces the idea—they are helpless.
  - Over time, they start feeling they are no good for anything and begin to think *the world would be better off without them.*
- For anyone in recovery, this negative emotional state leads to drug use or suicide.

Boredom

Boredom can derail a person in recovery by working all the time and not having any time for fun. Every day is the same—they eat, sleep and work, and then they start all over again. With the repetition and the daily grind, they start to wonder *if this is all there is to life?*

- When life becomes a routine—the sameness—can make those in recovery want to escape. They start remembering how exciting it was searching for drugs and then finding them. Their Stinkin-thinkin is blocking their recollection of all the pain and suffering they experienced while on drugs.
- The desire for adventure versus the monotony of their life can cause a powerful pull toward using drugs again.
- What people in recovery don't know—it takes time for their brain reward pathways to improve. In some people, it can take up to three or four years. As treatment providers, we need to let people know things will get better. They will not always feel everything is an effort and nothing is enjoyable.

Feeling lonely and isolated

Feeling lonely and isolated is hard on anyone, but it can become devastating for those in recovery and drive them back to using drugs again. Some say the treatment for addiction is connection. When alone, all they have to keep them company is their painful memories of past mistakes and what they had lost.

- Pain is something people with addiction avoid, whether this is mental or physical pain. Even the thought of pain triggers intense anxiety and the desire to escape.
- Loneliness can become unbearable. During the COVID-19 pandemic, a lot of people had relapsed and overdosed

during this time. Because of government restrictions and fear of spreading the virus, they couldn't:

- Go to work
- Go out to eat.
- See a movie
- Visit friends and families

- Loneliness can affect them in any stage of recovery and increases their risk for relapse. In the early stages of recovery, it is a lot worse. To avoid taking drugs, they have to abandon all their old friends when they haven't made any new ones. They are alone, isolated, and miserable.
  - The lack of companionship drives them to reach out to their previous contacts, just to make them not feel so isolated.
- Going to AA or NA meetings becomes a safe place for them to go.
  - The information helps, but the *companionship* and *acceptance* from the group is the true power.
  - No longer do they feel alone.
- Family members don't understand what people in early recovery are experiencing and their struggles.
  - All they hear from family members are complaints from all the wrongs they had done in the past. They can't talk to their family about their feelings and cravings because of the hysterical reaction that will occur. Family's fears keep them from understanding what their loved one is experiencing and is unable to help them.
- They need a safe place where they are accepted but also held accountable for their actions.

Lack of joy in their life

In recovery, if anyone is miserable and not happy about their work, spouse, or children, this makes them more susceptible to start using drugs again. In the past, whenever they had a problem, the answer was to escape the pain and avoid dealing with the situation by taking some drugs.

- In recovery, they have to *confront* their problems and look for a solution that does not involve taking drugs.
  - The desire to run away and escape associated with the accompanying anxiety reaction makes it difficult to redirect their thoughts. Practicing daily relaxation techniques will help reduce their anxiety reactions. They also need to develop ways on how to confront and fix issues.
  - Relaxation techniques will *not work* if they *only use* them when they are in the middle of a panic attack or crisis. They will only work when they do *daily* relaxation skills. The repetition creates pathways in the brain that causes an autonomic reaction for them to relax.
  - Also, frequent meditation allows information to pass quickly between the right and left hemispheres of their brain. By connecting to their creative mind they can develop unique solutions and perspectives to their problems.
    - When we give our creative mind free reign to solve a situation, it can find solutions that previously seemed impossible to the logical part of the brain. The logical part of the brain sees all the problems and struggles to find any answers. While the creative part of the brain sees all kinds of unusual solutions—this is called thinking outside of the box.

Strong emotions

Strong emotions happen when anyone becomes angry or in a rage that can lead them into making impulsive decisions and actions.

- In anger, they want to strike back and take drugs to *punish* the other person. They justify their drug use because the other person made them angry or hurt their feelings.

- o Not aware that the only person who can make us angry is our self and the only person we are truly hurting is ourselves.
- In extreme anger, people don't recall what they had said or what they had done. The rage took over and they no longer have any control over their actions or recall of what had transpired. It's like the brain had wiped the memory clean from their consciousness. This can be very dangerous for anyone who experiences this, and they need to seek professional help to prevent this from happening again.

Holding their feelings inside

When they keep stuffing their feelings into an ever-expanding balloon, eventually, it will burst. To keep from exploding, they feel like they need to take something to deal with all the pain, suffering, and any accompanying stress by taking a drug to avoid the conflict or situation.

- Commonly seen in people who constantly are doing things to help others at the expense of denying their own or family needs.
- When anyone doesn't set any boundaries and gives in to their kids, spouses, or co-workers' demands, they will become overwhelmed and *overreact* to any minor disagreements or situation.
  - o They get conflict at home because of all the time they are spending at work.
  - o At work they struggle to meet the ever-growing demands on their time caused by all the projects other people dump on their desk that they don't want to do.
  - o No matter how much they do—it's never enough.
  - o Eventually, they will explode over a minor incident or start taking drugs to cope.
- When anyone starts setting boundaries, there will be a lot of complaining and angry words. *But*, if they stay firm in

their convictions, the next time will be better. By *consistently* upholding the boundaries, eventually, the arguments will cease. Others have learned no means *no*.

- Life becomes calmer and even peaceful without constant power struggles, impositions, or inconsiderate demands on their time and energy.
  o They no longer have to keep holding their feelings inside, which caused so much of their emotional anguish.

People pleasing

Many people in recovery—especially those in early recovery try to make up for all the wrongs they had done while in active addiction. They expend most of their time and energy trying to please other people at the expense of what is good for them. They mistakenly believe their family will appreciate how truly sorry they are over their past behaviors and show them they are trying to turn their life around. Instead of receiving praise for their efforts, they get complaints instead. They double down and try even harder, but it doesn't matter how much they do—it's never enough. Eventually, they give up trying and return to drug use.

- To become a doormat for another person to like and accept them will never work. When they neglect their needs it builds resentments. Only by making choices that improve their self-esteem and relationships will allow others to see the changes they have made in their life.
- By suppressing their needs, they become exhausted, under-appreciated, and overwhelmed, setting them up for relapse.

Feelings of inferiority

Low self-esteem leads people to make a lot of poor choices. They feel like they don't deserve a loving mate or a considerate friend. They become drawn to those who confirm the same opinion they have of themselves.

- They get into abusive relationships and will never get out until they change their perspective on their value as a person.
- When anyone feels they don't deserve a second chance, they won't even try to get better. Why try? They have done so much wrong they deserve to live this miserable life. They are trying to punish themselves, and only God can take the condemnation away.
- Everyone makes mistakes. This is how we all grow. The only way to *success* is by making mistakes and sometimes *lots of them* in order to *learn* from them and change our ways.
  - A child would never learn how to walk if they tried just once and fell. Moving forward is a process of tri-al-and-error. There is no failure in a *mistake* as long as they learn from it.
  - Mistakes can sometimes turn out to be a blessing and is better than their original plans. Alexander Fleming accidentally discovered the antibiotic Penicillin by forgetting to put the cover on a petri dish that he had just swabbed with bacteria. The next day he saw mold growing in the dish and noticed a clear ring around it because none of the bacteria could survive near this mold.

Feelings of superiority

When anyone thinks they know more than their physician or counselor on what treatments they need. They feel the rules don't apply to them because they know what works best to treat their problem.

- It is difficult to help them because they are not willing to try any treatment that is different from what they want. They do not recognize their way will never work.
  - If they are so knowledgeable, then why are they still taking drugs?

- ○ Only by accepting, they have *no* control over their disease do they have a chance to get better.
- Their way of treating their addiction problem will always be doomed for failure.
  - ○ If it hasn't worked for them in the past, it won't work for them now.
  - ○ They have closed their mind to trying other options and keep recycling the same mistakes they made before.

Over-reacting to stressful events

When we catastrophe a situation and make it appear to be insurmountable—it gives us an excuse to not even try. When people in recovery exaggerate any problem, it causes a severe anxiety reaction from the overwhelming thoughts they created in their minds. Their thoughts intensify their anxiety and cause such anguish that they will take anything to make these thoughts and feelings go away.

- The anxiety reaction clouds their judgment and the ability to think clearly, which is needed to make good choices.
  - ○ Overwhelming urges to take drugs block their ability to focus on how to correct the problem.
- Anyone in recovery needs to practice coping mechanisms to reduce the stress response system.
  - ○ They can reduce their level of stress by changing the words they say to themselves. Rather than say *this situation is impossible*. They need to change the word from impossible to challenging. *I have succeeded in past challenges, and I can do it again in this situation.*
- Only by practicing *daily* relaxation techniques will help them deal with their anxiety and stress. So, that when they feel overwhelmed and do a meditation exercise to get their mind off the problem, they start to relax and calm down.
  - ○ Only by practice and repetition, their brain will become trained to relax. It's like teaching a dog to obey even when distracted.

○ At first, they find it difficult to relax, but by *repetition,* their brain develops an automatic learned response.
  ▪ Just like a pianist automatically moves their fingers when they perform. No thinking—they just play.
- When they *learn* how to relax, it frees their mind to put their problem(s) in its proper perspective and make better choices.

Compulsive and impulsive

Compulsive and impulsive behaviors make it difficult for them to stop and think things through before they act. They react instead of responding to any situation.

- If they start using drugs before the age of twenty-five, it can permanently affect the hardwiring needed to *connect* the impulsive areas to the logical parts of the brain that weighs the consequences of their actions.
- This impulsive reaction makes people do things they later regret. Impulsive action is like jumping out of an airplane with no parachute. It takes a lot of training and practice to slow this impulsive/compulsive reaction.
  ○ The ability to stop *before* they react makes it difficult and, for some people, impossible to accomplish without help.
- For a person to remain successful in recovery, they have to practice ways to *slow down* these impulsive actions.
- I had a patient tell me about leaving his home every night after his wife was asleep, so he could then sneak off to his friend's house to take drugs. He discussed different ways he tried to keep this from happening, but all his efforts were unsuccessful.
  ○ He asked, "*What can I do to stop this?*"
  ○ "You need to let your wife help you with this problem."
  ○ "*I don't want her to know. She'll get so upset with me.*"

- o "You have to give her the keys to the car every night and lock them up."
- o *"I really don't want to do this. She'll be so disappointed in me."*
- o "Better to be disappointed than bailing you out of jail. You have to put a *barrier* between the impulsive thought in order to slow down the impulsive action from taking place."
- He had his wife lock his keys in the safe, so he didn't have any access to them. Later that night, when he got the urge to use again, he walked over to his friend's house. It took him over an hour one-way to reach it. By the time he got back, he was exhausted. The next night, after only walking for fifteen minutes, he turned around and went home. After that, he no longer had any urges.
- When his wife locked-up the keys, his cravings and compulsive thoughts disappeared. A couple of months later, he was doing great and asked for his keys back.
  - o He couldn't believe it—those crazy urges came roaring back.
  - o The cravings disappeared when he had no immediate access to getting drugs but returned when he could get them quickly.
- For Recovery to become successful, *barriers* are needed to either *avoid* a situation or to find ways to *slow* down the impulsive/compulsive action from happening. Delaying the action gives them a chance to think through the situation by allowing enough time for the impulse to connect with the logical part of the brain. Now they can accurately assess the situation and give them a chance for a different outcome.

Thrill-seekers

They need constant stimulation or excitement in their lives, and the more dangerous the activity, the greater the thrill and the release of Adrenalin and Dopamine.

- Dopamine release is highly addictive. The exact same substance that's released when opioids stimulate the receptors in the brain and can trigger a person in recovery a desire to return to addictive behaviors.
- When anyone drives excessively fast, goes on dangerous rides or treacherous mountain climbs, they have an addiction to an adrenalin rush and the dopamine release.
- Thrill-seeking can also be manifested by having multiple sexual partners and can trigger the desire to use various drugs.
  - With their misguided thinking (Stinkin-thinkin), they start to believe it's okay *as long as it's not my drug of choice and think they are immune from becoming addicted to other drugs or behaviors.*
  - *Wrong thinking*, they are unaware their addiction can make them susceptible to other addictions and can *easily* trade one addiction for another.
- The more hazardous the activity, the more exciting it becomes, putting themselves and those around them in danger.
  - The thrill-seeker is unaware they are addicted to adventure as others are to drugs.
  - Thrill-seekers are at risk to experiment and take even more dangerous drugs.

The need to Celebrate

Celebrations are an unexpected emotional trigger that can lead many people to relapse. Getting promoted at work, landing a successful contract, any holidays, birthdays, anniversaries, or find we are going to be parents are all-natural reasons to celebrate. This need to celebrate on the surface appears to be justified, *but* in a person with addiction, it triggers the Stinkin-thinkin part of their brain.

- Previously their life revolved around searching for drugs, acquiring the drugs, and then taking them. The *reward* in their life was getting and taking drugs.
- So, when other rewards happen in their life, it brings them back to a craving for drugs.
- The brain equates taking drugs as the ultimate reward for good behavior.
- To break the associations between rewards and celebrations, we have to stop thinking about life in terms of right or wrong—reward or punishment—happy or sad and learn to view all days as good days.
  - They need to view life as a journey, and every day brings them closer to their destiny. Even when things don't turn out the way they want—there are lessons to be learned and keep moving toward their goal. They can think about certain problems as roadblocks and remain stuck behind the barriers, *or* they just see it as a scenic detour and enjoy the process of gaining new ideas and perspectives in their journey.
  - They need to learn how to become content in every second of their day. No matter what's going on in their life.
- The process of learning and growing from an experience allows us to help others who are stuck in the same problem. *Important* to note: Those in recovery should not *directly* help their previous drug-using buddies because their subconscious memories can trigger them to relapse. When they are around former associates, their subconscious mind is humming an old love song priming them for the right moment to relapse. They can always pray to have God guide their former friends to get help—but they can't be the one to do it. Their memories cause too strong of a pull toward drug use. But, they can help others with addiction (just not previous associates) when they are stable in their recovery.

To become stable, they need to have no slips, cravings, or desires for drug use for at least two to three years. It can take longer for some people for their brains to recover from all the insults drug use has had on their brain. They need to have stable relationships and a job they like or hobbies they enjoy. They can help others as long as they are not vulnerable emotionally or physically and realize they are at risk for relapse if any life conditions change. Whenever any stressful event happens, it is best if they step back and not help anyone with addiction until their emotional crisis has resolved.

Negative emotions

People with negative thoughts and feelings keep them from moving forward and affect their relationships with other people. Resentments, grudges, and un-forgiveness will hinder anyone, especially those in recovery. These negative emotions can consume their thoughts and block them from receiving the truth.

- ○ *I am responsible for my own thoughts and actions.*
- ○ Why not make them good ones?
- When they blame others, it gives them an excuse not to change. It also becomes a handy excuse to elicit other people's sympathy.
  - ○ What they really need is a reality check. How long are they going to blame others? When do they become responsible for their own actions and the mistakes they have made?
- It takes a lot of self-awareness to stop the blaming and excuses. For me, only God was able to reveal this truth about my own life. Only God could strip away my protective paint that covered my flaws and excuses. I felt vulnerable, exposed, and naked, but could finally see the truth and become healed from the pain I had inside me. Free from the excuses, the emotional garbage that held me hostage for so long.

- Only by *letting go* will anyone be able to *move forward*. Releasing all the excuses, the hurts and resentments, freed me to step out and build a better future full of hopes, dreams, and achievements.

ATTITUDES

People may not be able to change their circumstances, but they can change their attitudes about it. The attitudes they have about a situation have a powerful effect on whether they will become successful in their recovery or fail. While treating my patients with addiction, some of the common attitudes I encountered that made life more challenging for them are: *I don't care, Self-pity, Blaming others, Negative attitude, Judge mentality, Doing things my way, and Dishonesty.*

I don't care attitude

I don't care attitude is commonly seen in people who have given up on themselves and any hope they will ever change. When they experienced painful events that made them feel unimportant or worthless—they gave up trying. They had lost hope that anything could get better or that change is possible.

- Commonly seen in women in abusive relationships, and feel they have no way out of their situation. To combat their helplessness and negative encounters, they need positive experiences to balance the scales in order for them to make better choices.
- They have had years of emotional abuse from others and from their own self-sabotage thinking.
    o They need positive people who praise them for things they are doing right. Not to make things up, but to look for any positive event and focus on that.

- o Over time, they start to hope again, begin to believe things could change. Sooner or later, they get the courage to reach out and eventually leave the situation.
- o They need time to recover from all this negativity in their life. They need someone in their life who genuinely cares and encourages their efforts, and not judge them.
- As a treatment provider, it fills my heart with joy when I see people break free from the bonds that were holding them back and start making choices that give them hope and a future. When they discover what they love and make plans to achieve it—I feel honored to be part of the process of reclaiming their life back.

Self-pity and blaming

When they feel sorry for themselves and have all kinds of excuses why they feel this way is an attitude that keeps them stuck in the past. They never take responsibility for their own actions.

- I hear people who are over forty years old complaining about how their parents didn't give them the opportunity to go to college or include them in the family business.
  - o I gently inquire, *"What age are you going to start becoming responsible for your own life?"*
    - They can always go back to school and take evening classes to improve themselves.
- They are the *only one* that keeps them from achieving their dreams—by the excuses they give to themselves.
- It's easier to *blame* than to *change*.

A negative person

A negative person always sees what is wrong with every situation and never sees the positive. They dwell on the worst-case scenario and can never see any improvement.

- They are always complaining and cannot find any happiness. No matter how wonderful a promotion they get—it's never enough.
- They constantly exaggerate the negative and discount anything positive in their life.
  - It gets weary for people to continue listening to all their woes.
  - Negative attitudes make people avoid them, leading them into isolation and loneliness.
  - They feel what they are going through is always worse than what others are experiencing—even if it's the same problem.
- Isolation and loneliness is a common trigger for relapse.

The judge mentality

When they compare themselves to others will lead to feelings of inferiority or superiority.

- I'm not as bad as Joey. I only snort heroin and not inject it.
- I can't get any better because my addiction is a lot worse than theirs.

Do things my way

They resent anyone telling them what to do. It is extremely difficult to help anyone who refuses to try or even listen for ways to get better. Whether this is coming from someone who thinks they know more than their treatment provider about their problem or from a person who doesn't want to change. I find it easier to help a person who doesn't want to change compared to the one who knows it all and won't listen or try other options.

- If a person doesn't want to change, the treatment provider listens carefully to what the patient says. If they say anything negative about taking drugs—such as how costly they are to get. I have them explain more about it.
  - o I do not judge or tell them what to do, but intently listen and make statements that reflect what they are telling me in order for them to elicit how it's affecting their life.
  - o This process is called Motivational interviewing (MI), and it helps people go from ambivalence about drug use to considering getting help and seek treatment.
- Motivational interviewing is a slow process that lets a person *see* the negative effects of drugs in their life, rather than me telling them what to do. Allowing them to *discover* their own reasons why they want to change.
  - o As a treatment provider, it's easier and quicker for me to tell a patient what to do, but *not* as effective.

Dishonesty

A person is dishonest when they try to avoid the consequences of their behaviors by lying to themselves or to other people. In some ways, their attitude is a game of *what they can get away with*.

- They strive for the *appearance* of being in recovery but still have the mentality of an addict.
  - o Doing whatever they can get away with to continue using drugs without anyone finding out.
- I tell my patients if I find they are trying to *hide* drug use from me, they are not really interested in getting better. I don't kick patients out of my treatment program because they slipped up. I understand this is a disease, and it takes time to start making the right choices. But, if I have anyone

who sees this as a game, on what they can get away with—
that will cause me to terminate them from my practice.

- I've had people take heroin or methamphetamine and give
  me a fake urine sample, so I wouldn't find out about it.
  They can be very creative in trying to *fool me*. They don't
  know (but quickly learn) that God has given me a spirit of
  discernment, and when I feel something is not right, I have
  my staff do a mouth swab to compare the results with their
  urine drug test. We also do temperature checks to determine if they brought in someone else's urine and do other
  measures to detect fraudulent urine samples used to avoid
  finding out they have other drugs in their system or have
  been selling their medication.

- It's incredible how long they will persist in their lie, even
  when I have evidence to prove their wrongdoing. I see this
  scenario frequently.

  o "The urine you gave us has a temperature over one-hun-
    dred and four degrees. Yet, your body temperature is
    only ninety-eight degrees. How can this be?"

    ▪ They will shrug their shoulders and say, "*I don't
      know. This is my urine.*"

  o "It's impossible for your urine temperature to be a lot
    higher than your body temperature. Now, what really
    happened?"

    ▪ "*I tell you, this is my urine.*"

  o "I want you to know that I don't tolerate lies. You must
    think I'm an idiot to believe that your urine's tempera-
    ture can be higher than where it came from."

    ▪ "*I'm telling the truth. Why don't you believe me?*"

  o If I don't get a straight answer right now, you might as
    well not come back. It's obvious you're not interested in
    getting better and only interested in what you can get
    away with. I can only help a person if they are honest
    with themselves and with me."

- o Finally, they admit to using drugs and had given me someone else's urine to keep them from getting kicked out of the program.
- o "I won't kick a person out of treatment because of a slip, but I will kick you out if you ever try to give me another fake or adulterated urine again."
- The only way a person can get better is to figure out what caused the mistake and learn how to avoid it in the future.
- The lies people tell themselves and others in order to keep from becoming accountable for the decisions they make— only hurts the one who is making them.

CONTROL

Control is influenced by the addictive Stinkin-thinkin part of the brain. They manipulate or intimidate people or situations in order to get their own way or to blame others for their mistakes. In other words, they are making other people responsible for their behaviors by the excuses they make and allow them to continue in their problems. Some of the ways a person controls others or is controlled by wrong thinking involve: *Constant Nagging and whining, Verbal, Physical, or Emotional Abuse, Blaming, Justification, and Rejecting Help.*

Constant nagging and whining

Some people will constantly nag and whine to get their own way. They manipulate people by wearing them down until they relent and give in to their plans.

- Children have learned this behavior at a very young age.
  - o If they fuss and cry loud enough and long enough, their parents usually give in to their demands.

Verbal, Physical, and Emotional abuse

Verbal threats and physical attacks are used to keep other people in their place and avoid taking responsibility for their own actions.

- They manipulate others through intimidation and fear to whip a person into submission.
  - Their angry shouts, cutting remarks, and physical attacks are all done to keep them from having to change.
- They threaten the well being of their children by withholding money or support as means to control another person.
  - If you keep nagging, I'm leaving, and who is going to support you and the kids?
  - As long as they can keep other people from nagging or complaining about their behaviors—they don't have to change.
- If no one confronts them about a situation, then they can *fool themselves* into thinking they don't have a problem.
- Emotional abuse comes from making other people feel responsible for their behavior.
  - *"If you weren't so snippy, I wouldn't have to go to a bar for some friendly conversation."*

Blaming other people

When they blame other people or circumstances, it prevents them from taking responsibility for their behavior.

- I had a patient who wanted to see his favorite band play at a concert and had arranged a non-drug-using friend go with him to avoid a relapse. When questioned about the feasibility of his plan. He insisted his plan would work. At the concert, they got separated in the crowd, and my patient injected heroin. When asked why he relapsed, he immediately blamed his friend.

- ○ *"It's all my friend's fault for not staying by my side. He didn't do what he was supposed to do."*
- ○ "Let's be honest, you found a way to sneak off and take some heroin. It was your responsibility to not get separated—not his."
- *"If you weren't such a lousy mom, I would have never started taking drugs in the first place, and that's why I can't quit."*
  - ○ To blame her mom as an excuse, why she started drugs, and why she can't stop makes her feel like a victim.
  - ○ She uses her problem as a weapon to punish her mother and absolve any responsibility for her to even try to change by blaming others for her problem.

Justification

Justification is used to make others think they don't have a problem; therefore, they have no reason to change.

- Put other people down to make them look like they don't have a problem.
  - ○ *I'm not as bad as my neighbor—now he really drinks a lot.*
- Or justify their actions to make it appear acceptable behavior.
  - ○ *The only reason why I stole your money because I needed it more than you did.*
  - ○ *Just because grandma has cancer doesn't mean she can't share some of her pain pills with me. I'm in a lot of pain, too.*

Rejecting help

On the surface, it appears they are taking responsibility for their actions. In reality, they are allowing the problem to continue and *control* them.

- They are misguided to think they have the ability to change when their own brain is working against their efforts to stop taking drugs.
  - Blind to how the addictive mindset manipulates them into repeating the same mistakes over and over again and keeping them stuck in the same problems.
    - *I will try harder, or I will do better*, will never work when they keep trying to control their recovery program and refuse recommendations from their treatment providers.
- I have patients who refuse to take an antidepressant because they don't want any drugs in their system.
  - Yet, they had no problem with shooting up or taking all kinds of unknown street drugs.
- Clinical studies clearly show if they are not treated for their mental illness at the *same time* as their addiction, they will not be successful.
  - They tell me, '*they know what's best for them*."
  - I respond, "If you know what's best, then why do you still have the problem?"
- Sometimes their Stinkin-thinkin convinces them, they are cured and can now practice *controlled* drug use, which leads them back to active addiction.

RELATIONSHIP AND LIFE PROBLEMS

Relationships and life problems are one of the most common causes of relapse. There are whole books devoted to this topic. I am going to focus on common causes of relationship and life problems that can lead to relapse in the next chapter.

SURVIVAL TIPS

- Abnormal addictive thinking (Stinkin-thinkin) never goes away.
- Learning to recognize the false words and replace them with the truth is the only way to combat this problem.
  - Ask God for wisdom and to surround ourselves with people who understand addictive thinking to help guide us in this process.
- Stinkin-thinkin is a *subconscious* process. They are unaware and unprepared for the sudden attack of cravings and urges.
  - They have to guard their mind. What they see, hear, and smell can all be triggers. But when they focus on what God says in the Bible, rest in his peace and redirect their thoughts to whatever is true, what is right, pure, kind, or excellent. They are renewing their mind.
- Stinkin-thinkin is based on emotional thinking with its ultimate goal—for them to return to drug use.
  - They need to be discerning when their emotions are involved. There is nothing wrong with having feelings, but they can't let it guide them into making their decisions.
  - Find ways to lower our emotional temperature. Take a walk and distract our thoughts and look at all the beauty around us. But do not walk and keep going over our problems that will only intensify our anger. Do something fun, watch a funny movie work on a hobby, talk to a friend, but not about any of our problems. We can listen to music, read a book or the Bible, do a yoga exercise are other ways to distract our mind.
  - Try to put the problem in perspective. Does it really matter that he doesn't put a new roll of toilet paper in

the bathroom after he used the last sheet? Let petty items go and focus on what's important—life will become less stressful.

- Pay attention to the early warning signs to avoid a relapse.
  - o Every time a person relapses—they need to write down what happened on an index card. So, they will have reminders of what happened before and what they can to do next time a similar problem occurs.
  - o When they know the early warning signs, they are prepared and less likely to be taken by surprise.
  - o It's the *unexpected* that makes them most vulnerable.
- Believing in God can bring peace to our life. When we give our life to Jesus, we surrender our will to follow God's will for our life. Surrender means we stop fighting circumstances by complaining, blaming, and judging.
  - o Only by letting go and letting God fight our battles allows us to go through the problems and learn what is needed to resolve them. Learning how to be content in the moment, no matter what is going on in our life, makes every day a good one.
- There is nothing wrong with praying for circumstances to go away. Even Jesus did this when He asked His Father if there was some other way to fulfill His Father's will. He didn't want to drink the cup of sacrifice, but He confessed, have it be your will, not mine.
  - o The acceptance and surrender of what we want allows God the freedom to guide us toward our divine destiny and purpose.

SURVIVAL TIP # 14

TAKE CARE OF THE ME BEFORE THE WE

Whether a person just started the journey or has been in recovery for years, *Relationships* and *Life* problems are some of the most common causes for relapse. Over time, they can delude themselves into thinking they are cured or have outgrown their addiction, and it can no longer affect them anymore. *Important:* They must never forget the addictive thinking resides in the *subconscious* level of their brain and can suddenly pop up in unexpected and inopportune times in their life. Any *intense emotional* reaction primes the pump to *activate* the addictive pathways. Generating a torrential flood of stress hormones to surge through the unsuspecting and vulnerable person. Making it nearly impossible to think clearly or rationally.

The ability to *resist* drug use only works when they are satisfied with their lives and their relationships. If anything negative happens (a fight with their partner, tragic news about a loved one, or getting fired from a job), they become vulnerable. If they combine this with being around the wrong people, an intense craving hits them with such force that it overwhelms their ability to think clearly. They were not prepared for the sudden explosive cravings and how strong their urge was to escape their pain. The recipe ingredients that will guarantee a person to relapse are:

- A painful triggering event.

- The hyperactive cascade of stress-hormones that overwhelms them with anxiety.
- Being around people who can obtain or give them drugs.
- To change the recipe, they need to change the ingredients and *avoid* being around the wrong people at the wrong time.

Only with a lifetime of *avoiding* the wrong people, places, and things, along with doing a daily stress management routine, can guarantee a person for success. *Resistance* (the ability to say no) requires them to be in the right emotional, physical, and spiritual state to avoid drug use.

In this chapter, I'm focusing on areas that many of my patients had discovered to be the most challenging for them to maintain sobriety in their journey towards recovery. Relationships can be rewarding, but the loss of a relationship, either from death or any form of breakoff, can be devastatingly painful. Even if the relationship does not dissolve, it's stressful to deal with another person's emotions and reactions while trying to work on their own. Many people in recovery found their emotional and social development became stunted at the time they started taking drugs. Most of them never learned how to set healthy boundaries for themselves or for others. Many don't know what they are feeling or doing is healthy or inappropriate. Here are some basic principles that are necessary for a relationship to function for the well being of both parties.

We all need to be aware that other people are *not* going to meet all our needs. We have to abandon the *unrealistic* expectations to have other people or our partner become responsible for:

- Making us happy
- Taking care of all my financial needs
- Constantly praising, lifting us up when we are down
- Solving any minor problem(s)
- Having the same values and perspectives that I have and seeing things my way

Expecting our partner to meet all these needs puts a serious strain on any relationship we will have with one another. It's exhausting to be around such a needy person. Everyone has to be responsible for his or her *own* happiness. There will be times, we need encouragement, but we also need to learn how to encourage ourselves. To be around a woman, who constantly wants her husband to say how beautiful she is, can get old very quickly.

Sometimes, we become misguided into thinking that we are responsible for keeping the peace at all costs, even when unrealistic expectations and demands are placed on us. She works a full-time job, takes care of the kids, cooks, cleans, and goes to the store for groceries. When her partner comes home from work, he plops down on the sofa and doesn't move an inch but expects her to get me this and get me that all evening long. When it's time for bed, he becomes upset when she's too tired for sex. This is not a partnership. Relationships are established when *both* parties are committed to each other by finding ways to meet *both* of their needs. Some people have the mistaken idea that showing love to another person is to ignore their own needs. When our needs are not met, resentments build. If a relationship is controlling, at the expense of the other person's mental and physical health, then boundaries need to be established, or changes in the relationship need to be made.

A relationship needs to have the freedom of acceptance that will allow both parties to be honest about their feelings and vulnerabilities. The ability for each party to be *honest* about their needs and wants and be open to hearing what the other person is thinking or feeling creates a *bridge* to promote understanding. This is respecting the other person's views, and not just our own. We are not trying to make the other person think and be the same as ourselves. Open communication allows both parties to become closer by respecting their differences.

But, if we allow the disagreements to become a battlefield of who won or lost, it will only cause separation and the breakdown of the relationship. Only when we can express our feelings without judgment will an emotional bond develop between us. But, if one person thinks that their opinion is the only way to think or feel, this will only create division, and their issues will never get resolved.

If a woman has low self-esteem, she is drawn to a controlling, abusive person who confirms the opinion she has of herself. Even if she breaks free from this relationship, she will find another one who is just like (or worse) than the one she escaped from. We are all creatures of habit, and if we are drawn to a certain personality type, we will keep making the same painful mistakes. Unfortunately, I see this way too often in women I treat for substance abuse. For people to break the cycle of abuse requires changing the image they have of themselves. This process takes time. In order for them to change, they need help.

- By surrounding themselves with positive, uplifting people in their life.
- Counselors to deal with the emotional trauma and help them to move past the pain and fear.
- Friends who will encourage their efforts to improve.
- Social services to help with housing, childcare, and job placement.
- Life skills training such as how to balance a checkbook, budget their money, plan for the unexpected.
- To be successful, they will need to learn how to take small steps that give them the confidence to take the next step.

In a relationship, both partners need to feel emotionally and physically safe in order to have meaningful communication. They can't be anxious or fearful of what the other person will say or do. To always be on edge, not knowing if the other person will lash out physically or with painful words. Words can penetrate deep into their heart and keep them from revealing their needs and vulnerability causing a schism in their relationship. Trust takes *time*, and *consistent behavior*, so we can predict what their reactions will be.

A person has to become *selective* in who they *decide* to become emotionally attached. Many people jump into a relationship of convenience because someone is attracted to them. They never took the time to analyze what traits are important to them in a relationship and consider: Is this the right person for me? Only to discover years later that unfaithfulness was something they could never tolerate. If we want our house to have everything in order—then getting involved with someone who is messy, with clothes all over the place, will drive us nuts. This *difference will always* be a source of conflict. To become involved in any relationship that makes us feel we have to change them to fit into our standards is a guarantee for disaster. We are deluding ourselves to think we could make this relationship have a happy ending. If neatness is something important, then either end the relationship *before* becoming too emotionally attached or *accept* this is how it will be and *stop* complaining.

There is one personality type that can make anyone's life miserable. I see this a lot in women, but I am sure there are men out there with the same problem. Narcissistic people see themselves superior to others and are only concerned about their needs and wants. This type of personality has certain behaviors that, if encountered—the wise will run away and *never* get caught in their snare. Some of the signs a person is in a relationship with a Narcissist are the following:

- The Narcissist doesn't negotiate and has a way of twisting things around to make it appear the other person is at fault or flawed.
- They demand constant attention and admiration and only see people in terms of what that person can do for them.
- The Narcissist focuses on going to all the right parties and to be seen with the right people so that others can admire them.
- Their world revolves around superficial matters, such as their looks, what car they drive and house they live in.
  - It's okay to take care of our body and desire to be attractive, but if anyone is constantly preening in front of a mirror and wanting lots of attention—be wary.
- Many times the Narcissist is very attractive, and the other person is flattered and in awe of them. At first, they lavish a lot of attention on how beautiful the Narcissist is and stand

proudly by their side. Every wish the Narcissists demand, they try to fulfill.

- The Narcissist has a constant need for affirmations and attention from others. This puts their partner into an emotional roller coaster—high when smiled upon and dark deep lows when he/she clings to another person in order to punish their partner for *perceived* lack of admiration.
- The constant flirting with other men/women is used as a whip to keep their partner in line.
  o Even when they realize that no matter how much they do—it's never enough, but they still keep trying harder.
- This process of reward and punishment the Narcissist delivers keeps a person on the hook and will continue until the Narcissist finds someone *better* and breaks off the relationship.
- The emotional roller coaster the Narcissist creates, becomes as addictive as taking drugs. It's a powerful force, and the only way a person escapes is when the Narcissist moves on to new pastures.
- This is why, *never, never* get involved with such a person. A person in recovery won't remain that way very long. The mounting pain and stress the Narcissist creates makes them feel they have to take something in order to cope with their misery.

How can we find the right person for us and not get involved with the wrong ones? Rather than go with the flow of hooking up with anyone who seems attracted to us, I recommend my patients write down what attributes they would want in a partner. They need to prioritize what is important. Here are some ideas:

- What is the most important aspect for the relationship to continue? It can be he/she likes kids, likes sports, is loyal, truthful, kind to animals, or believes in God?

- What items could be negotiated in the relationship? It could be, he/she is not a good cook, messy or overly tidy, smokes cigarettes, or potential in-law issues?
- What would not be tolerated in the relationship? Not having a job, lazy, dishonest, takes drugs, promiscuous, hates animals, or does not believe in God?

Also, it's important to write what we can contribute to a relationship. It takes a lot of self-exploration to know our weaknesses and our emotional needs. It takes *time* to discover this facet of our personality. This is why anyone in early recovery, who is not married, is encouraged not to get involved with another person. Self-discovery is like peeling an onion. There are many layers that need to be exposed, analyzed and processed, before embarking into a relationship. To *know thy self* is more important than accepting whatever comes along.

Another important point many people miss. We are responsible for our own lives. Do not expect others to protect my interests better than I would. We have to take responsibility for our words and actions. We do not blame others or circumstances. Only by taking responsibility can we change and correct an action. We are not perfect. We all make mistakes, but we are all accountable for what we did *or* for what we didn't do. Do not make the mistake that self-care gives us the right to be selfish and do what we want, regardless of the other person's thoughts, feelings or discomfort. It's important to know our values and finding a partner who shares those same beliefs. If we love kids and want to have a big family and the other person doesn't want any kids. We are already on different tracks. We can't assume once we have kids, they will change their mind. We are only deluding ourselves, and that disaster is only a matter of time. If we love having lots of people come over to the house and be the epicenter of activity and the other person is reclusive and view their home as a sanctuary of peace and tranquility. This difference will always be a constant source of conflict. In the *early* stages of this relationship is the time to decide if this person is right for me. The earlier we break off a relationship that is not right for us, the easier it becomes.

Too many times I hear my patients tell me, "*I've wasted ten years of my life on this jerk.*"

In evaluating the criteria I made and comparing it with the person I am dating, I have to ask myself: Can I live and accept these differences without complaining about them? As a child, I heard my mom constantly griping about my dad smoking cigarettes. I remember telling myself—I will *never* date anyone who smokes. I did not want to spend the rest of my life trying to change someone who doesn't want to change.

Important: We need to know what we want in a relationship. To know what my needs are will eliminate a lot of future heartache and pain. The earlier we discover this, the easier it is to break off the relationship. In the discovery process, if anyone engages in sex, they need to use birth control. Do *NOT* trust anyone who says, '*I'm on the pill.*' I have found too many men get caught in a lifetime relationship with a person they no longer like because she got pregnant. He is now responsible for a child they created and has to deal with different parenting styles. Rule your life with your head by always using protection or be prepared for a baby on the way.

The *relationship* we have with *ourselves* will determine how our relationships will be with other people. Be aware that in addiction, the only thing that was important was taking and acquiring drugs. In recovery, they have to discover what they want and what their needs are before getting involved with another person. The need to connect is powerful, but it can also be painful, and *pain* is something that people with addiction strive to *avoid*. In the past, the only coping skill a person in recovery used was taking something to avoid feeling the pain. They never learned how to work through the difficulties and the un-comfortableness that is needed to resolve the issues.

It takes two people *both* working together (committed) rather than one person trying to make the relationship work. If one person is constantly compromising and giving in to the other person's demand and their needs are not met—any rational person would leave. But addiction is not rational. They double down and try harder—and harder—until they have to take something to cope with the emotional exhaustion, frustrations, and hurts. We can only *change our-selves*. We are *not* responsible for making the other person change.

I see people stay in a relationship because they remember how the relationship used to be and not what it is currently. Just like we have changed physically over the years, so does our relationship change with our partner and with our self. Sometimes people stay in a bad relationship because of the memories of how good it was before and think; *he or she will be back to who they used to be*. We have to be realistic and not live in the past but in the present. I have a patient who has been in recovery for over five years. He got his dream job, been taking classes in order to advance and make more money to provide for his family. One day, he accidentally answered his wife's phone and discovered she was having an affair with a co-worker for about a year.

Even though she had been unfaithful, he remembered how committed she was when he was in active addiction. He felt he 'owed' her a free pass on the affair and accepted the blame for her indiscretion because of his previous addiction problem. I could understand his attitude if this happened when he was actively using or when he just started recovery—but after five years? He is not responsible for her affair, nor is it unreasonable to ask her to change her job if she wants their relationship to work. She refused to quit her job and is reluctant to go to marriage counseling. He is trying so hard to keep from getting a divorce. He comes home early and cleans the house, takes care of the kids, and studies late at night, when everyone is asleep, so she won't feel deprived of attention. He doesn't want his kids to suffer. His biggest problem, he has trouble accepting that she is no longer *committed* to saving their family. He feels responsible for her actions and thinks by making things easy for her, she would want to stay.

It is so strange and counterintuitive to find when a person is actively using drugs; their partner stays in the relationship. But when they are turning their lives around—got a job—money in the bank—involved in family activities—their partner leaves them. Unfortunately, I see this dynamic way too often. I believe the reason for this behavior is: while their spouse was actively using drugs, their partner was getting a lot of sympathy and praise from other people. They got used to hearing:

You must be an angel to put up with his drinking.

You are so brave and strong to keep trying to help him.

You are so loyal, committed, faithful—fantastic.

The list of accolades continues from other people, as they complain about all their struggles dealing with their partner's drinking or drugging. But when their spouse is no longer taking drugs or alcohol, has a job, making money to buy a house, a car, helps around the house, and cares for the kids. They have nothing to complain about and are no longer getting all this attention and sympathy from family, friends, and co-workers. They feel deprived and latch onto anyone who flatters them and starts an affair. It's like the *sympathy* was as *addictive* to them as the drug was to their partner.

Conflict will come into any relationship. For a relationship to work, there are some principles that need to be followed. To resolve the conflict and improve the relationship, we need to learn how to communicate effectively.

- Communication starts before we even say a single word. Our body language and eye contact transmits vital information and can determine if we are being heard and understood or dismissed.
- To keep our eyes focused on our partner we can't be multitasking.
  - Put down the computer and turn off the TV, stop texting on the phone.
  - Give them our undivided attention.
- Both parties need to feel safe.
  - No verbal or physical attacks—even clinching of fists can be intimidating.
  - Judgmental words of—you should, or shouldn't, must or must not—put the other person on the defensive and the desire to strike back.
- We need to listen to the other person's point of view without interruption.

- Let them know, we are trying to understand their feelings and thoughts by asking questions such as:
  - I just want to make sure I got this right. You are upset because_____ and it made you feel like your time is not important. Is this correct?
  - By stating what we think the person said might clarify the situation.
  - Many times, we only hear *part* of what the other person is saying. Our *subconscious filter* processed the information *differently* than what they had *intended.* It is easy to get caught up in—who is right and who is wrong.
  - Our problems will never get resolved unless we learn to *clarify* if this is what they meant.

We all have different life experiences that color our viewpoints. For harmony to exist, we need to find ways to bridge these differences. We can only do this by understanding why a person feels or sees things a certain way. When we understand the *why* it helps us *emotionally connect* with each other. One way we can do this is by trying to step into the other person's shoes and see the situation from their perspective. A disagreement doesn't have to be, I am right—you are wrong. We can both be right or wrong, and sometimes we have to agree to disagree.

Our *emotions cloud* our ability to see things clearly and are a powerful force that keeps us stuck into seeing things from only our viewpoint. When we talk, we have to be honest about how we feel and *why* we feel that way.

An example: "Every time you shout, I want to run away because whenever my dad shouted, he started throwing things. See this scar on my arm is from the knife he threw at me." Revealing our feelings and *why we feel* that way brings understanding.

But if she screamed, "Stop shouting at me."

It would only make the other person yell even louder. For communication to bring unity into a relationship, both parties need to be truthful to each other and not make excuses or exaggerate the situation to justify their point of view.

One thing to remember—*timing* is important. It is never a good idea to have a major conversation if we are tired or have a lot of things that need to be done. Schedule a day and time to go over issues when both are not stressed and overwhelmed. We need to prioritize our issues (pick our battles). If a situation is a low priority matter, then go along with the other person's plans, but if it's very important, then it's necessary to say what needs to be said. Be aware, *emotions* can make us all become very *unreasonable*, and sometimes we may need to take a time-out to work through our feelings and the situation before we resume discussions.

Important to reiterate—the way we communicate can make or break a relationship. For communication to be effective, we have to first recognize what we want and how we feel before trying to express it to another person. It requires dedication and effort to develop these skills and involves spending time with a loved one to understand the needs of each other.

Finally, make sure that we are kind to ourselves and to others. Do not criticize or belittle our partners or our own imperfections. We need to accept we all make mistakes. If we focus all our energy on the negatives in our relationships—we will get more negatives. Our words have the power to change our relationships into a loving one or into one with constant strife. If we start focusing on the positives and encourage our partner—a shift in the dynamics occurs. It's inspiring what a few kind words can do in drawing us closer to each other. When we look at all the possibilities rather than the failures, it keeps our perspective clear. Not clouded by painful emotional reactions that hinder rather than help us move forward in our life.

For anyone in recovery, unexpected painful life events happen, throwing them off balance and create a need for them to escape the pain. It is so important for them to have a strong support system that consists of many people. If anyone in recovery only has one person who can support them through difficult times and that person leaves, it makes him or her susceptible for a relapse—the safety net is gone. There is strength in numbers. Even the Bible says a three-fold cord is stronger than one. We need to have an updated safety plan to help us during difficult times so when 'shit-hits-the-fan,' we have a plan for help during difficult times. It is always important to remember:

In life, anything or anyone can pitch a curveball and throw us off balance. Don't let that happen. Be prepared so that no one or any thing can take away what was so painfully earned—our life, our future, and our destiny.

SURVIVAL TIPS

- Effective communication occurs when both parties are honest about their feelings and vulnerabilities.
  - How a relationship survives depends on our relationship with ourselves.
  - To connect with another, we need to first connect with ourselves. We need to take the time to explore what is important to us in our life.
  - God will reveal His plan for us if only we ask. Have Him give us a heart of compassion, understanding, and the ability to express our needs in a way that brings us closer.
  - Give ourselves a time out when we become too emotional. Emotion clouds our judgment and ability to reason. There is nothing wrong with asking to discuss this later. Give a specific date and time, so the other person doesn't think we don't want to deal with the problem. We do, just not at this moment.
- Relationship issues are the main cause of relapse.
  - We need to pray first, then write down and prioritize what attributes we want in a partner.
  - We want to keep our physical attraction from camouflaging the true nature of a person. Appearances can deceive us.
  - When dating, we are both on our best behavior. We need to see how they act toward other people. Actions are more revealing than their words.

- Are they snide and snippy toward the waitress or cutting to people who are less fortunate?
- Do they make comments about other people that are crude or not kind?
- Remember, how they treat people who don't matter to them will likely be how they will treat us later on.
- *How they treat their family, friends and previous partners can be a real eye-opener.*
- Ask God to reveal their true nature and heart.
  - By their fruits we shall know them.
- We are responsible for making ourselves happy.
  - We can look at all the negatives in our life and be miserable.
  - Or, by praising God, we can look at all the positives and possibilities in life.
  - We lack because we don't ask. We need to ask God to:
    - Guide us
    - Provide the right resources and opportunities to achieve what He has placed in our hearts.
    - To open our eyes and see what is right before us.
    - If God takes care of the birds in the air that neither toil nor trouble—how much more will our Heavenly Father take care of us?

EMOTIONS ARE STRONGER THAN WILL-POWER

When anyone in recovery has strong emotions, it triggers and then intensifies their stress response system that contributes to their inability to resolve issues in their relationships. Coping with the stress that life brings can be extremely difficult for someone who has a drug problem. In the past, drug use was the only way they knew how to cope and numb their pain and discomfort. In recovery, this is no longer a viable option if they want to stay on the right path and to continue getting better. Since strong emotions are so powerful, I will be discussing each of them in sections. The quartet *of Anxiety, Depression, Fear, and Anger* can make anyone in recovery at risk for relapse at any stage of the recovery process.

ANXIETY

When people are stable in their recovery their addiction pathways go into a dormant state. But, when they are exposed to painful events, several addictive pathways become reactivated.

- The brain stimulates a flood of cascading hormones and chemicals to surge through their system that increases their stress and anxiety reaction.

213

- The memory circuits start firing, and they begin recalling all their previous painful events. This triggers the emotion center in their brain to magnify their anxiety, intensify their discomfort, and exaggerates their problems. This further inflames their discomfort, causing a release of even more chemicals and substances, resulting in a vicious *escalating* cycle of overwhelming stress and anxiety.

Overwhelmed by the tidal wave of emotional and physical reactions makes them feel like they are drowning. They will do anything to make it stop. Every cell in their brain is clamoring: I can't take it any longer. This intense emotional surge drives them to do the one thing they know that will eliminate all their distress in an instant. If they are around anyone who can give them something, anything, they will take it.

In order to stay on track with recovery, they have to know a very important *truth*: The addicted brain's *mission* will always try to get them back on drugs. The brain sees drug use as essential for survival because the addictive drugs stimulate the reward pathway more intensely than natural survival rewards can ever do. Drug use becomes more important than eating or drinking water, sexual activity, and parenting—even more important than their safety.

Once they learn that the battle to *remain* in recovery is waged in *their mind.* They have to find ways to *recognize these addictive thoughts* and *physical reactions early* in order to keep from relapsing. It won't be easy because this over-exaggerated stress response the brain creates makes it extremely difficult for them to handle stress—even minor stress. It is *not* a character problem. These biological changes make it extremely difficult for them to handle *any* stressful situation.

One of the chemicals the brain releases is Cortisol Releasing Factor (CRF). CRF is released when the brain perceives their life is in danger and triggers the fight or flight response. In the past, it was activated to avoid getting a person killed. It prepares them to either run away from danger as fast as they can to safety or to fight for survival. This system activates the adrenal system that increases their heart rate, blood sugar, and blood pressure. It channels how blood flows through the body by causing an increase in flow to the skeletal muscles that are needed for them to either run away or fight and less blood flow to their higher cortical areas of the brain, making it very difficult to think and analyze a situation. In order to survive a lion attack, they need to act quickly, either by running away or by fighting back. They do not have time to think the situation through and decide what would give them the best outcome. By the time they make a decision, they just became someone's dinner. These survival instincts do *not* involve thinking and reasoning things out. It is *impulsive, reactive, and instinctual.*

Unfortunately, a system that was used in the past for survival to avoid getting killed now *undermines* their ability to stay calm and figure things out. The stress response system doesn't allow those in recovery to think clearly by overwhelming them with anxiety and emotional reactions. The addicted part of the brain hammers in the message that the only way they can get through this is by taking something—anything to calm down. Once they relapse, it strengthens the addictive pathways by intensifying the discomfort the next time they want to stop. The *more a pathway is used, the stronger it becomes.* Think of it like lifting weights. The heavier the weight and the more reps we do—the stronger our muscles become.

How can they overcome such odds when their own brain is fighting against all their efforts to stop using drugs? These pathways will never go away, but that doesn't mean they can't retrain their brain to learn *new* pathways to *deal* with stress. When they *repeatedly practice daily* relaxation techniques, they develop an automatic response to relax. So, when they are in a stressful situation, and they start focusing on their breathing, the learned response helps them relax. This process of practicing daily relaxation techniques is the only way a person in recovery can *cope* with the *unexpected events* that plague all of us in life. In this process of training, it takes time and commitment to do it *daily*. They need to practice daily when they are *not* in a crisis in order for it to *work* when they are in one. The repetition creates super highway circuit pathways in the brain that will transport information quickly from one area of the brain to another rather than go through the usual snail mail information processing system.

So, that when overwhelming emotions occur and they start focusing on their breathing—they quickly become more relaxed because their brain has been *trained* to respond this way. It allows them the chance to distract their cascading thoughts that are overwhelming them by simply focusing on their breathing. A moment of peace (a pause) that gives them enough time for the thinking part of the brain to start analyzing the situation, not clouded by emotion or anxiety. When they have a variety of different coping mechanisms to learn helps relieve the monotony of the training process. Some of the stress-relieving coping mechanisms can include:

- Safe-place visualizations where they try to re-experience a place that is comforting to them. Try to be as concrete as possible.
  - I picked my mom's kitchen, where she is singing, Oh Suzanna, with her sweet Italian accent while stirring the tomato sauce in a pan on top of the cast-iron stove. The air is filled with the scent of bread baking in the oven while I sit at the old metal table with pink plastic seats that stick to my skin while I impatiently wait for the food to be done. Sunlight streams through the window over the sink that is filled with cups and plates sitting in a rubber tub filled with soapy water. My blue overweight parakeet is next to me, perched on the edge of the sugar bowl, and bends its head to take a few nips of sugar, then ruffles its feathers and sniffs the air. Pretty Bird (the name of my bird) would wobble over and climb up my arm to give me a gentle peck on my face and nuzzle its head against my skin and would coo, "*pretty bird, pretty—pretty—pretty bird is a good bird.*"
    Oh, how I loved that bird!
  - The more details to describe their safe place, the more real it becomes.
- Distraction techniques help redirect their thoughts, such as,
  - Doing puzzles
  - Watching a funny show

- o Listening to music
- o Focus on anything other than the anxiety that is causing their problem.
- Mind-body relaxation techniques such as Yoga or Qigong help ease the tight muscles in our body that stress causes. By practicing Qigong, it involves rhythmic-balanced movement with focused, mindful breathing meditation that relieves the tension in both their muscles and their mind. All these skills require a daily routine for them to avoid taking drugs that will make all these uncomfortable emotions go away in an instant.

Some people would like to think that over time these changes in the brain caused by addiction would go away and never bother them again. This is *dangerous*. It lulls them into thinking they are safe. Just what the addicted brain wants. It will play the waiting game until they are not so vigilant about doing all the things necessary to remain in recovery. Be aware of those addictive thoughts that can be reactivated faster than a speeding bullet during any unexpected painful event. Some of the situations that put people in recovery at risk are:

- When family members or partner start complaining about all the time they spend going to recovery meetings or practicing meditation exercises. All their complaining does is make them think they are being selfish and inconsiderate.
  - o Not realizing they wouldn't have a family if they relapsed and returned to active drug use.
- Their partner is upset that they are not helping them bring the kids to the multitude of sports practices, games, lessons, band, ballet, dance, or other activities.
  - o This makes them feel even worse like they are neglecting their family's needs. They know they require the meetings but start feeling their family needs them more.
    - I wonder do kids really need to be involved in so many activities that cause so much stress in the family? Maybe they need to consider limiting their child

to only one or two activities. This will reduce the
burden for everyone.

- A child doesn't want to spend the only time they have with
  their parents by being chauffeured from one activity to
  another. This chaos is not good for the child, the spouse, or
  anyone in recovery.

- Under so much pressure from too many commitments
  (rather than cut back on all the kids' activities), they begin
  to attend less and less recovery meetings until they stop
  altogether.

- The family has the mistaken belief that recovery is only
  about stopping drug use and think once their loved-one
  stops using drugs, they will be back to the same person they
  were *before* drugs took over their life.
  o The family and those in recovery start thinking they are
    cured.
  o The family becomes less diligent about not leaving any
    leftover pain medications in the bathroom cabinet and
    start going to celebrations and parties. During these cel-
    ebrations, a person in recovery sees some of their old
    drug-using friends. At first they do fine and have no
    cravings that further fuel their thinking, they are cured.
    ▪ *Until* a stressful event occurs and they are around
      the wrong person at a vulnerable moment—and
      relapses.

A slip can happen even twenty or thirty years into recovery. It is
important to know these addictive brain pathways lie dormant, just
like a seed—waiting for the right environment to sprout. Seeds can
remain dormant for *centuries* until they are planted, watered, and
then grows into a mature plant. Just like anyone in recovery having
the right environment created by stressful event(s) (job loss, death
of loved one, divorce, etc.) and watered by being around the wrong
people can activate the dormant addictive pathways and mature into
full blown addictive behavior at *any* time in their life. For the unprepared, it can be devastating. They no longer have the same tolerance

to drugs like they had before when they regularly used drugs. So, when they take the same dose as before, they overdose and can die.

In recovery, they have to maintain constant vigilance about the people they associate with and continue a daily mindfulness routine to deal with the unexpected, overwhelming emotional events that plague all of us in life. They need to stay connected by attending recovery meetings, going to counseling, church, or spiritual guidance in order to be around positive, uplifting people, but who will also hold them accountable for their actions. The advantages of attending recovery meetings give them a purpose in life. When they share their experiences with the group, it helps other people struggling with the same problems. It gives others hope that they can get better, too.

- Caution: Anyone in recovery should not try to help former drug-using buddies. When painful events happen, they are already triggered by their subconscious memories and primed to get overwhelming cravings that make them more susceptible for a relapse.
- Even if they think going to a support meeting is a waste of time. They need to be reminded they are only one slip away from a relapse. They have to always be on guard. There is *no* time off for good behavior.

DEPRESSION

Depression is common in people who have an addiction. Many were self-medicating themselves with drugs to treat or to cope with their depression. It's surprising to hear the responses I get when I ask people in recovery what their first reaction was when they first took an opioid. Many said they felt great, their anxiety was better, the empty loneliness had eased, and they had a lot more energy and could now get through the day. Many felt the pain of previous abuse lessened; while others felt confidence they never had before and could conquer any problem. Somehow, the opioid boosted their confidence, energy and reduced their fears, making them feel capable to face life head-on. Unfortunately, this state doesn't last very long. With chronic drug use, the brain stimulates chemicals to offset the pleasure and benefits that the drugs had created. Like a titter-totter, when pleasure goes up from drug use—the brain releases substances to bring the pleasure down. One of the substances the brain releases to offset the effects of addictive drugs is Dynorphin. Dynorphin stimulates the Kappa receptors in the brain to cause dysphoria—a state of being very unhappy, anxious, and dissatisfied. With chronic drug use, they no longer feel any benefit from taking the opioid drugs and only continue using in order to keep from experiencing the horrible and painful withdrawal symptoms from happening.

This is an important point that many people don't know, so I am repeating it to make sure everyone understands. After a person uses opioids for a while, *they no longer experience any pleasure from taking them and only continue the opioids to keep from experiencing the severe mental and physical withdrawal symptoms*. I have *never* heard of anyone physically dependent on an opioid get excited about going through withdrawal. Withdrawal symptoms cause severe muscle aches, heart-pounding anxiety, profuse sweating, intense abdominal cramping, nausea & diarrhea, and make them feel like they are going to die. These are experiences no one wants to go through again.

Remember—the addicted part of the brain's goal is for them to *never stop* taking drugs. So, with every withdrawal—the brain intensifies the dread, the overwhelming fear of going through another withdrawal and that makes them do *anything* to get more drugs. The addicted part of their brain pounds this message in with every attempt to get off them—drugs are needed for survival. This response is contrary to what many people think and feel that those who stay on drugs are taking them to get high or for fun. Not realizing over time, they are now only taking them to keep the pain of withdrawal away. *They are miserable.*

Knowing how painful it was to get off the opioids, it would be reasonable to think anyone with an addiction would do anything to avoid ever getting hooked on them again. So, why do they keep relapsing? When they stop taking any opioids, the addicted brain's mission is to make them feel so *wretched* that they will come begging on their hands and knees to start taking them again. The addictive brain releases chemicals that cause:

- Intense anxiety
- Depression
- Severe fatigue and body aches
- Emptiness and loneliness
- Makes everything they do an effort
- Nothing is pleasurable.

This elevated brain reward state can last in some people up to four years in recovery. So, It's understandable why they relapse so often in the early years of recovery. This elevated brain reward happens because opioids stimulate the reward center of the brain at least 200 times more intensely than the natural rewards can ever do. It takes a long time for the brain to *slowly return* for natural rewards to become pleasurable again. While waiting for the brain to recover, they are depressed. Nothing is pleasurable or rewarding, and they feel like they are going through the motions in life. Everything is a chore. It's hard to become motivated to do anything when nothing makes them happy, excited, or feel anything is worthwhile.

About six to eight months into recovery, they forget how miserable they were while taking drugs. Right now, they are tired of having to force themselves to get out of bed every day. Their life has become drab, dull, with no relief in sight. They begin to think: *Is this all I have to look forward to for the rest of my life?* They start recalling all the good times they had while taking drugs, and they forgot all the bad. This type of thinking is called romancing the high. The addicted part of the brain *blocks* their recollection of all the misery the drug use did to them and to others. They are in a game with the cards stacked against them. The addicted brain knows them better than they know themselves and what buttons to push to intensify the agony. It will even create injuries in order to get them back on drugs. The addicted part of the brain's mission is to win at *any and all* costs. Some get so tired of this merry-go-round of misery that they commit suicide by overdosing to end the horrible game that their life had become.

FEAR

Fear has many facets. For a lot of people, it can be extremely difficult for them to see how it's affecting their life. The first step with dealing with fear is awareness of its multiple medusa heads. When one head is cut off—it seems like another one pops up in its place. Their fears were already there but unrecognized—until now. Fear is subtle, and devious with its goal to keep them stuck in their circumstances and life. Fear keeps a person from reaching their full potential, and traps them in their problems.

Several people in recovery will tell me, *"I'm not afraid. I've had so many drug overdoses that I'm not afraid of dying."*

They may not be afraid of dying, but they certainly are afraid of living. Fear can be an emotion but most of the time it presents itself as a mindset. Fear deprives us of *hope*, and without hope, we are lost.

Fear is very subtle so how do people recognize if fear is in control of their life? How many *excuses* do they have for not achieving their goals or dreams? *For every excuse—there is a fear.* I don't have the finances, the connections, the right opportunities, the abilities, the personality, or the attractiveness. If anyone had my childhood, they wouldn't have succeeded either. They blame their parents, family, or friends—everyone but themselves for not doing what they feel in their hearts they want to achieve. They tell themselves they are too old, too young, or it's not worth the effort to excel. They are letting fear control their decisions.

Sometimes the fear of failure keeps a person from even trying. They fear what others would think if they tried and failed. Their fears deceive them and keep them stuck in their misery. They worry about all the time lost trying to achieve the impossible. They don't want to make any sacrifices to move forward unless the outcome is guaranteed. For every dream lost is filled with a mountain of excuses and fears. Their eyes are so focused on past mistakes and regrets that they can't see the opportunities right in front of them. Fear has them *dwell* on the *negativity* and not on all the *possibilities*.

When people are actively using drugs, fear can easily keep them stuck by reminding them of all their previous efforts to get off drugs and failed. They have tried so many programs before and kept returning to drugs again. They eventually reach the point of why try any more—nothing works. It's easy to lose hope and feel stuck in the never-ending cycle of relapses. Many have committed suicide because they could see no way out and were exhausted from the constant effort of finding more and more drugs to keep the pain away. They felt trapped with no hope for recovery. Their addicted brain has taken over their life, and they see no way to escape the constant searching for drugs and then taking them. Their life becomes limited to only three options.

1. Continue what they are doing until they die from an overdose or infection.
2. Commit suicide to end the cycle of pain.
3. Or realize they can't stop on their own and get help.

Getting help is a very difficult step to do. They have to overcome their fears of rejection by their family, healthcare, and their friends. Many people have no support to help them in this process. They have burned all their bridges from the multiple times their family had tried to help them and was unsuccessful. Unfortunately, the help the family was seeking was ineffective, expensive, and frustrating since it did no good. In a very short while, their loved ones had resumed taking drugs again. What was not recognized or treated was how strong this compelling urge the addicted brain creates to continue the cycle of taking drugs. Until the *urge* is *curbed,* they will relapse.

This is the absolute saddest part. The very treatments that have been *proven* to be successful in helping curb their intense cravings are discouraged or even ridiculed as trading one addiction for another. Remember, they are helpless to fight against this addictive pathway. They can't control it. This pathway sees taking drugs are necessary for survival. How long can any of us last if we could not eat any food or drink any liquids? Would we last one day, a week, a month, or a year? Eventually, the drive to eat or drink is going to overcome any resolution a person makes, especially if the food and water are right in front of them. The addictive pathway sees *drugs* as more important than surviving and is *more powerful than thirst or hunger.*

Once a person seeks treatment and is on a medication to help curb their cravings—fear strikes again. This is the fear of shame caused by all the lost time, mistakes, and hurts they had made to those they loved. A feeling of unworthiness crushes them from all the wrongs they had done. They can only break free of this *toxic* shame by learning the power of *forgiveness and acceptance.* No matter how they wish things were different.

- They can't change the past.
- They can't correct what has already happened.
- They have to learn how to forgive themselves.
- They have to let go of the guilt, condemnation in order to move forward.

It's already a difficult process to change, but it becomes almost unbearable when they are weighed down with all this emotional baggage that hinders every step they make in an attempt to get better.

Believing in a loving and forgiving God has an advantage over someone who doesn't believe. When they believe that Jesus had died for their sins and paid the ultimate sacrifice by the shedding of his blood. When they confess their sins and ask God for forgiveness, they become free from condemnation and the burden of their past mistakes. With the weight removed from their shoulders, it allows them to move forward in their life. They no longer have to live in the past but can live in the moment of possibilities with all things becoming new again. With eyes looking forward instead of back and the courage to follow their dream. Every day is a new beginning, a chance to *learn* from past mistakes instead of dwelling on them. This gives them the courage to proceed forward, relying on God, a power far greater than anyone's limited understanding to help them achieve the greatness that is in all who believe. Only by having hope, and believe for a better life spurs them through the rigorous, painful process of recovery and dealing with their problems. Without hope, they will not succeed. *Fear destroys all hope*, and it's one of the main causes of discouragement and failure. People fail because they *stop trying*.

As long as they keep bouncing back from their mistakes, they become unstoppable in fulfilling the dream that's instilled in them. They have to push the fear, disappointments, and discouragements to the side and stop focusing on their problems. Instead, they need to focus on the goals they want to achieve and allow it to guide them forward. The Bible says, without a vision, the people will perish. Without a dream, a goal, everything a person does becomes a heavy burden and becomes too difficult to bear. Part of my treatment in helping those in recovery is to discover what dreams have been left behind and give them the encouragement to pursue them.

Many people in recovery had lost so much to drug use. The drugs have taken away their love for life and filled it with love for the drug above everything that was important to them. They are lost, with no vision or dream for a better life—just having endless joyless days ahead. The drugs had taken away their dreams and happiness and made everything else meaningless—not worth the effort. They are fighting what they know they need (recovery) versus what the addiction process wants (more drugs). On their own, this is a losing battle. This is why it is so important to have a support team to get them through this struggle that can last longer than most people want. It can be a lifetime process. When they start thinking addiction is a temporary problem, they are priming themselves for a setback. Once they let their guard down, they slowly *unconsciously* start making wrong choices that eventually lead them back to a path they thought was long gone.

Remember, this is a disease in remission, but it is *not gone*. Addiction is like a seed that only needs the right environment (painful situation) and water (hanging around the wrong people) to allow it to sprout, grow and take over their life again. It doesn't take a month of dabbling in drugs for them to become hooked again like it did the first time. It can take only one drink, one snort, or one line of drugs for addiction to start controlling their life again.

Fear can be a good thing or a bad thing, depending on how they use it. Fear is good if they are terrified of returning back to drugs, and their fear keeps them away from any potential threats. As long as they avoid the problems, they will remain safe. On the other hand, if they walk around with blinders on and act like this addiction problem will never happen again. It allows their unconscious addictive thinking to take over. It does this by gradually having them make bad choices that will ultimately lead them back to becoming a slave to drugs again. If fear is used to avoid the wrong people, places, and things, then it can be extremely helpful in their recovery, *but* if fear keeps them from pursuing their talents and dreams, it can lead them back into drug use.

ANGER

Anger stimulates the stress response system, and it channels more blood to go to our muscles and less flow to our brain. This is why when we are angry, we make rash decisions that spearhead into impulsive actions that can lead to serious problems. Adding problems to anyone in recovery is like adding gasoline to a fire, making it extremely difficult for them to cope. Also, anger has a way of distorting reality, making them feel justified for their actions. When anyone in recovery has a fight with their partner—it can trigger their addictive Stinkin-thinking. It can make them feel justified to take drugs as an excuse to get back at their partner for making them upset. They use their anger as a whip to keep other people in line by implied intimidation—don't argue with me, or you'll be responsible for my relapse.

Anger makes people not listen to good advice and makes them unreasonable. With all those chemicals surging through their system, they can't think clearly or rationally. Emotional thinking has taken control, and their anxiety intensifies to the point that all they can think about is the need to take something to calm down.

Later, they justify their action. "*If they didn't make me so mad, I wouldn't have gotten drunk and got arrested for drunk driving.*"

Naturally, in their mind, if anything goes wrong, it's not their fault, and they relinquish any responsibility for their problems. Anger isolates a person. The need to connect is powerful for all of us. Yet, there are certain behaviors angry people do that drive others away.

- Name-calling is a common culprit. When they call other people bitch, stupid, or an idiot does not promote cooperation or connection.
- When they are unhappy. They want everyone around them to be unhappy by causing unreasonable, petty arguments to provoke a fight that will justify their need to go out and take drugs.
- They get irritated easily and are unpredictable in their actions. They might throw their drink in a co-worker's face, dump food in their lap, or shout and create a commotion.

What anyone says—can't be unsaid. When they keep apologizing repeatedly for making the same mistakes, it grows old very quickly, and other people stop believing them anymore. Lashing out verbally and/or physically does not bring people together but pulls them apart. The only way they can deal with their anger is to *accept I have a problem* and not blame it on other people or circumstances. They need to recognize one vital truth: *They can only change themselves and their reactions.* They cannot change other people. Only with recognition, I have a problem will give them hope for a different future. Awareness that *I am the problem* is difficult because in the past, their mindset was other people were the problem and responsible for my actions and the way I feel.

So what are some of the symptoms and signs that anger is in control of our life? How many friends do I have? Anger has a way of isolating us because people avoid being around anyone who makes them feel miserable or fearful. No one likes to be called terrible names—lazy, worthless, stupid, or to be criticized all the time. Who wants to be around someone who is irritable all the time?

Complain—complain—complain and blaming other people or circumstances, rather than take responsibility for their own actions.

- They will never find a solution to any of their problems due to their misguided belief that other people or circumstances are the problem—not them.
- People stop talking to them because of fear of their reaction. Either they blow up and make molehills into mountains or give the silent treatment by pouting and slamming things around the house.
  - To constantly be blamed for everything that is wrong in the world and in their life makes people want to avoid them.
- So, how many friends do they really have? Or have they lied to themselves by saying, "*I prefer the solitude?*"

Finally, when they recognize they might have an anger problem—what can be done to change it? Anger is a *learned* behavior. In the past, they learned that anger was an effective weapon for them to cope with stress or deal with change. Anger cannot be unlearned, but it can be channeled into learning *new* behaviors that are less destructive towards other people and to themselves. Learning requires *daily repetition* of the new behavior for this to work. This takes time and is not a quick fix on changing how to react to situations they don't like.

Anger is an impulsive reaction. So, how can a person manage this response? I find that anger has two main components that can be addressed for treatment.

1. Anger creates a *physical reaction* that is caused by the survival fight, flight, or freeze response system. This primitive system was used to keep us alive but now has become the source for impulsive actions and thinking.
2. Anger causes *emotional thinking* by having more blood flow going to their muscles and less to the higher cortical areas of their brain (the logical thinking part of the brain.). This change in blood flow allows the emotional area of the

brain (amygdala) that is right next to the survival area of the brain to control their thoughts and feelings. *Emotional thinking* is *irrational*. It is difficult for them to control these repetitive thoughts that escalate their anger and physical reactions they are experiencing. This triggers them to say and do things that cause problems in their relationships, work environment, and possible legal issues to develop.

Once anger reaches a certain point, it triggers an automatic cascade of chemicals to bombard their mind and body. Having any discussion about a problem during this time only makes matters worse. When emotions are *not* engaged, it's like stopping a car only going one mile an hour. But once intense anger is triggered it causes a cascade of chemicals to surge through their system. Once this happens, it's like trying to stop a run-away-train going two hundred miles an hour, and has no brakes. The train will destroy anyone or thing in front of it. Just like the run-away-train, when anger strikes, they have lost control. This is why it's so important for them to *recognize* the *physical reactions* to anger *before* they reach the point of no return. These physical symptoms are an early warning signal that *uncontrollable* anger is about to take over. It is like a sign in the road that says: Bridge out ahead. If they ignore the information, they will crash, and can cause serious problems in their life: a break-up of relationships, the potential loss of a job, or fighting that can result in jail time. Anger causes an adrenalin rush, and these are some of the physical signs that anger is about to take over.

- Their heart is beating fast.
- Their breathing becomes quick and shallow.
- Their hands become clammy, and their body begins to sweat.
- They feel jittery, anxious, and nervous.
- Their pupils dilate
- Many get a spurt of energy or an increase in strength and a reduction in feeling pain. So, when they smash their fist

into the door, they have a diminished sensation of pain until most of the adrenalin gets out of their system.

All these symptoms are due to the fight-flight-freeze survival response system that channels blood to the skeletal muscles and less to the organs of the body and the higher cortical areas of their brain. The survival response system increases blood flow to the primitive parts of the brain that involve: Alertness, reward, memory, emotion, and motor centers. This allows them to become *hyper-focused* on only their side of the situation. The stress response system can make any uncomfortable event or argument as if it's a *life or death emergency*. Their breathing becomes quick and shallow in order to increase oxygen to their muscles that tighten and clench, ready for action. They are geared for action to either speak with snappy cutting remarks, to physically attack, or run away. In this life or death *mental* moment, they become unreasonable (remember the thinking part of the brain is shut off) for discussion since *their viewpoint* is all they can *see* or *understand* at this time. When they are in this stage, they struggle to control their words and actions. This is why it is *imperative* that they learn how to recognize their symptoms *before* they reach this state.

How can anyone gain control of a situation before it becomes too late? Anger is an impulsive reaction. Any way they can slow down the process gives them time for blood to flow and reach the thinking—logical part of their mind. Some people find taking a time-out when they start to feel their heart rate increase, their breathing becomes rapid, or feel their muscles tightening, such as gritting their teeth or clenching their hands into a fist. They need to calm down before continuing, and they have to *leave* the situation—for now. They can distract their mind by taking a walk and count the number of trees, watch something funny on television, count backwards or only focus on their breathing, and not let other thoughts intrude. The time away only works if they focus on *other things* and not on their problems. If they ruminate about their problems, it only magnifies their anger and worsens the situation.

Other ways to help reduce their anger is making sure they get plenty of sleep every night. The ability to cope with problems is compromised when they are tired or hungry. A regular routine of exercise, food, and sleep can help them deal with issues in a more positive way. Aerobic and stretching exercises release hormones that reduce stress, but combative exercises such as punching a bag can intensify the anger response. Aerobic exercise for thirty minutes a day, such as walking (preferably outdoors), riding a bicycle, or swimming release oxytocin, endorphins, and serotonin in the brain that improves their mood, reduces anxiety and stress.

Other ways people can reduce their stress level is by learning how to delegate some of their work to other people or set boundaries to avoid becoming overwhelmed with responsibilities. If a person works all day, then cooks, clean, do the laundry, mow the yard, and trim the bushes. When someone asks them to do another task or errand, they explode. It is like the straw that broke the camel's back. They reached the breaking point and are not able to handle one more thing. To keep from becoming overwhelmed, they have to find ways to delegate some of their work to others by hiring a cleaning service once a month or a lawn service to do the yard work. All these responsibilities elevate their stress level, making them irritable, snippy, and angry all the time. People need time just for themselves in order to relax. When they go to sleep, the body rests, but the brain does not because it's still processing the events of the day. Some ways the mind can get *rest* is by doing some type of meditation that focuses only on the moment and provides the mind peace, rest, and tranquility. There are books or U-Tube meditation practices they can access and learn. Meditation has been shown to release hormones in the brain that increases happiness and reduces stress and anxiety.

Some people think they have no control over their anger. They blame other people or circumstances as an excuse for why they became angry. Blaming others takes the responsibility off themselves to change. One compelling fact: We all have limited control over what *happens* to us, but we do have the ability to change the way we *decide* to *react* to a person or situation. We have the *power* to change. Sometimes we require professional help to guide and help us to take back our power to change. We all have blind spots and need instructions on how to handle a problem. Some areas a professional can assist people learn how to control of their anger are:

- First, what are their triggers?
  - What situations or certain people make them angry?
  - Then they need to *practice* different ways to respond to these situations and work on a less emotional outcome.
    - Role-playing is very helpful guide in this process.
- Have a daily routine of practicing some activity that reduces stress.
  - Mindful breathing exercises, safe place visualization, mind-body connection, such as yoga or Tae Chi.
  - A professional can help assist in teaching these techniques and encourage the need to continue doing them to get the full benefit for anger control.
  - When they reduce their stress level, it also raises their anger threshold, making it more difficult for them to become angry.
- The words they say to themselves has a way of escalating or diminishing their anger response.
  - How they *interpret* a situation has a big impact on how they will *respond* to it. When a person goes to work and says "Hi," to a fellow worker, and they don't say anything back. They have many options on how to respond based on what their thoughts are.
    - If their thought is: *I can't believe she ignored me after all the help I did for her the other day. The bitch thinks she's better than me.* These thoughts are likely to lead to an angry outburst.
    - Instead, if they choose to think on: *She must have a lot on her mind, or she didn't hear me say hi or did I see tears in her eyes?* This response would be much different than the previous one.
  - When they learn to *step back* and *relook at other possibilities* for other people's actions, they can develop new ways of responding to it and take control of their life.

- How to let others know how they feel can be a balancing act. When they resort to name-calling or labels, it will magnify their disagreements and block the ability to find any resolution to their problem(s).

When they simply state, "*I am so upset because you forgot to call and tell me you were going to be late. The special dinner I spent all day making is ruined. I've been worried sick if something horrible has happened to you.*"

This response is so much better than screaming, "*You are such a jerk for not calling and telling me you were going to be late. I'm not interested in any more excuses. You are so inconsiderate,*" as she throws the dinner plate at him, then storms out the door, yelling, "*I don't know why I bother with such a stupid, liar like you.*"

It takes time to change how we will respond to people and situations. It does not happen overnight. For those with an anger problem that is causing trouble in their relationship with their partner or at work, they would benefit from seeing a counselor. The counselor can guide their anger responses and help them gain much healthier relationships.

To change a behavior or a reaction, they have to make an action plan and figure out: Why did I react the way I did? Here are some considerations to implement.

- Recognize the physical signs that I am getting angry. I need to make a plan on finding ways to calm down *before* I explode.
  - Take a time out by:
    - Distracting my thoughts by watching a funny movie or doing a puzzle.
    - Doing mindful breathing, or muscle relaxation exercises to release my tension.
- Discover what are my triggers? What buttons are being pushed that seem to always lead me to lose control?
- What are my thoughts? What am I thinking about or feeling that is causing this surge of anger to explode? How can

I divert my thoughts into a *new direction* to change the outcome?

- How I reacted in the past is where I need to figure out what I could have done differently to avoid the outburst.
  - Could I have *stopped* reacting in anger when she threw the dinner plate at me?
  - Could I have stopped getting angry when she yelled at me?
  - Could I have avoided the fight if I apologized right away and explained the emergency?
  - Or could I have called and let her know I was going to be late?
- Practice looking at the situation from the other person's perspective. When I change my viewpoint, it allows me to see the situation differently. When I *change my thoughts* and opinions, it broadens my understanding and changes the way I respond.
- Find ways to keep calm during a discussion.
  - Focus on what they are saying and *not* on what I am going to say.
  - Repeat what I think they are saying to make sure I understand their concerns. This also allows the other person to know that I am listening.
  - The ability to keep calm can be challenging. They need to develop a plan on how to *daily* reduce stress, and it will immensely help them reduce the anger response.
  - Seek professional help—nothing to be ashamed about—we all need help at some stage in our life. The smart ones get help.

What is important is to learn how to do things *differently* and make a plan, and then keep tweaking the plan until it meets their needs.

SURVIVAL TIPS

- Fear makes us dwell on all the negatives instead of the possibilities.
  - Fear keeps us stuck and blocks our ability to consider other options.
  - God has *not* given me a spirit of fear but of power and of love and a sound mind. When fear attacks, we need to fight that fear with what God says about us. We have the power, the ability, and the mental capacity to overcome our obstacles—when we rely on God.
  - Fear has us focus on the problem and not on our all-powerful, knowing, loving God. Just waiting for us to call out to Him. Just like we rush over to protect our child, God is there. Now our battle has become God's battle.
    - We know that God has us in this situation for a reason. We can't lose sight God has a purpose for everything I am experiencing. I need to trust Him to turn everything for my good because He Loves Me.
  - As long as we keep our eyes on God by praising Him despite our circumstances and trusting God—He will do what He says He will do.
- Anxiety amplifies any painful event and makes it difficult for people in recovery to keep from taking a drug to ease their discomfort.
  - We gain peace in our life when we hand over our lives to God. God is now in control. Nothing can stop God from fulfilling His purpose in our life as long as we follow His lead.
  - We no longer have to worry about other people trying to sabotage our efforts or become someone else to fit in. King Saul tried to kill David. He used all his authority and men to hunt him down to destroy him. But God protected David, and he became the next king.
  - God is our protection, our shield. As a Christian we need to make sure we do any job to the best of our

ability. We are representing Our Father. God does not approve of sloppy, don't care attitudes, wanting to do as little as possible, show up late, leave early, and spend most of our time gossiping instead of working. He will not bless our efforts unless we strive for excellence.

- If we don't have God heal our hearts, the pain will never fully go away.
  - o God wants to set us free. We can't get better on our own—we need God's power and direction to get better.
- God is a creative God. Since we are made in His image, our mind is creative, too. When we seek medical help, God has allowed people to invent medicines, glasses, hearing aids, and false teeth. Do we criticize the medical treatments, but find it acceptable to wear glasses or clothing to protect us from the elements? God provides answers to problems in His own and unique, creative ways. Just like Jesus did not heal everyone the same way. Some He told to reach out their hand, another He spit in clay and put it over a blind man's eyes and told him to wash it in the pool of Siloam, another He touched the man's eyes, another He said to stand up and take your bed with you, and another—your sins are forgiven. They were all healed.
  - o God loves to reveal His uniqueness and power.
  - o Don't prevent a healing by what our expectations should be. The *perceptions* we have about things keep us from utilizing what God provides for us. Let God be God and let Him do things in His many myriad ways.
- Anger can destroy relationships and keep them isolated in their misery.
  - o To take back control of their anger issues, they need to discover their triggers, practice daily stress reduction and change the way they talk about their problems or the situations they encounter.

LIVING A BALANCED LIFE—A ROADMAP TO A HAPPY LIFE

The earth, moon, sun, and our bodies function and move in an organized, consistent manner. For trillions of years, the earth has followed the same path as it orbits the sun. There is a rhythm, a purpose for the patterns, just like our body has a rhythm in order to function at peak performance. When we alter this rhythm, we work at less than peak efficiency, and over time, our systems start to not function properly and cause problems. Just like when we stop putting any oil into our car or doing any maintenance on our vehicles that it needs to run at peak efficiency.

When our system starts to break down, it alters our immune and stress response systems, and we begin to develop mental and physical health problems. Over time, these changes make us more susceptible to developing chronic diseases such as Alzheimer's, hypertension, heart problems, diabetes, or even cancer.

As I had mentioned in previous chapters, the body has mechanisms in place to regulate our temperature, our blood sugars, our moods, sleep-awake cycles, and a whole host of other processes. The ability to *adapt* is built into our bodies, but at the *expense of other systems* down the line if we don't return to the factory-made settings. This adaptability is a blessing for the moment, but if not corrected, it can become a curse to our system over time.

Balanced living requires structure, a routine, and fun. When we have an erratic eat, sleep-wake cycle, this causes our body not to perform at peak efficiency. We feel sluggish, tired, have difficulty concentrating, and struggle with our emotional regulation. We become irritable that causes discord for us at work and at home. We become unpredictable in how we respond to a problem. We are like an open bottle of nitroglycerine, sitting next to a lit match about ready to explode. We are unhappy, and we make everyone around us miserable with our bad attitudes and actions. We need to get back to our normal *body* routines.

Our body is finely tuned with a controlled, *coordinated* release of hormones that either rise or drop during certain parts of the day. This is called a Circadian rhythm. The Circadian rhythm is like an airplane control tower that directs all the planes flying in the area to avoid crashes and near misses. When we don't take care of our bodies, there are consequences that over time can become irreversible. We need to have a schedule and go to bed, eat and wake up at the same time every day. We can't skip meals and eat at random intervals because our body will be releasing hormones at the wrong times leading to exhaustion, feeling overwhelmed, and emotional distress. When our ability to cope has been compromised, we resort to drugs as a means to deal with our problems. We take something for pain (rather than stop doing what is causing all the pain). We take something to sleep, for our anxiety, our depression, and stimulants (caffeine, energy drinks, Adderall, Methamphetamine) to give us energy. We keep taking *things* to fix us. Yet, the power to make us feel better is already built into our body by keeping the patterns that make us function at peak performance. Living a balanced life can offset these stressors and gives us the ability to cope with our problems in a more healthy way.

Living a balanced life also requires a *mental* routine. What we think has a powerful effect on our body. Learning to *block* random thoughts that are negative, judgmental, or critical is important. Negative thoughts can stimulate stress hormones to be released that cause an anxiety reaction and a depressed mood. We need to become free from these stressors for us to live a fulfilled life. Focusing our thoughts to be *positive*, uplifting, kind, and merciful thoughts takes practice and *consistent discipline*. In the beginning, it seems like all our thoughts default to the negative. We focus on what we don't want to happen or worry about what will happen, making us upset because things didn't turn out the way we thought they should. We spend a lot of *emotional energy* on things we have *no control* over, and the things we do have control over, we fail to see what we can do to change the circumstances. When we focus on positive, uplifting, kind, and merciful thoughts, our mood changes, our outlook on life shows us the *possibilities* and reduces the stress that change and uncertainty happen in all our lives. Thinking positive is seeing the good in a situation and *learn* from it, rather than focus on all the wrongs and feel overwhelmed from it. It takes a lot of practice and consistent discipline to change the way we think, but the *quality* of our life depends on it.

At first, it is hard. It may seem like every thought is critical or negative. In the past, I never knew that I had the power to accept or reject a thought. How does a person accept or reject a thought? That was the question I asked myself when I became aware I had this power. Accepting a thought is dwelling on that thought and believing it to be true. Rejecting the thought is telling myself that I don't know or understand the whole situation, and I am not going to spend any emotional energy by dwelling on it, thinking about it, or allowing it to influence any of my actions. In other words—I *ignore* it.

The primitive survival part of our brain consists of our reward pathways along with the memory, emotional and impulsive (need immediate action) systems that collectively create our Stinkin-thinkin misguided thoughts. This is where our first thought about a situation hits our consciousness. It's reactive, emotional, selfish, and not logical. It takes a while for the information to reach our reasoning, the logical part of the brain that weighs the consequences of our actions. If a person dwells on the first thoughts, their actions will be influenced by emotion and past problems, leading them to another negative outcome. But more importantly, they will *never* develop a fast track to the reasoning, thinking part of the brain.

Neuroplasticity is the ability of the brain to modify circuits to transfer information to pass quickly from one area to another. This occurs in *repetitive* learning. When I first learned to type, I had to think about where every letter was and what finger I needed to hit it. Over time and with lots of practice, I no longer think about what my fingers are doing. They just type, but at a much faster rate than if I try to 'think' about what they need to do. The brain has made a *superhighway* to quickly move information from the brain to my fingers and type. Anytime I *repetitively* think a certain way, the brain becomes *hard-wired* to continue thinking that way. So, the more I practice thinking positive thoughts, at first, it takes a lot of effort, but with repetition, a superhighway develops, and it becomes easier and quicker. Many times the negative and positive thoughts almost hit me at the same time. Every time I choose positive thoughts, that pathway gets stronger. Just like when we keep lifting weights, our muscles get stronger the more we do it.

What a wonderful discovery: I can't control what happens to me, but I can control how I will respond to it by the *thoughts* I decide to *dwell* on.

People with addiction and their families struggle with living an emotionally balanced life. Guilt has a way of eroding reason and make people respond in ways that cause more harm for themselves and their loved ones. They have difficulty setting boundaries and become so emotionally entangled (co-dependent) that their happiness depends on how the other person is performing. That careful balance between caring and helping and letting go is difficult to achieve. There is a thin line between helping and enabling. When we have a loved one who has a substance use problem (addiction), we want to help them. What kind of help is going to be useful, and what would be harmful? To make this an even more difficult challenge is the timing. What can be helpful in one stage of their recovery can become harmful to them at a different stage. If I could've, should've, would've plagues us into feeling helpless and trapped with no right answer or direction to follow.

The best advice I can give for the family is to seek counseling for themselves and for their family member who has a substance use disorder. To learn how to balance the needs of self with the need to help another—either extreme is harmful. To become self-aware of a problem is difficult because the memories and emotional center in the brain are making it challenging for us to step back and analyze the problem. Unfortunately, we keep repeating the same actions-reactions with the same predictable responses. To develop balance in our lives, we need to spend time taking care of ourselves. This is not being selfish. This is self-care. How can we love another person if we can't love ourselves? How can we love God that we can't see and not our neighbor who we can see? How can we help another—if we are in need of help?

In the Bible, Jesus said, *"First take the plank out of our own eye, and then you will see clearly to remove the speck from your brother's eye."*

In our efforts to help, we can actually cause more problems. We need to learn how to take care of our problems before we try to help another. So, the first step in leading a balanced life is learning how to take care of our needs. Many of us have forgotten or never learned how to take care of us. We have spent most of our life focused on other people's needs and not our own. First, it was pleasing the husband, the kids, and then the boss at work with no time to find out how to please ourselves. Many of us have forgotten how to have fun, develop new talents, or just enjoy the moment without worrying about cleaning the house, doing the laundry, or making dinner. There is nothing wrong with completing daily chores, but we also need to have something enjoyable to look forward to do.

Learning how to tap into our creative side brings joy and happiness to our lives. A young child has no problem with finding fun things to do, whether it's banging on the pots and pans with a wooden spoon or hiding under a blanket to make a tent. Tapping into our creative side teaches us how to have fun again. Our creative side has been suppressed by our logical mind for way too long. The creative mindset has no boundaries and loves to explore new ideas and adventures. It is what some people call thinking outside of the box. It's freeing our imagination to discover *new* possibilities. The more we tap into our creative minds, the happier we become and the more motivated we are to try new things. Creativity has no right or wrong way to do things. We can follow the rules of making a musical chord or not follow them, allowing our imagination to run free and to explore other possibilities. Finger painting is not all about the outcome, but the sensation of feeling the ooey-gooey paint ooze between our fingers and toes.

The creative mind defies logic. The logical mind says, you have no talent, no training, or have the right connections to succeed. The creative mind sees the situation from a different perspective: As an exciting challenge, something enjoyable to do, an opportunity to grow. See the difference! The logical looks at the outcome, the creative looks at enjoying the process. There is a reason why we have a left and right side of the brain. We need the balance of the fun part of the brain coupled with the logical steps and discipline needed to accomplish our goals. We can't be creative all the time and not have the discipline to finish a project. We can't be so disciplined—there is no fun or joy in our life. Part of living a balanced life is to *avoid* extremes. We can't be 'me' centered all the time, nor can we be a people-pleaser all the time. We need to find a middle road for fulfillment and the ability to interact with other people. Many people in recovery don't know how to interact with other people in a balanced way. They are either a people-pleaser or self-centered—both extremes cause stress for themselves and for others. Unfortunately, people in recovery have a heightened stress reaction, and any little criticism can make them upset, anxious, and go into immediate catastrophic thinking. This negative emotional state is coupled with depression symptoms that make nothing is pleasurable; everything is an effort causing it to be even more difficult to balance this heightened emotional dysregulation.

To reduce this emotional reaction, it's important for us to start enjoying life again. I do this by encouraging my patients to tap into the creative parts of their brain. In order to jumpstart their emotional recovery, it's necessary to explore ways to make them happy to offset their elevated reward system caused by *prolonged* withdrawal symptoms that makes nothing pleasurable or enjoyable. Think of it as priming the pump, so when the brain starts to recover, everyone is already running with the ball. In early recovery, it is difficult for anyone to think of a single thing they would like to do, even after I give them a list of over one hundred different activities to try.

When this happens, I ask, "What did you enjoy doing before drugs became part of your life?"

These are the activities I have them become involved in, hoping their memories of previous pleasures will resurface. It takes time to start enjoying any activities, but slowly it returns as the brain reward system slowly resets and improves. Also, I explore other ways to stimulate the brain by learning something new. It is difficult at first to concentrate and focus, but gradually, it becomes easier for them to do.

I had a patient who worked as a welder and was bored with his life and his job. I encouraged him to try making some metal art. He made flowers out of old spoons and was surprised at how many people wanted to buy them. He was very gifted and talented and decided to start a business creating different types of flowers and was exploring making other types of metal art projects. He would come into the office with pictures of new items he made and had a big grin on his face. He was excited and proud of his work, whereas, previously, it was humdrum, just another boring day. I had another patient who wanted to learn how to paint. He couldn't afford to take any lessons and went on YouTube to learn how to paint. Since then, he has sold some paintings and is excited about painting more pictures. If anyone can tap into the creative side—life becomes fun again. The happier a person is, the less likely he or she will be susceptible to relapse.

Part of living a balanced life focuses on how to deal with strong emotions. In the past, people with addiction had a sure-fire way of dealing with painful situations. Only one pill, one snort, or one injection was all it took to numb their feelings and make all the pain go away. For a person in recovery this is no longer an option. They have to learn new ways to counterbalance these painful emotions.

To balance painful emotions or to deal with stressful situations requires developing coping skills. Stress is a *huge* trigger for anyone in recovery, and it comes in many different packages.

- Finding a job can be overwhelming for a person in recovery.

- Even wearing appropriate clothing to work can become a stumbling block.
- Keeping a job can be equally difficult.
- Something as simple as getting to work on time can be a struggle for those who never had a routine.
- To learn how to interact with other people without resorting to drug use can be challenging.

This is why it is so important for anyone in recovery to have a "safe zone." A place where they feel accepted, encouraged and can be honest about their struggles without getting yelled at or feel ashamed over their feelings. In this safe zone, they are free to explore options and discuss their thoughts and feelings. This allows them time to discover their own motivation for recovery. When the motivation to change comes from *within*, they are more likely to form a *lasting* recovery, with fewer slip-ups in their journey toward wholeness.

Addiction in a family causes stress for everyone. To maintain balance in the home, everyone would benefit from counseling. Unfortunately, most family members don't think they have any need for counseling. Family members view the situation as their loved one has the problem, and I don't. They are in as much denial as a person who says they don't have a problem with drinking or taking drugs. Denial keeps everyone stuck in this repeating cycle of doing the same things and expecting a different outcome this time. Why would this time be any different from last time? A change is needed, but sometimes we are caught in this emotional rollercoaster, and we can't think past anything other than how can I fix this? In our efforts to fix a problem, we only make things worse. It's like trying to perform brain surgery without any medical training. I would hate to see the outcome of that mess. Therapy would be helpful for both the family members and their loved one in recovery. They need to learn ways to cope with their own stress in dealing with their loved one's addiction and finding workable solutions that can benefit both of them.

Sometimes, I recommend people to attend a family support group. It's beneficial, as long as it doesn't become just a complaining session with people comparing notes to see who has it worse than the other person. It's good to have an outlet for our frustrations and discouragements, but a family support group needs to be more than that. It needs to be balanced, so we can focus on our successes in dealing with certain situations and what we did to make them happen. We need to focus on balancing:

- Our problems with solutions
- Our emotions with reasoning
- Worry with acceptance
- Blaming with forgiveness
- Anxiety with peace
- Unrealistic expectations balanced with reality
- Enabling with setting healthy boundaries
- Coping mechanisms for a person with an addiction and for the family members dealing with it

Many people in recovery struggle with sleep. Either they want to sleep all the time or sleep in the daytime and be awake all night. Some find it extremely difficult to fall asleep, and when they finally get drowsy, the alarm rings thirty minutes later. Time to get up. This sleep dysregulation is common in early recovery, but for people with an alcohol use problem (alcoholic), this problem can persist up to two years. Many times, this lack of restful sleep causes them to become irritable, angry, and anxious, making it difficult for them to be around other people. Sometimes this irritability and anxiousness cause them to start drinking again in order to get some sleep. There is a medication available that can treat the underlying cause of the sleep disturbances, and it does *not* involve taking highly addictive sleeping pills or benzodiazepines that create a new problem for them. Gabapentin (can be addictive in some people but is less addictive than the alternatives) has been shown to help reduce this protracted withdrawal from alcohol that can help them sleep and ease their turbulent emotional state without using harmful, highly addictive substances.

There are ways to help people who suffer from insomnia (either they can't fall asleep, stay asleep or not feel rested in the morning.)

Here are a few tips on how to retrain the brain to sleep. Like training a puppy, it takes consistent effort for it to become effective.

- They need to have a consistent time for sleep and wake cycle. They never deviate from their schedule and stay on the same routine—even on weekends, holidays, or days off.
- Do not take any naps.
- Have the bedroom cool, lights off, and quiet (can use white noise if unable for it to be quiet).
- Do not eat a heavy meal or exercise close to bedtime. Both of these activities can increase their body temperature and make it too hot for them to sleep.
- Not to watch anything with a blue screen for at least one hour before bedtime. This means no computers, watching TV, or being on the phone. The light stimulates the alert center in the brain, making it hard for them to sleep.
- Avoid any stimulate medication(s) or other drugs that can affect the sleep cycle.
  - Caffeine that includes no decaf coffee (it only has twenty percent less caffeine than regular coffee.)
  - Nicotine (is a stimulant)
  - Decongestants (is a stimulant)
  - Alcohol affects the sleep cycle
  - No sleeping medications such as Ambien, Lunesta, Halcion, Restoril. Taking these medications for more than a week worsens the insomnia issues.

After thirty to sixty minutes, if they still can't sleep, they need to get up and go into another room. Keep the lights dim. Do not watch TV, use a computer or talk on the phone. Read a boring book, listen to soft music, drink four ounces of milk, or eat one slice of turkey (do not eat a lot). When they start to feel drowsy, go back to bed. If their mind still doesn't let them sleep, then practice doing a mindful breathing exercise that focuses on their breath. Breathe in to the count of five, hold to the count of four, and then out to the count of nine. They need to continue breathing in, holding and counting the breath out until they fall asleep. If they continue with sleep problems and have racing thoughts that won't shut down or have multiple awakenings, they should see their treatment provider and be evaluated for possible thyroid issues, depression, bipolar depression, or other types of health problems.

Learning to achieve balance in all of our life helps us go from crawling to running again. It gives us the energy and strength to make it through the day. Focusing on only today gives us the courage to try new things. Letting *go* of the *old* is needed for any of us to *grasp* onto the *new*. Think of it like a gymnast who is on the uneven bars and swings from one bar to the other. They can't swing to the next bar without letting go of what they are holding onto.

Balance improves our ability to learn by keeping our emotional and physical energy in check, by not overextending or overwhelming ourselves. We can all benefit from learning how to live a balanced life. Focusing our spiritual, physical, and emotional energy in the same direction gives us the strength, ability, and joy to live the life we were destined to achieve.

SURVIVAL TIPS

- Living a balanced life requires structure, routine and fun.
  - Our God is a God of structure. He has a plan and a timetable for everything He has created on Earth.
  - He knows what is best for our body, and maintaining consistent times we eat, sleep, and wake is part of His plans to optimize physical and mental health.
- Learn to balance the needs of self with the needs to help another.
  - Even Jesus left everyone to spend time alone with His Father. We need time alone to restore our mental, physical and spiritual strength. We need to fill our life jar with what is important and not have it all filled with sand that allows no room for our destiny.

- We need to tap into the creative side of our brain to learn how to have fun.
    - God made us in His own image. God is a creative God. When God created the earth, it gave Him happiness, and He said it was good.
    - We gain satisfaction when we do something new.

FILL THE HOLE INSIDE TO KEEP ADDICTION AWAY

The need to rediscover joy and fulfillment help makes the power of drugs less attractive. It sounds easy but so difficult for people in recovery to achieve. When anyone takes opioids on a regular basis, the body starts adapting in a process called homeostasis. The body is trying to bring the brain receptor responses back into a more normal range. Every time they take more and more drugs, the brain counterbalances to respond less and less to its effects. The brain does this by reducing the number of receptors that will react to the drug presence, and the body releases chemicals to offset the pleasure the drugs give. Then they take more drugs to get the previous effect, and the brain counter-punches by releasing more and more chemicals and reduces of the number of receptors even more to lower their response to the drugs taken. This process keeps escalating. When anyone *suddenly stops* taking drugs, it takes a long time for all those negative chemicals and changes in the brain to return to a more normal state. It is unknown if the brain will ever completely become restored to normal.

How long it takes for this process to normalize is unknown at this time, but I suspect it can take more than three years. The reason why I say more than three years is based on the number of people who remain in treatment. Those who are in treatment for more than two years do better than those who are only in for one year. But, people in treatment for three years do better than those in treatment for only two. The findings show, the longer a person stays in treatment, the better the outcome.

In my experience of treating patients, I have observed after they have been in recovery for more than three years, a significant change in motivation occurs. In the beginning stages of recovery, my patients would tell me that everything is an effort. Nothing is pleasurable, and after six to nine months into recovery, some of them give up trying. The memory about how bad everything was before they started recovery has faded, and the chore of the daily boring grind has set in. They start thinking, *this drab existence will never go away, and they can't tolerate living this way for the rest of their life.* They are miserable and don't want to continue living this way. They give up trying.

This is why; I tell my patients in *early recovery* that it takes time for the receptors in their brain to reset. We have to find ways to reconnect with previously enjoyable activities they did before becoming addicted to drugs. I had a patient decide to be an assistant soccer coach at his son's school. Before he started drugs, he was very much into sports and thought he could re-connect with his previous passion. In the beginning, he had to force himself to do this. His son loved it, his wife was proud of him for spending time with his kids, but he struggled putting a smile on his face. He felt so miserable inside, but he kept coaching.

One day in our group addiction meeting, he told us, "*The strangest thing happened to me today. When I went outside, I heard the birds chirping. I never noticed them before.*"

I asked, "How long did it take for you to start enjoying things?"

He said, "*It has taken me more than three years before I even started to look forward to doing things again. Before, I was just going through the motions.*" Gradually his interests and joy returned.

It can take a long while for the brain to heal. People who started taking drugs before the age of twenty-five may never have a brain that will function normally. Why that magic age of twenty-five? That is the time the brain has finally connected all the circuits between the impulsive—got to have it now part of the brain with the cognitive—

thinking of the consequences part of the brain. This is why teenagers are so impulsive and at times engage in risky behaviors because the connection between the impulsive parts of the brain has not been fully connected to the part that says this is a bad idea.

When anyone takes an addictive drug chronically, it stimulates the impulsive part of the brain and blocks the information from reaching the thinking part of the brain. This explains why they struggle trying to stop taking drugs. If anyone starts taking addictive drugs before the age of twenty-five, the connections between the impulsive and cognitive (thinking part) of the brain is stunted. They may never fully develop the connections necessary for them to make good choices in their life. This explains why it takes a lot *longer* for anyone who started drug use before the age of twenty-five to quit compared to those who started using drugs after that age.

Chronic drug use blocks *this is not a good idea response* and allows the impulsive part of the brain to reign and creates havoc in their life. The impulsive part of the brain *acts* on:

- What it sees.
- What it wants.
- What it feels.
- What it will do regardless of the consequences.
- This type of thinking leads them into adverse circumstances.

This impulsive reaction is why they keep making the same mistakes over and over again. The need for the drug overtakes the natural reward system that is used for survival. They are *not* a bad person. They have no control (without help) because the *reasoning* part of the brain is *turned off,* and the impulsive part of the brain has a green light that says, *go—go—go.* It doesn't matter how bad the consequences were the last time they took drugs; when their addictive survival system is activated, it makes them feel like they are going to die if they can't get any drugs to take. It's not logical, but then again, the *logical* part of the brain is *disconnected.* It is like a computer that has a virus. When we type one word or command—the computer does something else. It's so demoralizing for anyone trying to get off drugs and promises never to take them and ends up using them again. All their efforts are lost because their *brain has a different agenda* than what they want to do.

Some people like to think, those who have an addiction have a choice. They choose to take drugs. They think this way because they have no problem saying no to drugs. Even those who have an addiction mistakenly think they have control over their disease.

When I talk to my patient who had just slipped-up and took some drugs I ask, "What are you going to do different next time?"

Inevitability, I hear, "*I'll try harder next time.*"

They are misguided to think they have control over this process and every time they try harder they fail. They are powerless when they experience an intensely painful event that triggers an urge to take something, anything to ease their pain. Their brain has switched from the logical part that says I want to get off these drugs that are ruining my life. And yields to the impulsive part that says, I got to have something right now to ease these horrible, anxious, heart-pounding, racing thoughts and feelings. They feel like they're drowning and the only life jacket that can save them is to take something.

Even though they had every intention of staying off drugs, the hi-jacked brain reward system had a different plan and made them go in an unwanted direction. Shame builds when they lose control over and over again. They have a conscience, and the feeling of despair and desperation leads them into wilder behavior. I wonder how the criminal justice system can incarcerate anyone who has no control over their behavior? We let people who are insane be free from the repercussion of their behaviors, and yet, those with addiction are sentenced to ten to twenty years in prison. Some say, we only send drug dealers to prison. Many people with addiction are buying and selling drugs to support their habit. They can't keep a job, and their families no longer support their habit, while their mind says drugs are needed to survive. So they either rob people, sell their bodies or *drugs* to get the help they need. Instead of penalizing a person because of the consequences of their disease, we need to get them into treatment. In prison, it's difficult to get any treatment, and if they do, they and are placed back into the prison environment, and it does them no good.

There is *no* transition to get back into society, and they still have the addiction that was not addressed or treated while in prison. A large percentage of those with an addiction had within three months after being released either died from an overdose or were back in prison. This proves prison does not help people recover (or change their behavior) caused by their disease. We need to stop criminalizing them for a disease they have no control over and get them the help they need.

People may not be aware that the definition of a drug dealer varies from state to state. If anyone *gives* or *advises* another person how to get a controlled or illegal drug, they can be considered a drug dealer. If a person has a certain amount of drugs in their possession (in their house, car, or on them), even if they had no intent on selling it—they are considered a drug dealer. If they have drugs on them and are found near a school, they are considered a drug dealer, and their penalties are even higher. So, if a friend or co-worker says I have a horrible headache and we give them one of our pain pills. We are now considered a drug dealer. *No* money has to exchange to be considered a drug dealer.

If an individual asks another person, "Do you know anyone who can sell me some drugs because I'm in a rough place?"

The girl is shaking and sweating profusely from withdrawal. Having experienced withdrawal before, compassion fills their heart, and they suggest the man down the street might have some. Even *suggesting* where they can get drugs is considered being a drug dealer, and they just committed a felony in some states.

Our society needs to focus on treatment for anyone addicted to drugs rather than focus on the "War on Drugs." Billions of dollars have been spent on this losing battle. Despite all this effort, we have more drugs in the streets than ever before. Like any commodity, the principle of supply and demand drives the market. If the demand is low, the price for drugs will be low and will not be profitable enough to offset the risks and expenses of bringing drugs into the country. If the demand is high, the price for drugs will be high and will be worth the effort to smuggle more drugs into our country.

The only way we can beat this problem is to *reduce* the *demand*. Right now we have over 223 people in our country dying from an overdose *every Day*. These are our children, brothers and sisters and our future as a nation being destroyed by drugs. The only way we can combat this problem is by focusing on treatment and prevention. Only by having fewer people wanting to take drugs will the demand drop, and make it become less profitable to smuggle more drugs into our country. We have seen this happen in Portugal when they started treating people for addiction and significantly reduced the amount of drugs in their country. Proving, if there is no profit, the need to provide illegal drugs will dramatically decrease.

Our treatment focus needs to be *long-term*. If anyone has diabetes or hypertension, we don't tell them: They only have to follow their diet, exercise, and medication for only a year or two. Yet, we tell people on medication to treat their addiction that after two years of treatment, they need to stop taking the medications that are helping them. When they stop, many of them relapse. We need to change the way we treat those in recovery and realize they might need a lifetime of treatment and monitoring, just like those who have diabetes. There is a reason I say a lifetime. Many people can remain abstinent from drug use for several years, some as long as twenty years, and relapse. We hear in the news how a celebrity overdosed on heroin after twenty years in recovery and died. I wonder if they would be alive today if they had stayed in treatment? The risk for overdose increases dramatically the longer they are abstinent from drug use. They no longer have the same tolerance to the drugs they had before. With the advent of extremely potent synthetic opioids flooding the market (Fentanyl), the risk for overdoses has dramatically increased. Addiction is a chronic and potentially *deadly* disease. From April 2019 to May 2020, overdose deaths in the United States increased eighteen percent, with 81,230 people who died in this twelve-month period. To gain some perspective, in 2020 United States had 16,650 deaths from motor vehicle accidents and 140,730 deaths from lung cancer (most likely caused by people addicted to smoking cigarettes) compared to 22,000 people who died from influenza. Addiction overdose deaths are escalating, and we need to stop thinking addiction is a criminal offense and a temporary problem like the common cold and start thinking about addiction as a lifetime disease and needs lifetime treatment.

How do we keep people from relapsing after several years in recovery? Sometimes, people with substance use disorder (addiction) begin to think:

- They are now cured of addiction. They stop going to meetings or support groups and get busy with their life. They stop becoming cautious and protective of who they talk to or activities they engage in.
- A long time has elapsed from their struggle with addiction, and they don't think it will affect them now. They even forget they ever had an opioid use disorder (addiction). If they need to have surgery, they think nothing about taking an opioid for pain.
  - What makes this situation even worse their own treatment provider thinks this would not be a problem for them to take the opioids for pain.

What their medical provider and people who have addiction fail to understand: Those addictive pathways will *never* go away. It takes very little to reactivate addictive pathways and start the cravings all over again. It's like riding a bike. A long time can elapse since the last time anyone rode a bike. But when they start peddling, their legs automatically move. In the beginning, their balance may be a little wobbly, but in a very short period of time, they are riding like they had never stopped. This learned behavior has not been extinguished. It is latent like breast cancer. It can be in remission for thirty years, and then suddenly, she develops metastatic breast cancer. Women with breast cancer will never be cured. This is why they need continued monitoring to determine if the disease has returned. The same principle applies to addiction. Anyone in recovery needs to monitor the people they associate with and continue practicing healthy coping mechanisms to deal with stress, anxiety, and disappointments to avoid a relapse. Relationship problems are a *huge* trigger for people who have been in recovery for years. Many times they are unaware they are at an increased risk for relapse. When an unexpected loss occurs, they are not prepared to deal with the sudden surge of anxiety, racing thoughts, and their inability to cope, making them very susceptible to taking a drug to ease their discomfort.

It's important for everyone to have a purpose, a goal that they enjoy doing. Recovery is a journey. It is not a quick fix. It's a journey of self-discovery and achievement. Along this journey, we need to add fun into the mix. We all need to have periods of rest and relaxation. The creative part of our brain is where all the fun is located. The creative part of the mind has no boundaries, limitations, or expectations other than—it must be enjoyable. I encourage people to try painting, music, dancing, decorating, writing, or fixing a car. It is so rewarding to create something from nothing and see the outcome. It doesn't have to be perfect. It will improve with practice. Just enjoy the process. We need to tear down those fences in our mind that say, I have no abilities or talent and step out to create something new. Whether it's a painting that previously was a blank canvas, a written song on a blank sheet of paper, a new dance move, or decorating a room. We need to become free from the expectations of other people and our own critic. Just enjoy the moment is when we do our best work by connecting with God, ourselves, each other, and the universe.

Some experts say the opposite of addiction is *not* sobriety but connection. In addiction, they become isolated from other people and themselves. The need to reconnect is part of the healing process. Healing takes time. We need to take time to discover who we are and not listen to what other people told us to be. We need to explore what we want and what we enjoy doing. Taking this time to explore our needs is not being selfish, but it's self-care. When we do what we enjoy, we become better at it, and if we continue, we eventually become an expert. I feel that God has put special gifts into each of us and when we explore and develop those gifts, not only will it give us joy, but it will also give us financial stability in our life. When we excel at those gifts, then opportunities and money will follow.

If we don't learn how to connect with ourselves, how can we connect with other people? When we connect with our inner needs, we learn to accept our strengths and our limitations. We are not per-fect. When we accept our imperfections and begin to love ourselves, we become less judgmental toward others. The way we think and feel about ourselves is *reflected* in how we think and feel about other people.

Some people think I am crazy when I tell anyone who has an addiction problem that they have been blessed with an opportunity to grow. Most people spend their whole life just wandering around and do not spend any time to determine what they really want or need. They are going through the motions of life. They have not learned how to *mold* their life into what they want to achieve.

The recovery process makes all those seeking help exam how their thoughts can influence their emotions and actions.

- They learn to control what they think.
- How to avoid situations that would not be beneficial.
- Develop skills on how to evaluate a plan that failed. Analyzing a situation is a tool they can use for any aspect of their life.
- Take one day at a time.
- Learn how not to become overwhelmed and deal with the challenges that today brings.

To live in the moment is the only thing we have control over, and learning how to *manage* those moments to achieve our goals is *a powerful skill to develop*. We learn to avoid people in our life who drags us down and associate more with those who challenge us to become more than we think we can achieve. We all stumble in our life, but it is what we *learn* from the circumstances that make the difference between:

- Success and failure.
- Happiness or sorrow.
- Love or bitterness.

Those in recovery have to learn valuable lessons to succeed. All of us have to take *control* of our destiny. Nobody else will do it for us.

- We have to adjust the words we say to our self to be uplifting and not critical.
- We need to spend time with positive people.
- How to learn from our mistakes.

In the beginning, it is difficult to change learned repetitive behaviors—but not impossible. For recovery to become sustainable, we have to spend the time needed to evaluate what is special and unique about us and to discover ways to develop those special gifts. When we pursue what comes easy for us, and we love doing it— we create a wonderful life that we never thought possible. Let us all enjoy the journey of self-discovery and fill the hole inside with meaningful experiences and joys. Having a meaningful life is like getting a beautiful brand new vehicle with all the bells and whistles. I doubt very many people would want to trade that wonderful car for a rusted, broken down crumpled piece of junk that is sitting in the junkyard. Recovery is a journey of self-discovery. Enjoy the process.

SURVIVAL TIPS

- The need to rediscover joy help makes the power of drugs less attractive.
  - A positive outlook sustains us, and Joy makes the journey worthwhile.
  - Joy is contagious, just like negativity can be spread to all those around us.
- It takes time for the brain to recover from drug use.
  - Don't give up on our loved ones, but more importantly, for them not to give up on themselves.
  - Family members need to understand anyone with addiction needs time to recover. If they broke their leg, we wouldn't expect them to run a marathon the next day.

- ○ As family members, we need to give our loved ones time to heal. Stop demanding perfection. Slips happen, but as long as they become less and less, progress is being made.
- The way we think and feel about ourselves reflects how we think and act toward other people.
  - ○ If we are having problems in our relationships, maybe we need to look and see what problems do we have with ourselves.
  - ○ Problems give us the opportunity to change.
- Addiction is a chronic disease and potentially deadly. We need to stop thinking addiction is a temporary problem. If we sustained multiple fractured bones, torn ligaments, and lacerations all over our body. We would not look or function the same.
  - ○ Why would we think with all the insults the brain sustained, it would function like it did before they ever started taking drugs?
  - ○ Damage has been done. Healing takes time. Everyone will change as a result of the trauma they had sustained—family included. With God's Grace, He can turn any negative into a positive for those who believe and trust in him.
  - ○ Thank you, God, for making a way when I could not see a way out.

RECOVERY REQUIRES COMMITMENT

Desire is NOT enough.
Wishing is NOT enough.
IT takes Work.

Recovery requires constant *action*. This is where I find a lot of treatment programs fail. Many people are voluntarily or coerced through drug courts to participate in an addiction treatment program. Most of the programs are I.O.P. (Intensive Outpatient Program) that involves attending meetings and counseling sessions several times a week. Once they complete the program, they 'graduate' and have a ceremony of completion. The treatment providers are doing a great disservice to their clients by making them think they are done. It is like telling a first grader that they have now completed all their education. Addiction is a lifetime disease, and they need to have a lifetime commitment toward handling their problem. The other issue is the graduation ceremony. In a previous chapter, I had discussed that any type of celebrations is a trigger for them to relapse. The brain has made powerful associations between getting and taking drugs as the ultimate reward, so when other events are rewarding, it triggers a craving for drug use. I have seen so many people relapse after they completed a program and graduated from it with some type of certificate of completion. In a very short time later, they relapse.

This is why they have to consistently strive to learn from their mistakes and not get bogged down in discouragement. Those in recovery need to monitor the people they are around and spend very little time with those who can drag them down. When they make a poor choice, they need positive people to uplift and encourage them, especially when they feel down or disappointed with themselves. When they slip up, they need people to remind them—it was a mistake, not the end of the world. It's important for them to understand why it happened. So, they can avoid making the same mistakes in the future. Everyone learns by trial and error. If they don't analyze why they slipped up—they can never learn from the experience and change the outcome the next time they encounter a similar problem. As long as they don't get bogged down in discouragement, life becomes a continuous learning and growing process. When an outcome is not what they wanted, they need to figure out what happened and what they can do differently the next time they encounter a similar situation. This is the only way they can fix the situation. For them to grow, they need to understand the *associations* that caused a poor choice. They also need to know what worked for them to achieve their goals. Life is all about options. The choices they make today determine what options they will have in the future. If anyone steals and goes to prison, their options have shrunk, making it difficult when they get out to find employment in certain occupations, such as banking, working as a cashier, or companies concerned about a loss of inventory.

To be successful, they have to stay surrounded by positive people and those who understand what they are experiencing. This is why AA, NA, Celebrate Recovery, Smart Recovery meetings, and having a Recovery Coach have been so helpful for people to stay on the right track. Those who have experienced addiction know what needs to be done to help them stay away from drugs or alcohol. They know how to guide them back onto the recovery train. Meetings help them stay motivated. Recovery can become very exhausting because:

- They always have to be aware of their surroundings, looking for any clues that might lead them into making a bad choice.

- They need to monitor and regulate their emotions, to keep negative feelings from influencing their behavior.
- They have to keep analyzing where did this thought come from? Is it the Stinkin-thinkin part of my mind trying to influence my decisions, OR is it the logical reasoning part of my mind in control?

Thoughts are contagious. If anyone is around a lot of negative people—their thoughts will become my thoughts. Those in recovery need to stay around positive people who can encourage their successes and can lift them up if they slip. They need to understand everyone makes mistakes. It's what they do with their mistakes that can bring success or failure. When they use their mistakes as a learning tool to gain a better understanding, then they can follow a new path. They have to keep encouraging themselves, so they can achieve their goals. Mistakes can bring life or death to their dreams. It's all a matter of how they view the situation and act on it.

The process of Recovery takes commitment. It doesn't happen on its own. Anyone in recovery has to *change* their *life*. It takes effort and constant vigilance of their environment (people, places, and things) in order to make better choices and to avoid situations that put them at risk to take drugs. Addiction is impulsive and putting a space between the thought, *I have to have it now*, and by adding a pause to delay the action, allows enough time for the information to reach the thinking of the consequences part of the brain to kick in and remind them of all the problems they had while taking drugs.

Recovery needs to have a *daily* routine of repetitive relaxation activities to practice in order for them to reduce stress. Stress is a *huge* trigger for relapse for a person at any stage of recovery. Any way they can stop focusing on the concerns they have about the future or the mistakes they made in the past can lower their stress levels. Stress reduction can be done by exercising, meditation, or practice mindfulness techniques that keep them focused to live in the moment.

- The right kind of exercise is a great stress reducer if it involves stretching, walking, or running—as long as they don't focus on their problems. They need to give their mind a chance to rest by just enjoying the activity or distracting their thoughts onto other things.

- o Do not do any contact sports such as boxing, wrestling, or karate. They can all stimulate their adrenalin system and can actually increase their anxiety and stress levels.
- Meditation can involve a lot of different activities that are geared to calm them and to release their concerns, worry, and fears.
  - o I have found when I pray to God about my concerns helps tremendously as long as I don't rush off after praying and do other things. I used to pray and wondered why I still didn't have any peace in my heart about the situation. I kept worrying and never had any confidence that anything would change. Even at times, I wondered if God even heard my cry for help. God heard me, but I rushed off so fast that I never got to hear what God had to say. I needed to sit still and open my heart and mind to listen and hear what God has to say. A verse would pop into my mind, or I would hear the soft, quiet voice that knows exactly what I needed to hear to comfort me during this time. It could be I will never forsake you or stop fighting because the battle is mine to do. When I wait and listen is when I get peace in my heart. My Heavenly Father will personally take care of my problems.
- Some people relax by practicing mindfulness, by focusing their mind on their breathing and not allow intrusive thoughts to distract them as they breathe in—hold—and breath out.
  - o Living in the moment with no worries about the future or the mistakes they made in the past. They have just this moment to concentrate on, as they breathe in and breathe out, giving their mind a chance to rest.

- Some people do mind-body connections that ease the tension in their body by gently stretching and allows their mind to focus on rhythmic balanced movements.
  - Some examples of mind-body connection exercises are Tai Chi, Yoga, or Qigong.

A trained therapist can teach these techniques, or they can learn them by buying books, videos, or watch YouTube demonstrations. Because stress is one of the most common causes for relapse, it's essential to have a *daily* relaxation routine to counteract the effects stress is having on their body and mind. For anyone in recovery, they need to realize doing a daily relaxation routine is as *important as eating*. Many people take care of their cars better than they do themselves. They will put the right kind of gas in their car to run at top performance, get oil changes and periodic tune-ups. For anyone, not reducing the effects of stress in their life that is causing havoc on their mind and body is like never putting any oil in their car. Eventually, it will break down. *Stress reduction* is like a *vaccine to prevent future relapses*. Much like the flu vaccine is used to protect us from catching the flu.

Daily relaxation helps keep the mind from getting overwhelmed and reduces the chance for them to feel they have to take something in order to calm down and release their anxiety. Relaxation is like defragmenting the memory chip in a computer. If it's not done over time, the computer will eventually freeze and crash. If daily stress is not managed, it can accumulate and cause a *toxic* stress state that leads to health problems such as diabetes, heart problems, cancer, and addiction. *Stress* has to be managed, or it will *eventually destroy us*.

To stay in recovery, everyone needs to recognize the early warning signs that show they are at risk for a relapse. They need to be aware that *relapse* begins *long before* a person ever starts taking drugs again. For people with addiction, when they encounter an early warning sign, they need to change their course *immediately* before the relapse happens. Just like when they see a sign that says, *road out* ahead. They need to stop, turn around and go in a different direction. Everyone is different so that not all the warning signs may apply to him or her, but it's important when they do slip to write down what happened by describing:

- What they were feeling?
- What they were thinking?
- Who were they with?
- Where were they at?

They need to analyze all this information to help them recognize what caused them to use drugs again. Sometimes they have to work backward to figure out where they could have said no or been able to avoid drug use. They have to learn what their unique or common causes are for relapse. So, they can learn how to avoid them or plan a different path to follow in order to deal with these situations. So, the next time they encounter a similar problem, they have an action plan. Some of the main culprits that caused many of my patients to relapse are: *Stop going to support meetings, Resentments with unrealistic expectations, Romancing the high, Isolation, Bipolar depression, External triggers, Internal triggers, and Spiritual growth, Purpose, and Fulfillment.*

Stop going to counseling or support meetings

I have found this to be a common cause for a person to relapse. In recovery, everyone needs someone to hold them accountable, to be supportive, and understand their struggles. They desperately need acceptance and connection. Rarely, family members can provide this for them. A lot of times, the family members are the ones who want them to stop going to so many meetings and are complaining about all their past mistakes. They can't separate their *frustrations* and *fears*, to become supportive and listen to them when they talk about wanting to start using drugs again. Family has this inability to *detach their emotional reaction* that is needed to delve deeper, to understand why they are feeling this way. When those in recovery breaks off their connection for help:

- They start to isolate themselves and stop talking about their feelings, anxiety, depression, or loneliness.
- They become irritable and upset that no one appreciates how hard they are trying.
- They start neglecting their responsibilities like getting to work on time, paying bills, or helping with household tasks.
- They have no one who understands how they feel and how difficult it is to stay motivated when nothing is enjoyable and everything is an effort.
- They are bored with their routine and have nothing to look forward to doing.
- They feel alone and have no friends.

Resentments with unrealistic expectations

Sometimes those in recovery feel under-appreciated and have *unrealistic expectations* that everyone should be focusing *all* their attention on them.

- *Doesn't my family know how hard I am trying?*
- When others don't praise all their efforts, they feel ignored.

They are struggling with recovery, and they have no one to talk about all these crazy thoughts and feelings bombarding their mind. Their resentments grow like a forest fire. All it takes is one disagreement, one argument, for them to erupt, and they explode into an angry inferno. I see this commonly happen when they get into a fight with their partner. They will storm out of the house and run to the nearest bar or previous hangouts to take alcohol or drugs. They blame their partner for making them angry. In twisted Stinkin-thinkin mentality, they want their partner to feel guilty for causing them to relapse. They are only hurting themselves and are blinded from the truth. They are unaware of the hidden subconscious addictive agenda that is constantly looking for *any* excuse for them to return to drug use. People in recovery need to be around those who are aware of how the addictive mind works and help them learn how to recognize their distorted thought patterns. How the addictive part of the brain actually can cause them to have even more fights and give them an excuse to use drugs again. Friends and family who have never dealt with having an addiction cannot understand, recognize or help them *see* what is really happening. This is why it is so important for people in recovery to stay connected to their counselor or go to recovery meetings and to nip these thoughts early *before* a relapse occurs.

Romancing the high

Alarm bells should be ringing when anyone starts recalling how good it was when they took drugs and forget about all the negative outcomes drug use had caused. I commonly see this happen when people in recovery see an old drug-using friend they accidentally encounter at the grocery store, the gas station, or in the mall. They start chatting and gradually their conversation changes *from*: How are you doing? *To*: Do you remember when? They start laughing about some crazy antics they did when they were high. Even though both of them are now in recovery, their old memories of taking drugs together are lurking *below* the surface of their conscious thoughts. They are unaware, what is really happening. Their addictive mind makes their time together *extra* pleasant. They enjoyed their time visiting. If only they knew, they were both being primed for a relapse—but not necessarily at this moment. The addictive mind is patiently waiting for the right opportunity to strike—like a tiger ready to pounce on its victim. They call each other and make plans to see a movie. But, when they got together, they impulsively decide to go over to a friend's house and smoke some weed. They had a great time and later started using other drugs, but not their *drug of choice*. Lying to themselves, they haven't relapsed, thinking (Stinkin-thinkin), *it's only weed with a touch of meth, no big deal. They never had a problem with it in the past—just something to do and have a good time.*

As they continue to see each other, they start planning ways to use more drugs without anyone knowing. Slowly they start putting themselves in more risky situations by visiting old drug-using friends or going to places where people are using even more drugs. They did not recognize how just being around a former drug-using buddy would be such a trigger for them to relapse.

A lot of people in recovery tell me, "*If I get rid of them, I won't have any friends.*"

I tell them, "Time to make new ones." In recovery, they can't go back again. To succeed, they can only go forward.

Isolation

Being lonely can make a person at *any* stage of recovery start using drugs again. It is not uncommon when a man's wife dies for him to start drinking or taking drugs. Being alone and lonely are very different. Loneliness rips into a person's soul to the very core of their being. Some people say the treatment for addiction is connection. Loneliness isolates a person and keeps them from reaching out and connecting with others. They feel like they don't fit in and withdraw. They don't share, what they are feeling, and avoid talking to others about their anxiety or depression. Instead, they are irritable, angry, and have a way of making everyone around them miserable. I have seen that behavior occur when a spouse decides to stop smoking. Smoking a cigarette was how they connected with other people. They would congregate in the break room to have a smoke and chat. They had something in common with another that bridged their differences. Smoking smoothed over awkward moments in conversation by taking a few puffs. But, when they stopped smoking, they can't go to the break room and chat. They feel out of place and don't know what to do with their hands since they don't have a cigarette in them. A few weeks later, their partner hands them a pack of cigarettes because they can't stand hearing all the bickering, complaining and angry outbursts.

Withdrawal from any addictive drug creates negative emotions to emerge. If these feelings persist and don't go away, they need to be evaluated to determine if any underlying problems are causing these symptoms that need treatment. Many times, this is why they started using drugs to deal with these uncomfortable emotions. A lot of people who use drugs had previous multiple Adverse Childhood Experiences (ACEs). The only way they could cope with these painful experiences and feelings of unworthiness, low self-esteem, and anxiety was to use drugs.

Bipolar Depression

A lot of people addicted to opioids have bipolar depression. When they took an opioid it made them feel better by reducing some of their racing thoughts and agitation. Treatment providers need to look for any underlying problems that might have caused anyone to start taking drugs to deal with their emotions by asking their patients, what *benefits did the drugs provide for them*? If the provider does not treat the underlying issues, they will not respond well to treatment. Inadequate treatment will affect their efforts to stay in recovery. Studies have shown if the mental illness is not treated at the *same time* as the addiction, both conditions will not do well. Bipolar depression is one of the most commonly missed mental health diagnoses. One study showed it could take over ten years for a person to be correctly diagnosed with this problem. Many times, they are incorrectly diagnosed as having both depression and anxiety. The provider prescribes the patient Xanax (which is extremely addictive). Now their problem has multiplied. They now have an underlying mental health problem (bipolar depression) combined with a benzodiazepine addiction (Xanax) caused by their treatment provider along with their opioid addiction. Remember when I mentioned if the mental health issues have not been treated at the same time as the addiction? They will not do well if they are only treated for one of these conditions. This person will not get better until they are *correctly diagnosed* and *treated* for both the mental health condition and their addiction(s) at the same time.

Why is the diagnosis of bipolar depression so easily missed? In the general population, bipolar depression is not as frequently encountered (I do wonder if it is more common than what treatment providers believe, and people are incorrectly diagnosed with depression and anxiety.) But in people with an opioid addiction, a high percentage of them have bipolar depression. Some people think they may have started taking opioids as a way to cope with their mental illness. Opioids have been shown to help reduce some of their symptoms. When a person goes into an abstinence treatment program for their opioid addiction and *stops* taking any opioids, most of the time, their mental illness will flare. If this mental illness is not treated properly, they will relapse.

Even in a population of people who have an increased percentage of bipolar depression, the diagnosis is still missed. Here are some clues that I have found to be helpful in making this diagnosis. I call them red flag signs that make me do a more detailed mental health evaluation. When I have someone tell me that antidepressants don't work for them or it made them feel worse makes me very suspicious something else is going on. There can be several causes why an antidepressant medication does not work, and I need to explore every one.

Sometimes they may have a problem with metabolizing the drugs to their active ingredient that makes the drugs work. An example: Yeast needs to be activated in order for bread to rise. If the yeast is killed by too hot water, it won't work, and we'll be eating crackers instead of bread. Gene testing evaluates how an individual's metabolic enzymes work. Until gene testing became available, I never knew people could metabolize their antidepressant medications so differently. I thought they all worked the same. But I discovered, just like people are different on the outside, they are equally different on the inside.

Later, I found how useful this genetic test was in helping my son. It took a long time for my son to eventually become diagnosed with having bipolar depression. It seemed like all the medications his physician prescribed him did not work. He would be released from the mental hospital, and within days, his symptoms of mania would escalate. He couldn't sleep, and he talked non-stop about grandiose delusions of being invincible coupled with paranoid thoughts that the mafia or the government was after him because he had a super-computer in his brain. Unfortunately, no one would admit him back into the mental health unit until he became at risk of hurting himself or others. He almost got killed when he was found lying in the middle of a busy highway, thinking he was invincible and could never get hurt. What became extremely frustrating that every time he was released from the hospital, he started lowering the dose of his medications because he didn't like the way it made him feel. I thought his non-compliance with medication was due to his denial that he had a problem. After a few years, I had lost count of the number of times he had been admitted to the mental health hospital.

Finally, the turning point my son needed was when I had read an article about doing genetic testing on people who were unresponsive to their medications used for treatment. I contacted the company that did the testing, and they sent me a kit. I swabbed my son's cheek and sent the sample to the lab. When I got the results of the test back, I was stunned and ashamed of my earlier thoughts. I found every medication that he previously took did not work for him and had high side effects. I gave the results to my son's psychiatrist and suggested he consider changing his medication.

The psychiatrist at first was resistant and said, "*I'm the specialist and know what I am doing.*"

I responded, "You have already tried all of these medications that the report says won't work for him and causes him a lot of side effects. Why don't you pick from the ones that say would work?"

He reluctantly changed the medication to one that said would work for my son. On the new medication, my son quickly improved and was released from the hospital four days later. For any of my patients who have been on more than two to three medications to treat a mental illness, I always recommend gene testing. I still find it incredible that all the medications my patients had tried and failed were exactly the ones that the test showed didn't work for them.

The gene tests can also detect if they can convert folic acid (a B vitamin) into L-Methyfolate. L-Methylfolate is used in the brain to recycle neurotransmitters. If they cannot recycle the neurotransmitters, then the levels of neurotransmitters in their brain will always be lower than in people who can recycle. Neurotransmitters affect our mood, and low levels cause depression. Antidepressants increase these neurotransmitters, but if they cannot recycle them, it makes the antidepressants less effective or not work at all. If they have this problem, I have them take L-Methylfolate for life (this is a genetic problem and will never go away). I did not know if L-Methylfolate would really make a difference. Since it is a B vitamin, I knew it was safe and would take a while for the neurotransmitters levels to increase. So, I prescribed it to my patient who suffered from depression for years, and none of the antidepressants worked for her. I scheduled her to see me back in three months. Six weeks later, I saw her in the grocery store and she came up and hugged me. She had a big grin on her face (I almost didn't recognize her because she had never smiled before in the past).

She said, "*I have never felt this good in my entire life. This has changed my life, and I've told everyone in my family to take it, too.*"

In my assessment, why an antidepressant does not work for a person, I also need to consider if the diagnosis is correct. Do they really have depression and anxiety, or do they have another condition that can mimic those symptoms, such as bipolar depression? Now, I do *not* ask them, do you have bipolar depression? For some reason, the diagnosis of bipolar depression makes people afraid and wondering, *does she think I'm crazy?*

I need to explore *why* they are feeling a certain way in order to get to the bottom of their problem. I need a more detailed history and ask if they have any of the following symptoms?

- I do *not* use labels to describe their symptoms. So, I *never* ask them if they are anxious, have panic attacks, or insomnia. I want *details* on how they are feeling.
  - I want more description of their symptoms to *avoid the buzzwords* they have used in the past to get more Xanax.
  - Rather than say do you have insomnia, I ask, do you have trouble sleeping because your mind keeps racing and won't stop? Or, you can fall asleep fine but wake up multiple times throughout the night? Do you take a nap

during the day or take any energy drinks to stay awake? How long does it take to fall asleep?

- Do they have episodes of having lots of energy and trouble sleeping, and other times, they want to sleep a lot?
  - Are they up for days or weeks at a time and then want to sleep all day long?
  - Have trouble sitting still? Constantly on the move?
- Do they feel irritable, and everything bothers them, and other times, it doesn't? Do they *start* lots of projects but never finish most of them?
- Have problems with concentration due to racing thoughts and jump from one thought to another?
- Are there times when they feel like other people want to hurt them?
- Do they see or hear things that other people don't hear or see?
- Does anyone in their family have lots of mood swings or been diagnosed with bipolar depression? (Notice I ask this toward the end—I do not want them to adjust their answers because of fear of being diagnosed with bipolar depression)

They will struggle with their recovery if I don't make the right diagnosis and provide the correct treatment for their problem. I need an accurate diagnosis to treat any condition that caused them to start taking drugs. For those who have a lot of symptoms of bipolar depression I give them a trial of a medication to see how they respond. I have used the medication Vrylar since it can lift their mood if they are in the depressive phase of bipolar and can calm the anxiety and racing thoughts if they are in the manic phase. Also, I like it because, within one week, a lot of people start feeling better, and the medication has fewer side effects compared to other medications used to treat bipolar. When they come in for their return appointment, it's heartening to hear them say, "*I can't believe how much better I feel.*"

External triggers

To sustain recovery, they have to *change their life* to avoid drug use. In the beginning, it's hard to avoid external triggers such as people, places, and things—Old friends, old haunts, old activities, and paraphernalia. The more anyone holds onto their past life, the less likely they will be able to sustain recovery. The addictive brain creates powerful emotional connections and urges, making it almost impossible to avoid a relapse. Logic cannot overcome these obsessive urges, and the only way to win is to *avoid* the triggers.

Internal triggers

Internal triggers can undermine their recovery at any stage of the process. Just like the external triggers can affect their recovery by being around the wrong people, places, and things can. The four internal triggers are: *Hungry, Angry, Lonely, and Tired.* Many use the acronym HALT to remember the internal triggers.

H stands for *Hungry*

Food is a natural survival re-enforcer. Eating increases dopamine in the brain that causes pleasure. When people are craving certain types of food, they actually want that dopamine surge to make them feel better. This is the same dopamine that is released when a person is craving drugs but in greater quantities in the brain.

A stands for *Angry*

Strong emotions are a huge cause for relapse. Addictive thinking is *emotional thinking.* The emotions keep them from looking at the situation in a *logical* manner. The emotions blind a person to options, to think through the situation, or even consider the potential consequences of an action. Emotional thinking triggers the impulsive part of the brain that wants to stop these painful feelings *now.* They are already set up for a relapse *unless* they have been practicing *daily* ways to reduce stress and coping skills to handle their strong emotions. I see this commonly in people who have been in recovery for years. A couple gets into a fight and breaks up. People with addiction can't stand the pain and take drugs to numb their feelings. A loved one dies, and they take drugs to ease their grief.

Learning relaxation skills and *doing* a relaxation skill *are very different*. During a crisis, if people try to perform a relaxation skill, such as mindful breathing, and they have not been doing them *regularly*— *It will not work*. When anyone does a repetitive behavior, the brain develops super-highway circuits that transmit information quickly from one area to another. When they practice daily meditation, and a crisis suddenly occurs, and they start doing mindful breathing exercises, their mind and body will relax due to the automatic behavior acquired through repetitive learning.

This automatic response happened when my husband taught our kids how to play basketball. Because my kids were short for their age, they got fouled a lot in a game. He had them practice shooting free throws daily, and follow the same routine before they could release the ball. First they had to bounce the ball three times, followed by bending their knees twice before they could go up on their toes to shoot and release the ball. While playing in a basketball tournament, one of my kids got fouled again. Standing at the free throw line I could tell immediately before my son even released the ball if he would get it into the basket. As long as he did the same routine during the game as he did in practice—he got it in every time. But, if he changed the routine and just aimed for the basket, the ball would always hit the rim and miss the basket. This is the same learned behavior we have when we walk. It becomes an automatic behavior because we no longer have to think about or concentrate on balancing on one leg while we stretch our other leg out and land on our heel, then roll onto the ball of our foot and then prepare for the other leg to swing forward. If we had to think about every movement, I wouldn't be surprised if we fell. When we walk, we just move our legs *automatically*—no thinking involved—we just do it. The more people in recovery practice ways to relax, the faster this super-highway becomes and the quicker they learn how to relax.

L stands for *Loneliness*

Remember, the treatment for addiction is connection. When they are isolated and feel that no one understands them—it triggers a relapse. Loneliness coupled with too much time on their hands is like turning on a propane tank and letting the gas build—all it takes is one spark to blow up. Inactivity for those in recovery allows the emotional part of their brain *room to grow and explode*. For anyone in recovery, it's never good for them to have too much free time. In early recovery, they are easily bored, and nothing is pleasurable, making this isolation unbearable. Even in people who have been in recovery for years, when the COVID-19 pandemic occurred and they were told to stay home, a lot of them struggled during this time. Very few people were allowed to work, so the majority of them had a lot of free time. Free time is never good for anyone in recovery. When I saw my patients, I stressed the importance of not deviating from their usual routine. I had them act like they were still going to work. They had to get up at the same time, get dressed, eat, and go to bed the same time like they did before they were laid off from work. I had them make a list of repairs or projects they needed to complete and do it. They had to stay active. Unfortunately, a lot of them did not follow my advice, and many of them had relapsed.

T stands for *Tired*

When a person is tired, that is when they are most vulnerable. It takes energy to redirect their thoughts and defuse their emotions. When exhausted, they don't have the energy, drive, or desire to keep fighting. When we are exhausted, all we want to do is go home and rest. To deal with any more problems can make us want to explode. This is the same with anyone who has an addiction. When they are tired, all they want to do is rest and not have to keep struggling with their thoughts. This desire to rest makes them at risk for making a poor choice. Anyone in recovery needs to avoid getting exhausted or extremely tired. They are more susceptible to slip-ups.

I have seen this happen to some of my patients when they had a rough day at work, and all they wanted to do was go home for some peace and quiet. Instead, they were greeted at the door with yelling and screaming kids, the house is a mess with toys everywhere, a sink full of dishes, and everyone shouting, "What's for dinner?"

Remember, recovery is not one huge step that looks impossible to achieve, but rather making a lot of small steps (choices) needed to take care of themselves. Self-care is not being selfish. It's taking time to take care of their needs. A man had a large jug of water and filled everyone's glass that was thirsty. At the end of the day, when he went to get a drink for himself—he had no water left. When a person gives and gives and gives—they have nothing more left to give. They can't even help themselves for their own needs. They no longer have the strength to fill the pot with water again.

People in recovery need to take the time to determine what is important to them. What traits do they want in a friend or partner? They need to discover what job they would like to do and plan on what steps they need to take to reach their goal. Drugs took away their life, and now they have to reclaim it back. Time is needed to discover what their values are and learn to set boundaries, so they can achieve their goals. Boundaries are difficult for people in recovery to do. They feel such guilt (condemnation) over what they had done while in active addiction. They think being a doormat to every whim a family member or partner has them do will show how remorseful they are for past behaviors. This toxic shame is poisonous to them and to their relationships. They cannot change the past no matter how hard they wish it were different. They can only demonstrate their remorse by their *current* actions of:

- Not taking any drugs
- Going to work
- Paying the bills
- Being honest in their answers.

These actions show they are making a tremendous effort to change. They cannot make-up for *past* behaviors. They only have *this moment*, this day—the power to *change*.

Boundaries are guidelines that they create to let other people know what behaviors they expect and what actions they will do if someone cross those boundaries. It helps them to set limits on what they will or will not tolerate. It's time for a boundary to be set when everyone is placing demands on their time, and they are exhausted from trying to meet them. Just like the jug was empty when it came

278

time to meet their need for water. It's essential for them to have the time to fill the jug and quench their thirst before trying to help others. This is not being selfish. This is self-care. One of the triggers for relapse is exhaustion. It's important to have time to explore what is important and take steps to achieve them. This is not ignoring other people's needs, but it can't be all about others, and they have nothing left for themselves. A *balance* has to be made. This is what boundaries are for: Not doing everyone's work at the expense of their mental and physical health that can keep them from achieving their goals.

Spiritual growth, Purpose, and Fulfillment

The final part of recovery treatment is spiritual growth, finding purpose, and fulfillment in life. Also, they need to add some fun into their life. They need to tap into the creative part of their mind and have it balanced with the practical (logical) part of their mind, and believing the impossible can be possible. This is *faith in action*. Moving forward toward their goal, even when circumstances may look bleak. They do *not* give up on their dreams. This push to move forward is spiritual. It is not logical, and at times, it's not fun, but eventually, it will bring them fulfillment. Having an open mind is essential to walk in this spiritual journey that involves connecting to other people, to nature, and most importantly, to God. Connection is what will break the isolation that addiction creates. Having all three parts: The logical, the creative, and the spiritual working together allows them to build a life worth living and makes living the life of taking drugs less appealing. This is what recovery is all about—discovering their hidden potentials and developing them.

My prayer for all who read this book: God, guide everyone in this journey toward self-discovery and fulfillment. To open their heart and mind to the endless possibilities and give them the courage to step out and the faith to achieve all the wonderful gifts that are in store for them. To live a life that will make a difference in other people's lives and in their own. Give them joy and satisfaction for a job well done.

SURVIVAL TIPS

- We all make mistakes. It's what we do with them that lead to success or failure.
  - When we believe and trust in God to turn all things for good gives us the drive to keep pursuing the desires of our heart—no matter what happens along the way.
- Anyone in recovery has to change their life. The real life-changer is when we give our life to God. When we *surrender* and stop fighting and do what God wants—the doors will open. I remember, as a little girl, I wanted to be a doctor. My dad was a medic in World War II and was in the very first experimental prototype mash hospital unit similar to the ones adopted in the Korean War. The defense department was hoping to save more soldiers' lives by providing them with more prompt medical care. They created a makeshift hospital to be placed less than a mile from the front line, where all the battles took place. When the troops advanced forward or back, the hospital could be immediately dismantled and put back together quickly and efficiently. In the day, my dad would crawl on his belly into the trenches, squat down, and hauled injured men back to safety while bullets whistled past his ears. Once out of firing range, he would run and carry them into the makeshift surgical tent. In the afternoon, he assisted the surgeons during surgery and did all the bandages and dressing changes. At night, when he was supposed to be sleeping, he would get up at two in the morning and check on all the patients he risked his life to save. Many times, he found them hemorrhaging. He alerted the surgeon on call and assisted with the operation to save their life. After the war was over, these men that God had my dad save would come by with their wife and baby to thank my Dad for saving their life. That made such an impression on me as a young girl that I wanted to become a doctor. So, when I surrendered my life to Christ, God told me to give up my

desire to become a doctor. It wrenched my heart, but I did what God asked. Two years later, God told me to go back to school and become a doctor. I argued with God, but He wanted to make sure there was nothing more important than Him in my life. God found a way and provided for all the finances and the opportunities for me to become a doctor.

- When we surrender, we give up on all our dreams and hopes, and God fills them with new ones or gives us the desires of our hearts when we are willing to give them up for Him.

- We have to manage stress, or it will eventually destroy us.
  - God gives us His peace that surpasses all our understanding and will guard our hearts and minds through Christ Jesus. When we rely on and rest in the comfort of God's protection, we *stop* looking at our circumstances but look to the one who can change them.

- If a mental illness is not treated at the same time as the addiction, they both won't do well.
  - A large percentage of people with addiction also suffer from some type of mental illness.
  - If we want to be successful in our treatments, we need to be accurate in our diagnoses to provide the correct treatment for the problem.

- Relapse begins long before a person starts taking drugs.
  - We make a lot of little choices that can affect the outcome of a situation. Little foxes destroy the vine.
  - We think little things don't matter, but they do to God.
    - Little things grow into bigger things and can take over a person's life.

BIBLE VERSES

Then God said, "Let us make mankind in our image, in our likeness, so that they may rule over the fish in the sea and the birds in the sky, over the livestock and all the wild animals, and over all the creatures that move along the ground."

"So God created mankind in his own image, in the image of God he created them; male and female he created them"

Genesis 1:26-27 (NIV)

And they heard the voice of the LORD God walking in the garden in the cool of the day: and Adam and his wife hid themselves from the presence of the LORD God amongst the trees of the garden.

Genesis 3:8 (KJV)

So he said, "I heard Your voice in the garden, and I was afraid because I was naked; and I hid myself."

And He said, "Who told you that you were naked? Have you eaten from the tree of which I commanded you that you should not eat?"

Then the man said, "The woman whom You gave to be with me, she gave me of the tree, and I ate."

And the LORD God said to the woman, "What is this you have done?"

The woman said, "The serpent deceived me, and I ate."

Genesis 3:10-13 (NKJV)

"And Abraham stretched out his hand and took the knife to slay his son"

Genesis 22:10 (NKJV)

And it came to pass after these things that his master's wife cast longing eyes on Joseph, and she said, "Lie with me."

But he refused and said to his master's wife, "Look, my master does not know what is with me in the house, and he has committed all that he has to my hand. There is no one greater in this house than I, nor has he kept back anything from me but you, because you are his wife. How then can I do this great wickedness, and sin against God?" So it was, as she spoke to Joseph day by day, that he did not heed her, to lie with her or to be with her But it happened about this time, when Joseph went into the house to do his work, and none of the men of the house was inside, that she caught him by his garment, saying, "Lie with me." But he left his garment in her hand, and fled and ran outside.

Genesis 39:7-12 (NKJV)

And Moses said to the people, "Do not be afraid. Stand still, and see the salvation of the LORD, which He will accomplish for you today. For the Egyptians whom you see today, you shall see again no more forever. The LORD will fight for you, and you shall hold your peace."

Exodus 14:13-14 (NKJV)

Then the LORD said to Moses, "Leave this place, you and the people you brought up out of Egypt, and go up to the land I promised on oath to Abraham, Isaac and Jacob, saying, 'I will give it to your descendants.'"

Exodus 33:1 (NIV)

Then it shall be, because he has sinned and is guilty, that he shall restore what he has stolen, or the thing which he has extorted, or what was delivered to him for safekeeping, or the lost thing which he found.

Leviticus 6:4 (NKJV)

And you shall consecrate the fiftieth year, and proclaim liberty throughout all the land to all its inhabitants. It shall be a Jubilee for you; and each of you shall return to his possession, and each of you shall return to his family.

Leviticus 25:10 (NKJV)

"Because they have not followed me wholeheartedly, not one of those who were twenty years old or more when they came up out of Egypt will see the land I promised on oath to Abraham, Isaac and Jacob—not one except Caleb son of Jephunneh the Kenizzite and Joshua."

Numbers 32:11-13 (NIV)

Then the LORD said to him, "This is the land of which I swore to give Abraham, Isaac, and Jacob, saying, 'I will give it to your descendants.' I have caused you to see it with your eyes, but you shall not cross over there." So Moses the servant of the

Lord died there in the land of Moab, according to the word of the Lord.

Deuteronomy 34:4-5 (NKJV)

But the Lord said to Samuel, "Do not consider his appearance or his height, for I have rejected him. The Lord does not look at the things people look at. People look at the outward appearance, but the Lord looks at the heart."

1 Samuel 16:7 (NIV)

[8] Goliath stood and shouted to the ranks of Israel, "Why do you come out and line up for battle? Am I not a Philistine, and are you not the servants of Saul? Choose a man and have him come down to me. [9] If he is able to fight and kill me, we will become your subjects; but if I overcome him and kill him, you will become our subjects and serve us." [10] Then the Philistine said, "This day I defy the armies of Israel! Give me a man and let us fight each other." [11] On hearing the Philistine's words, Saul and all the Israelites were dismayed and terrified.

1 Samuel 17: 8-11 (NIV)

[25] Now the Israelites had been saying, "Do you see how this man keeps coming out? He comes out to defy Israel. The king will give great wealth to the man who kills him. He will also give him his daughter in marriage and will exempt his family from taxes in Israel."

[26] David asked the men standing near him, "What will be done for the man who kills this Philistine and removes this disgrace from Israel? Who is this uncircumcised Philistine that he should defy the armies of the living God?"

27 They repeated to him what they had been saying and told him, "This is what will be done for the man who kills him."

1 Samuel 17: 25-27 (NIV)

2 From that day Saul kept David with him and did not let him return home to his family.

1 Samuel 18-2 (NIV)

"The LORD rewards everyone for their righteousness and faithfulness. The LORD delivered you into my hands today, but I would not lay a hand on the LORD's anointed"

1 Samuel 26:23,(NIV)

"The God of my strength, in whom I will trust; My shield and the horn of my salvation, My stronghold and my refuge; My Savior, You save me from violence"

2 Samuel 22:3 (NKJV).

Hezekiah's Illness

In those days Hezekiah became ill and was at the point of death. The prophet Isaiah son of Amoz went to him and said, "This is what the LORD says: Put your house in order, because you are going to die; you will not recover."

Hezekiah turned his face to the wall and prayed to the LORD, "Remember, LORD, how I have walked before you faithfully and with wholehearted devotion and have done what is good in your eyes." And Hezekiah wept bitterly.

Before Isaiah had left the middle court, the word of the LORD came to him: "Go back and tell Hezekiah, the ruler of my people, 'This is what the LORD, the God of your father David, says: I have heard your prayer and seen your tears; I will heal you. On the third day from now you will go up to the temple of the LORD. I will add fifteen years to your life. And I will deliver you and this city from the hand of the king of Assyria. I will defend this city for my sake and for the sake of my servant David.'"

Then Isaiah said, "Prepare a poultice of figs." They did so and applied it to the boil, and he recovered.

Hezekiah had asked Isaiah, "What will be the sign that the LORD will heal me and that I will go up to the temple of the LORD on the third day from now?"

2 Kings 20:1-8 (NIV)

So Saul died for his unfaithfulness which he had committed against the LORD, because he did not keep the word of the LORD, and also because he consulted a medium for guidance. But he did not inquire of the LORD; therefore He killed him, and turned the kingdom over to David the son of Jesse.

1 Chronicles 10:13-14 (NKJV)

And he said, "Listen, all you of Judah and you inhabitants of Jerusalem, and you, King Jehoshaphat! Thus says the LORD to you: 'Do not be afraid nor dismayed because of this great multitude, for the battle is not yours, but God's.'"

2 Chronicles 20:15 (NKJV)

"And you, my son Solomon, acknowledge the God of your father, and serve him with whole-hearted devotion and with a willing mind, for the

LORD searches every heart and understands every desire and every thought. If you seek him, he will be found by you; but if you forsake him, he will reject you forever."

1 Chronicles 28:9 (NIV)

Eliphaz Accuses Job of Wickedness

Then Eliphaz the Temanite answered and said:
"Can a man be profitable to God,
Though he who is wise may be profitable to himself? Is it any pleasure to the Almighty that you are righteous?
Or is it gain to Him that you make your ways blameless?
"Is it because of your fear of Him that He corrects you,
And enters into judgment with you? Is not your wickedness great.

Job 22:1-5 (NKJV)

"And the LORD restored Job's losses when he prayed for his friends. Indeed the LORD gave Job twice as much as he had before"

Job 42:10 (NKJV)

"In peace I will lie down and sleep, for you alone, Lord make me dwell in safety"

Psalms 4:8 (NIV)

"The LORD is my shepherd; I shall not want"

Psalm 23:1 (NKJV)

Then I acknowledged my sin to you
and did not cover up my iniquity.
I said, "I will confess

my transgressions to the LORD."
And you forgave
the guilt of my sin.

Psalm 32:5 (NIV)

"I waited patiently for the LORD, he turned to me
and heard my cry"

Psalm 40:1 (NIV)

He will cover you with his feathers.
He will shelter you with his wings.
His faithful promises are your armor and
protection.

Psalm 91:4 (NLT)

He will cover you with his feathers,
and under his wings you will find refuge;
his faithfulness will be your shield and
rampart.

Psalm 91:4 (NIV)

O Lord, You have searched me and known me.
You know my sitting down and my rising up;
You understand my thought afar off.
You comprehend my path and my lying down,
And are acquainted with all my ways.
For there is not a word on my tongue,
But behold, O Lord, You know it altogether.
You have hedged me behind and before,
And laid Your hand upon me.
Such knowledge is too wonderful for me;
It is high, I cannot attain it.

Where can I go from Your Spirit?
Or where can I flee from Your presence?
If I ascend into heaven, You are there;

If I make my bed in hell, behold, You are there.
If I take the wings of the morning,
And dwell in the uttermost parts of the sea,
Even there Your hand shall lead me,
And Your right hand shall hold me.
If I say, "Surely the darkness shall fall on me,"
Even the night shall be light about me;
Indeed, the darkness shall not hide from You,
But the night shines as the day;
The darkness and the light are both alike to You.
For You formed my inward parts;
You covered me in my mother's womb.
I will praise You, for I am fearfully and wonder-
fully made;

Psalm 139:1-14 (NKJV)

"Lazy hands make for poverty, but diligent hands bring wealth"

Proverbs 10:4 (NIV)

"All a person's ways seem pure to them, but motives are weighed by the LORD"

Proverbs 16:2 (NIV)

"Death and life are in the power of the tongue, And those who love it will eat its fruit"

Proverbs 18:21 (NKJV)

"Do you see a man skillful and experienced in his work? He will stand [in honor] before kings; He will not stand before obscure men"

Proverbs 22:29 (AMP)

"Do you see a man who excels in his work? He will stand before kings; He will not stand before unknown men"

Proverbs 22:29 (NKJV)

"A sluggard buries his hand in the dish; he is too lazy to bring it back to his mouth"

Proverbs 26:15 (NIV)

My Son, Be Wise
Do not boast about tomorrow,
For you do not know what a day may bring forth.

Proverbs 27:1 (NKJV)

"Where there is no vision, the people perish"

Proverbs 29:18 (KJV)

"Though one may be overpowered by another, two can withstand him. And a threefold cord is not quickly broken"

Ecclesiastes 4:12 (NKJV)

"Catch us the foxes, The little foxes that spoil the vines, For our vines have tender grapes"

Song of Solomon 2:15 (NKJV)

The Lord says:
"These people come near to me with their mouth and honor me with their lips,
but their hearts are far from me.
Their worship of me
is based on merely human rules they have been taught."

Isaiah 29:13 (NIV)

But those who hope in the Lord
will renew their strength.
They will soar on wings like eagles;
they will run and not grow weary,
they will walk and not be faint.

Isaiah 40:31 (NIV)

"Forget the former things;
do not dwell on the past.
See, I am doing a new thing!
Now it springs up; do you not perceive it?
I am making a way in the wilderness
and streams in the wasteland."

Isaiah 43:18-19 (NIV)

But He was wounded for our transgressions, He
was bruised for our iniquities; The chastisement
for our peace was upon Him, And by His stripes
we are healed.

Isaiah 53:5 (NKJV)

For I know the plans I have for you," declares
the LORD, "plans to prosper you and not to harm
you, plans to give you hope and a future. [12] Then
you will call on me and come and pray to me,
and I will listen to you.

Jeremiah 29:11-12 (NIV)

At the same time that my sanity was restored, my
honor and splendor were returned to me for the
glory of my kingdom. My advisers and nobles
sought me out, and I was restored to my throne
and became even greater than before.

Daniel 4:36 (NIV)

²Therefore, if you are offering your gift at the altar and there remember that your brother or sister has something against you, leave your gift there in front of the altar. First go and be reconciled to them; then come and offer your gift.

Matthew 5:23-24 (NIV)

"This, then, is how you should pray:
'Our Father in heaven,
hallowed be your name,
your kingdom come,
your will be done,
on earth as it is in heaven.
Give us today our daily bread.
And forgive us our debts,
as we also have forgiven our debtors.
And lead us not into temptation, a
but deliver us from the evil one.'"

Matthew 6:9-13 (NIV)

"For if you forgive men their trespasses, your heavenly Father will also forgive you. But if you do not forgive men their trespasses, neither will your Father forgive your trespasses"

Matthew 6:14-15 (NKJV)

"Look at the birds of the air, for they neither sow nor reap nor gather into barns; yet your heavenly Father feeds them. Are you not of more value than they?"

Matthew 6:26 (NKJV)

"Which of you by worrying can add one cubit to his stature?"

Matthew 6:27 (NKJV)

"Do not judge, or you too will be judged. ² For in the same way you judge others, you will be judged, and with the measure you use, it will be measured to you"

Matthew 7:1-2 (NIV)

Why do you look at the speck of sawdust in your brother's eye and pay no attention to the plank in your own eye? How can you say to your brother, 'Let me take the speck out of your eye,' when all the time there is a plank in your own eye? You hypocrite, first take the plank out of your own eye, and then you will see clearly to remove the speck from your brother's eye.

Matthew 7:3-5 (NIV)

¹⁶ By their fruit you will recognize them. Do people pick grapes from thornbushes, or figs from thistles? ¹⁷ Likewise, every good tree bears good fruit, but a bad tree bears bad fruit. ¹⁸ A good tree cannot bear bad fruit, and a bad tree cannot bear good fruit.

Matthew 7:16-18 (NIV)

Jesus Forgives and Heals a Paralytic

So He got into a boat, crossed over, and came to His own city. Then behold, they brought to Him a paralytic lying on a bed. When Jesus saw their faith, He said to the paralytic, "Son, be of good cheer; your sins are forgiven you." And at once some of the scribes said within themselves, "This Man blasphemes!" But Jesus, knowing their thoughts, said, "Why do you think evil in your hearts? For which is easier, to say, 'Your sins are forgiven you,' or to say, 'Arise and walk'? But that you may know that the Son of Man has power on earth to forgive sins"—then He said to the paralytic, "Arise, take up your bed, and go to your house." And he arose and departed to his house.

Matthew 9:1-7 (NKJV)

"But the very hairs of your head are all numbered"

Matthew 10:30 (NKJV)

"Then He said to the man, "Stretch out your hand." And he stretched it out, and it was restored as whole as the other"

Matthew 12:13 (NKJV)

And Peter answered Him and said, "Lord, if it is You, command me to come to You on the water."

So He said, "Come." And when Peter had come down out of the boat, he walked on the water to go to Jesus. But when he sawthat the wind was boisterous, he was afraid; and beginning to sink he cried out, saying, "Lord, save me!"

And immediately Jesus stretched out His hand and caught him, and said to him, "O you of little faith, why did you doubt?"

Matthew 14:28-31 (NKJV)

...Thus you nullify the word of God for the sake of your tradition. You hypocrites! Isaiah was right when he prophesied about you:

"'These people honor me with their lips,

but their hearts are far from me. They worship me in vain;

their teachings are merely human rules.'"

Matthew 15:6-9 (NIV)

But the things that come out of a person's mouth come from the heart, and these defile them. For out of the heart come evil thoughts—murder, adultery, sexual immorality, theft, false testimony, slander. These are what defile a person; but eating with unwashed hands does not defile them."

Matthew 15:18-20 (NIV)

A Canaanite woman from that vicinity came to him, crying out, "Lord, Son of David, have mercy on me! My daughter is demon-possessed and suffering terribly."

Jesus did not answer a word. So his disciples came to him and urged him, "Send her away, for she keeps crying out after us."

He answered, "I was sent only to the lost sheep of Israel."

The woman came and knelt before him. "Lord, help me!" she said.

He replied, "It is not right to take the children's bread and toss it to the dogs."

"Yes it is, Lord," she said. "Even the dogs eat the crumbs that fall from their master's table."

Then Jesus said to her, "Woman, you have great faith! Your request is granted." And her daughter was healed at that moment.

Matthew 15:22-28 (NIV)

"So the multitude marveled when they saw the mute speaking, the maimed made whole, the lame walking, and the blind seeing; and they glorified the God of Israel"

Matthew 15:31 (NKJV)

"His master replied, 'You wicked, lazy servant! So you knew that I harvest where I have not sown and gather where I have not scattered seed?"
Matthew 25:26 (NIV)

"Then Jesus came with them to a place called Gethsemane, and said to the disciples, "Sit here while I go and pray over there"
Matthew 26:36 (NKJV)

"And Jesus came and spoke to them, saying, "All authority has been given to Me in heaven and on earth"
Matthew 28:18 (NKJV)

"Therefore I say to you, whatever things you ask when you pray, believe that you receive them, and you will have them"
Mark 11:24 (NKJV)

"And when you stand praying, if you hold anything against anyone, forgive them, so that your Father in heaven may forgive you your sins"
Mark 11:25 (NIV)

Peter's Mother-in-Law Healed

Now He arose from the synagogue and entered Simon's house. But Simon's wife's mother was sick with a high fever, and they made request of Him concerning her. So He stood over her and rebuked the fever, and it left her. And immediately she arose and served them.
Luke 4:38-39 (NKJV)

Do Not Judge

"Judge not, and you shall not be judged. Condemn not, and you shall not be condemned. Forgive, and you will be forgiven"

Luke 6:37 (NKJV)

And that very hour He cured many of infirmities, afflictions, and evil spirits; and to many blind He gave sight. Jesus answered and said to them, "Go and tell John the things you have seen and heard: that the blind see, the lame walk, the lepers arecleansed, the deaf hear, the dead are raised, the poor have the gospel preached to them. And blessed is he who is not offended because of Me."

Luke 7:21-23 (NKJV)

"Salt is good, but if it loses its saltiness, how can it be made salty again? It is fit neither for the soil nor for the manure pile; it is thrown out"

Luke 12: 34 (NIV)

A Spirit of Infirmity

Now He was teaching in one of the synagogues on the Sabbath. And behold, there was a woman who had a spirit of infirmity eighteen years, and was bent over and could in no way raise herself up. But when Jesus saw her, He called her to Him and said to her, "Woman, you are loosed from your infirmity." And He laid His hands on her, and immediately she was made straight, and glorified God.

But the ruler of the synagogue answered with indignation, because Jesus had healed on the Sabbath; and he said to the crowd, "There

are six days on which men ought to work; therefore come and be healed on them, and not on the
Sabbath day." The Lord then answered him and
said, "Hypocrite! Does not each one of you on
the Sabbath loose his ox or donkey from the stall,
and lead it away to water it? So ought not this
woman, being a daughter of Abraham, whom
Satan has bound—think of it—for eighteen
years, be loosed from this bond on the Sabbath?"

Luke 13:10-16 (NKJV)

"Is it lawful to heal on the Sabbath or not?" But
they remained silent. So taking hold of the man,
he healed him and sent him on his way"

Luke 14: 3-4 (NIV)

"Jesus said to him, 'Rise, take up your bed and
walk'"

John 5:8 (NKJV)

"She said, "No one, Lord."

And Jesus said to her, "Neither do I condemn you; go and sin no more"

John 8:11 (NKJV)

"Then you will know the truth, and the truth
will set you free"

John 8:32 (NIV)

So if the Son sets you free, you will be free indeed"

John 8:36 (NIV)

When He had said these things, He spat on the
ground and made clay with the saliva; and He
anointed the eyes of the blind man with the clay.
And He said to him, "Go, wash in the pool of

Siloam" (which is translated, Sent). So he went and washed, and came back seeing.

John 9:6-7 (NKJV)

"He replied, 'The man they call Jesus made some mud and put it on my eyes. He told me to go to Siloam and wash. So I went and washed, and then I could see'"

John 9:11 (NIV)

"When Jesus heard that, He said, 'This sickness is not unto death, but for the glory of God, that the Son of God may be glorified through it'"

John 11:4 (NKJV.

Jesus Promises the Holy Spirit

"If you love me, keep my commands. And I will ask the Father, and he will give you another advocate to help you and be with you forever—the Spirit of truth. The world cannot accept him, because it neither sees him nor knows him. But you know him, for he lives with you and will be in you. I will not leave you as orphans; I will come to you.

John 14:15-18 (NIV)

"Peace I leave with you; my peace I give you. I do not give to you as the world gives. Do not let your hearts be troubled and do not be afraid"

John 14:27 (NIV)

"These things I have spoken to you, that in Me you may have peace. In the world you will have

tribulation; but be of good cheer, I have overcome the world"

John 16:33 (NKJV)

"The word which God sent to the children of
Israel, preaching peace through Jesus Christ—He
is Lord of all"

Acts 10:36 (NKJV)

Free from Indwelling Sin

"There is therefore now no condemnation to
those who are in Christ Jesus, who[a] do not walk
according to the flesh, but according to the Spirit"

Romans 8:1 (KJV)

You, however, are not in the realm of the flesh
but are in the realm of the Spirit, if indeed the
Spirit of God lives in you. And if anyone does
not have the Spirit of Christ, they do not belong
to Christ.

Romans 8:9 (NIV)

In the same way, the Spirit helps us in our weakness. We do not know what we ought to pray for,
but the Spirit himself intercedes for us through
wordless groans. And he who searches our hearts
knows the mind of the Spirit, because the Spirit
intercedes for God's people in accordance with
the will of God.

Romans 8:26-27 (NIV)

"And we know that all things work together for
good to those who love God, to those who are
the called according to His purpose"

Romans 8:28 (NKJV)

"What then shall we say to these things? If God is for us, who can be against us?"

Romans 8:31 (NKJV)

"Nor height nor depth, nor any other created thing, shall be able to separate us from the love of God which is in Christ Jesus our Lord"

Romans 8:39 (NKJV)

If you declare with your mouth, "Jesus is Lord," and believe in your heart that God raised him from the dead, you will be saved. For it is with your heart that you believe and are justified, and it is with your mouth that you profess your faith and are saved. As Scripture says, "Anyone who believes in him will never be put to shame."

Romans 8:39 (NKJV)

"So then faith comes by hearing, and hearing by the word of God"

Romans 10:17 (NKJV)

"And do not be conformed to this world, but be transformed by the renewing of your mind, that you may prove what is that good and acceptable and perfect will of God"

Romans 12:2 (NKJV)

Do not conform to the pattern of this world, but be transformed by the renewing of your mind. Then you will be able to test and approve what God's will is—his good, pleasing and perfect will.

Romans 12:2 (NIV)

For I say, through the grace given to me, to every-one who is among you, not to think of himself more highly than he ought to think, but to think soberly, as God has dealt to each one a measure of faith. For as we have many members in one body, but all the members do not have the same function, so we, being many, are one body in Christ, and individually members of one another.

Romans 12:3-5 (NKJV)

The Law of Love

"I know and am convinced by the Lord Jesus that there is nothing unclean of itself; but to him who considers anything to be unclean, to him it is unclean"

Romans 14:14 (NKJV)

But as it is written: "Eye has not seen, nor ear heard,

Nor have entered into the heart of man

The things which God has prepared for those who love Him."

But God has revealed them to us through His Spirit. For the Spirit searches all things, yes, the deep things of God. For what man knows the things of a man except the spirit of the man which is in him? Even so no one knows the things of God except the Spirit of God. Now we have received, not the spirit of the world, but the Spirit who is from God, that we might know the things that have been freely given to us by God.

1 Corinthians 2:9-12 (NKJV)

"But he who is spiritual judges all things, yet he himself is rightly judged by no one. For "who has known the mind of the LORD that he may instruct Him?" But we have the mind of Christ"

1 Corinthians 2: 15-16 (NKJV)

Those who are spiritual can evaluate all things, but they themselves cannot be evaluated by others. For, "Who can know the LORD's thoughts? Who knows enough to teach him?" But we understand these things, for we have the mind of Christ.

1 Corinthians 2:15-16 (NLT)

If I speak in the tongues of men or of angels, but do not have love, I am only a resounding gong or a clanging cymbal. If I have the gift of prophecy and can fathom all mysteries and all knowledge, and if I have a faith that can move mountains, but do not have love, I am nothing. If I give all I possess to the poor and give over my body to hardship that I may boast, but do not have love, I gain nothing.

1 Corinthians 13:1-3 (NIV)

Love is patient, love is kind. It does not envy, it does not boast, it is not proud. It does not dishonor others, it is not self-seeking, it is not easily angered, it keeps no record of wrongs.[6] Love does not delight in evil but rejoices with the truth. It always protects, always trusts, always hopes, always perseveres. Love never fails. But where there are prophecies, they will cease; where there are tongues, they will be stilled; where there is knowledge, it will pass away.

1 Corinthians 13:4-8 (NIV)

The Thorn in the Flesh

And lest I should be exalted above measure by the abundance of the revelations, a thorn in the flesh was given to me, a messenger of Satan to buffet me, lest I be exalted above measure. Concerning this thing I pleaded with the Lord three times that it might depart from me. And He said to me, "My grace is sufficient for you, for My strength is made perfect in weakness." Therefore most gladly I will rather boast in my infirmities, that the power of Christ may rest upon me. Therefore I take pleasure in infirmities, in reproaches, in needs, in persecutions, in distresses, for Christ's sake. For when I am weak, then I am strong.

2 Corinthians 12:7-10 (NKJV)

But he said to me, "My grace is sufficient for you, for my power is made perfect in weakness." Therefore I will boast all the more gladly about my weaknesses, so that Christ's power may rest on me. That is why, for Christ's sake, I delight in weaknesses, in insults, in hardships, in persecutions, in difficulties. For when I am weak, then I am strong.

2 Corinthians 12:9-10 (NIV)

"I have been crucified with Christ and I no longer live, but Christ lives in me. The life I now live in the body, I live by faith in the Son of God, who loved me and gave himself for me"

Galatians 2:20 (NIV)

Freedom in Christ

"It is for freedom that Christ has set us free. Stand firm, then, and do not let yourselves be burdened again by a yoke of slavery"

Galatians 5:1 (NIV)

"In your anger do not sin": Do not let the sun go down while you are still angry"

Ephesians 4:26 (NIV)

Therefore God also has highly exalted Him and given Him the name which is above every name, that at the name of Jesus every knee should bow, of those in heaven, and of those on earth, and of those under the earth, and that every tongue should confess that Jesus Christ is Lord, to the glory of God the Father.

Philippians 2:9-11 (NKJV)

"For it is God who works in you to will and to act in order to fulfill his good purpose"

Philippians 2:13 (NIV)

Brothers and sisters, I do not consider myself yet to have taken hold of it. But one thing I do: Forgetting what is behind and straining toward what is ahead, I press on toward the goal to win the prize for which God has called me heaven-ward in Christ Jesus.

Philippians 3:13-14 (NIV)

Be anxious for nothing, but in everything by prayer and supplication, with thanksgiving, let your requests be made known to God; and the peace of God, which surpasses all understanding, will guard your hearts and minds through Christ Jesus.

Philippians 4:6-7 (NKJV)

Finally, brothers and sisters, whatever is true, whatever is noble, whatever is right, whatever is pure, whatever is lovely, whatever is admirable—if anything is excellent or praiseworthy—think about such things.

Philippians 4:6-7 (NKJV)

I know what it is to be in need, and I know what it is to have plenty. I have learned the secret of being content in any and every situation, whether well fed or hungry, whether living in plenty or in want.

Philippians 4:12 (NIV)

"I can do all things through Christ who strengthens me"

Philippians 4:13 (NKJV)

"In every thing give thanks: for this is the will of God in Christ Jesus concerning you"

1 Thessalonians 5:18 (KJV)

"For God has not given us a spirit of fear, but of power and of love and of a sound mind"

2 Timothy 1:7 NKJV)

For the word of God is living and powerful, and sharper than any two-edged sword, piercing even to the division of soul and spirit, and of joints and marrow, and is a discerner of the thoughts and intents of the heart.

Hebrews 4:12 (NKJV)

For the word of God is alive and active. Sharper than any double-edged sword, it penetrates even to dividing soul and spirit, joints and marrow; it judges the thoughts and attitudes of the heart.

Hebrews 4:12 (NIV)

"Let us therefore come boldly to the throne of grace, that we may obtain mercy and find grace to help in time of need"

Hebrews 4:16 (NKJV)

"For I will be merciful to their unrighteousness, and their sins and their lawless deeds I will remember no more"

Hebrews 8:12 (NKJV)

"How much more shall the blood of Christ, who through the eternal Spirit offered Himself without spot to God, cleanse your conscience from dead works to serve the living God?"

Hebrews 9:14 (NKJV)

God Disciplines His Children

In your struggle against sin, you have not yet resisted to the point of shedding your blood. And have you completely forgotten this word of encouragement that addresses you as a father addresses his son? It says,

"My son, do not make light of the Lord's discipline,

and do not lose heart when he rebukes you,

because the Lord disciplines the one he loves,

and he chastens everyone he accepts as his son." Endure hardship as discipline; God is treating you as his children. For what children are not disciplined by their father? If you are not disciplined—and everyone undergoes discipline—then you are not legitimate, not true sons and daughters at all. Moreover, we have all had human fathers who disciplined us and we respected them for it. How much more should we submit to the Father of spirits and live! They disciplined us for a little while as they thought best; but God disciplines us for our good, in order that we may share in his holiness. No discipline seems pleasant at the time, but painful. Later on, however, it produces a harvest of righteousness and peace for those who have been trained by it.

Hebrews 12:4-11 (NIV)

Let your conduct be without covetousness; be content with such things as you have. For He Himself has said, "I will never leave you nor forsake you." So we may boldly say:
"The LORD is my helper;
I will not fear.
What can man do to me?"

Hebrews 13:5-6 (NKJV)

"If any of you lacks wisdom, let him ask of God, who gives to all liberally and without reproach, and it will be given to him"

James 1:5 (NKJV)

You desire but do not have, so you kill. You covet but you cannot get what you want, so you quarrel and fight. You do not have because you do not ask God. When you ask, you do not receive, because you ask with wrong motives, that you may spend what you get on your pleasures.

James 4:2-3 (NIV)

"Submit yourselves, then, to God. Resist the devil, and he will flee from you"

James 4:7 (NIV)

Meeting Specific Needs

Is anyone among you suffering? Let him pray. Is anyone cheerful? Let him sing psalms. Is anyone among you sick? Let him call for the elders of the church, and let them pray over him, anointing him with oil in the name of the Lord. And the prayer of faith will save the sick, and the Lord will raise him up. And if he has committed sins, he will be forgiven.

James 5:13-15 (NKJV)

"Casting all your care upon Him, for He cares for you"

1 Peter 5:7 (NKJV)

My little children, let us not love in word or in tongue, but in deed and in truth. And by this we know that we are of the truth, and shall assure our hearts before Him. For if our heart condemns us, God is greater than our heart, and knows all things. Beloved, if our heart does not condemn us, we have confidence toward God. And whatever we ask we receive from Him, because we keep His commandments and do those things that are pleasing in His sight. And this is His commandment: that we should believe on the name of His Son Jesus Christ and love one another, as He gave us commandment.

1 John 3:18-23 (NKJV)

ABOUT THE AUTHOR

Dr. Theodora Saddoris was a practicing Internal Medicine specialist in Columbus, Indiana for over thirty years, until she transitioned her practice to only treating substance use disorders (addiction). She is American Board-certified in Internal Medicine since 1983 and in Preventive Medicine—Addiction Specialist since 2018. She has been actively treating patients with addiction since 2014. She is a Fellow of the American Society of Addiction Medicine (FASAM) and an active member and treasurer of the Indiana Society of Addiction Medicine (ISAM).

She has been involved in speaker programs to educate the public. She has given a presentation for Desperate Housewives in Columbus, Indiana to help those in her community to understand more about addiction. She had assisted with educating people at Good Samaritan Health and Wellness Center in Jasper, Georgia, on the need for an addiction program and how to start an opioid treatment program at their facility. She was involved in helping her community get a grant for Columbus Regional Hospital to begin an addiction treatment center called TASC (Treatment And Support Center) and was a consultant and an educational speaker for the program.

She has been actively involved in her community, trying to reduce the stigma of addiction and helping with resources and treatments to help those with a substance use disorder. In the past, she has done monthly addiction education on a local radio station 1010 WCSI and has written several articles to a local newspaper, the Republic, about addiction issues.

Since 2015 she has done free to the public weekly addiction group cognitive behavior and mindfulness counseling and been involved with helping family members deal with loved ones suffering from an addiction problem.

She gives all her successes to her Lord and Savior who has guided her path into helping those lost to this disease called addiction.